T0318189

Spontaneous Venturing

Spontaneous Venturing

An Entrepreneurial Approach to Alleviating Suffering in the Aftermath of a Disaster

Dean A. Shepherd and Trenton A. Williams

The MIT Press
Cambridge, Massachusetts
London, England

This book was set in Palatino LT Std by Toppan Best-set Premedia Limited.

Library of Congress Cataloging-in-Publication Data

Names: Shepherd, Dean A., author. | Williams, Trent, 1981- author.
Title: Spontaneous venturing : an entrepreneurial approach to alleviating
  suffering in the aftermath of a disaster / Dean A. Shepherd and Trenton A.
  Williams.
Description: Cambridge, MA : MIT Press, 2018. | Includes bibliographical
  references and index.
Identifiers: LCCN 2018010474 | ISBN 9780262038874 (hardcover : alk. paper),
ISBN 9780262546768 (paperback)
Subjects: LCSH: Disaster relief. | Social entrepreneurship.
Classification: LCC HV553 .S477 2018 | DDC 363.34/8--dc23 LC record available at
https://lccn.loc.gov/2018010474

Contents

Acknowledgments

Dean would like to acknowledge his inspiration, his father, John Mervyn Shepherd; his Aunt Shirley Tregent; and his wife, Suzie, who is always looking to help people (whether they want it or not).

Trent would like to acknowledge his wife, Natalee, who has been a living example of grace, patience, and resilience to the adversity of physical trauma. He would also like to acknowledge his grandfather, Colonel Gail S. Halvorsen, the "Berlin Candy Bomber," who has devoted his life to always acting when he felt called on to help, even when what he offered seemed small and simple.

Dean and Trent both thank Ali Fergusson for her work copy editing the book.

Introduction

This book is by two entrepreneurship scholars who are interested in understanding the various ways in which entrepreneurship and venturing shape and improve our lives. In particular, this book on venturing to alleviate suffering emerged from our personal experiences with crises and the challenging and inspiring situations that followed.

The story of the book began soon after the first author was exposed to the violence and destruction of a natural disaster that struck his home state of Victoria, Australia, in 2009. Moved by a deep desire to learn more about the disaster and the people caught in its path, both authors began an inductive exploration of how some of the victims responded to the crisis in real time. The result was the discovery of the extraordinary capacity for compassion unleashed in the form of venturing to alleviate suffering, or, as we call it, compassionate venturing. This discovery led to a number of projects that formed the early foundations for this book, including publications in management journals, a dissertation, and field research in Haiti. Both authors continue to study compassionate venturing with ongoing projects across a number of contexts.

The discovery of compassionate venturing as a response to crisis resonated with both authors. For the first author, it solidified many of the experiences he had observed firsthand in Australia and helped contextualize the compassionate responses exhibited by victims of the disaster. For the second author, it helped explain some of the actions of his grandfather (Gail Halvorsen, the "Candy Bomber"), who, in the aftermath of World War II, was instrumental in responding to the humanitarian crisis of the Berlin Blockade by participating in the Berlin Airlift and beginning a candy-bombing initiative to drop candy and chocolate to destitute children. From this beginning, the co-authors explored a range of topics on compassionate venturing, seeking to understand the personal costs of disasters and suffering, the human capacity for resilience, and the role of venturing in alleviating the suffering of both rescue agents and victims. This exploration eventually expanded beyond the Australian context to include exploring compassionate venturing in a least developed economy, Haiti, after the devastating earthquake that struck near Port-au-Prince in 2010.

That is the brief explanation of why we are interested in compassionate venturing. Why should others also be interested? Because disasters and crises affect millions of people each year, and organizational scholarship holds great potential to add to the conversation of how to more effectively anticipate and respond to crises. Furthermore, individual efforts to organize a response to a crisis have been described as an inevitable outcome when disasters strike, suggesting that spontaneous, compassionate, impromptu responses to crisis are a normal and important component of organizing and disaster response. Our hope is to reach as many scholars, individuals, and organizations as possible to generate additional knowledge that might better equip individuals, organizations, and communities to alleviate suffering due to disaster. In doing so, we hope to continue to expand the scope of entrepreneurial venturing and the ways it shapes human experience.

Dean A. Shepherd and Trenton A. Williams

1   Disaster and Suffering

You cannot fight 100-foot flames with a garden hose. Don't try to be a garden-hose hero. Don't wait until it becomes really scary and then think you'll be able to escape. Because you may not.

—Sandra Millers Younger, *The Fire Outside My Window*

Despite living in the United States for many years, I (the first author of this book) am fortunate to be able to head back home to Australia each North American winter. This means I can celebrate my birthday with family and enjoy the Southern Hemisphere's summer. In 2009, my parents planned a birthday party at their house for Saturday, February 7. It was hot! So hot that my brother decided he could not attend the party. That was fine with me, but I did not want his children to miss out on all the fun, so I drove to my brother's house to pick them up. While I was there, my brother asked about my fire plan. I told him that if there was a fire, I would take the children to the beach (about one mile away) and stand in the water. My plan seemed to satisfy him, and my nieces and I headed for the party. It was a great party, but later in the evening, Dad kept going in and out of the room and spending a lot of time on the phone. When I eventually asked him what was going on, he responded, "Shirley is alive! Shirley is alive!" I had no idea what he was talking about, but he slowed down his nervous circuits around the phone and told me what had happened. A firestorm had hit country Victoria and ripped through Clonbinane.

Clonbinane is where Auntie Shirley lived alone on a small farm (ranch). That night, she was at the local community hall playing bingo. If she had been home, she almost certainly would have died. The bush-fires destroyed, along with many other properties, her home, sheds, and equipment and killed her dog and horses. Nothing was salvageable. Dad picked Shirley up the next day. She was still in shock. She had the clothes on her back and nothing else. Auntie Shirley lived with Mum and Dad for three months. She decided to move back to country Victoria but not to the property; she now lives in an apartment in a country town.

Like most people from Victoria, I remember vividly where I was on Black Saturday. Before we present and discuss effective disaster response, it seems useful to provide a closer look at the devastation wrought that day through some firsthand accounts of those who faced its fury.

Devastation of Black Saturday

The Black Saturday fires of February 7, 2009, were the worst in Australia's history and forever altered the lives and livelihood of many Australians. On Black Saturday, hundreds of fires burned out of control across the state of Victoria in South Eastern Australia. Conditions that day were ripe for fire risk: a high-pressure system in the Tasman Sea was causing record-high temperatures across Victoria ranging from 40 to 48 degrees Celsius (104 to 118 degrees Fahrenheit), as well as gale-force winds. These conditions, coupled with the normal bushfire danger in the Victorian bushlands, presented an extraordinary threat that resulted in hundreds of fires. According to the Victorian Bushfires Royal Commission, at the peak of the conflagrations on Black Saturday, more than four hundred fires burned across the state (see Teague, McLeod, and Pascoe 2010).

While many rural residents were somewhat prepared for bushfires, no one was ready for the Black Saturday fires' virulence. In traditional bushfires, grass and other bush burn uncontrollably, the fire moving across the land in search of more fuel. Although these storms are very hazardous, traditional bushfires are not as dangerous as firestorms. In firestorms, the fire itself generates and maintains its own wind system, which produces fire whirls and fireballs that can be hurled substantial distances. On Black Saturday, a vicious firestorm ravaged Victoria, with trees, grass, and other flammable material often catching fire twenty to thirty minutes before the primary fire front came through. Unlike other fires, this firestorm was unique, as the fires crowned in forested areas, thus hampering ground control, and large columns of gas, smoke, and ash developed above the fire, burning fuel in their path and launching fiery bark downwind for several miles. The fire reached a temperature of 1,200 degrees Celsius (2,192 degrees Fahrenheit) at its worst and

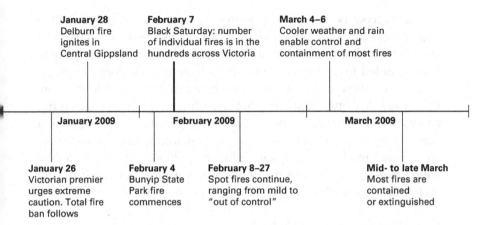

Figure 1.1
Fire Timeline, Black Saturday, Victoria, Australia

traveled at speeds up to 121 kilometers per hour (75 miles per hour), leaving in its wake widespread devastation.

The Black Saturday firestorm wrought extreme destruction. It destroyed more than 3,500 structures and killed 173 people, leaving many others injured, displaced, or otherwise incapacitated. In just a few hours, entire townships were wiped out, acres of farmland were destroyed, and billions of dollars' worth of damage was caused (Teague, McLeod, and Pascoe 2010). Additionally, more than one million animals, wild and domestic, were estimated to have perished in the fires. Figure 1.1 shows the timeline of the firestorm.

Personal Stories of Black Saturday

Though statistics provide some insight into the devastation caused by the Black Saturday bushfires, we want to start this book with a deeper insight into the disaster event by introducing and reflecting on the stories of those who experienced it firsthand. The following excerpts of accounts from those in or near the disaster zone provide a richer picture of what happened that day (though some of the stories of lost family members were so wrenching we decided not to include them in the book). We felt it was important to give a human face to the events of that day lest we forget that the primary goal of disaster response is to alleviate human suffering. Moreover, it was these stories that first prompted us to explore the topic and drove our efforts to better understand the variety of responses to overwhelming loss.

These accounts are primarily firsthand accounts provided as written submissions to a government inquiry into the disaster (a few have been very lightly edited for punctuation here). As the Black Saturday bushfires included fires in multiple locations in country Victoria, we highlight the location of each actor. As we connected response to location, it quickly became apparent that bushfire response communities emerged in response to "their" fire, or the specific fire that struck a community with which the recorder self-identified. Later in the book, we advance models that explain resilience and recovery, but even then we try not to lose sight of the personal suffering experienced during and in the aftermath of a disaster.

Leave Early or Stay and Defend

To set the scene for these personal stories, it is important to explain residents' choice of fire strategy, either "leave early" or "stay and defend." The fire strategy is important to understand because an individual's choice could have serious implications for the nature and the level of suffering, which in turn triggered the types of spontaneous ventures created to alleviate suffering. But we also have another motive for discussing the "leave early or stay and defend" fire strategy because, even though the primary purpose of writing the book is to highlight and better understand spontaneous venturing as a compassionate response, the larger purpose is to reflect on how we as a collective can reduce the amount of suffering in the aftermath of a disaster. To further this larger purpose we highlight the choices people had, the choices they made, and the consequences of those choices in terms of their personal suffering and the suffering experienced by loved ones.

Wayne Haggar of Kinglake explained the reasoning behind the choice of options local residents faced:

Two years ago we attended a CFA [Country Fire Authority] meeting held in our street and collected the pamphlets being distributed. This is how we knew about the "Leave Early or Stay and Defend policy" and, more specifically, that if we could see flames from our property, then it was too late to leave. … We supported the "Leave Early or Stay and Defend policy" because many rural communities and towns have limited road access which, combined with the scale of evacuation, would make compulsory evacuation impossible and, more importantly, dangerous. While some individual properties are sited in heavily bushed, poorly accessed and likely indefensible areas there are others, like ours, in generally cleared areas where defence can be reasonably expected. We also believe people can become complacent when they know government policy involves compulsory evacuation and equip themselves less thoroughly for fire fighting.

Jess Odgers of Kinglake explained how her fire plan was to leave early:

I implemented my fire plan by leaving Kinglake with my children in my car on Friday 6 February 2009. ... It was early in the afternoon (Saturday 7 February 2009), after I came back from a swim at approximately 2pm, when I first heard of the fires. I turned on the radio and heard accounts of fire in Kilmore. Then I started to worry about my friends in Upper Plenty because they are so close to Kilmore.

A friend from Upper Plenty rang me at about mid-afternoon and she said that they had got off the mountain, that they were driving towards Whittlesea and they could see the fires heading up towards Kinglake. My friend said that the flames were so massive that the whole of the mountain, including Kinglake, would be next on fire, and therefore my place too.

At about 6 pm I got a text message from a next-door neighbour in Kinglake, saying that he had just got out of the house. An hour later he texted me again and said our homes were both gone. Initially I went into denial at the loss of my house, but within half an hour of the initial text notification from my neighbour, l received many other texts from friends still in Kinglake and Yea that affirmed my worst fears that our home and town were burnt. My friends were alive, but others did not survive. It was at that point that my grieving began and l became very emotional.

Others did not leave their property as early as Jess. More representative of those who left their properties were Karen Ward and her husband of Mudgegonga. Karen recalled the journey:

When we saw the fire at the top of the hill and saw what it was that we were facing, my husband said to me, "I don't think we should stay." We both walked around to the front of the house. There was a police officer on our front veranda and he asked us whether we were staying or going. We said that we were going to go. He said, "Well get out and get out now." I could hear in his voice that he was very concerned. I then thought that we could not fight the fire, based on the tone of voice of the police officer, what we had seen at the back of the house, as well as the fact that there was still no smoke, embers or ash falling around the house.

We got the animals into our two cars and drove off the property. The police officer had warned us that there were cattle on the roads. When we drove out, a paddock on the side of our house was burning, and we had to drive out through flames on our property. There were also flames on the road that we had to drive through and we saw cows on the road. I stopped briefly because of a cow in front of the car and then drove around. I got through that area and then it was clear with no smoke, no ash, and no embers. I couldn't see my husband's car behind me and so I drove slowly down the road until I could see him. He had hit a cow coming out. We both stopped and he got out and fixed his vehicle so it was driveable. ...

So when we got to the bottom of the road we turned right onto Myrtleford-Yackandandah Road towards Wodonga. We drove for another 5 minutes until we got to the top of the hill on the Myrtleford-Yackandandah Road when we stopped again. We both got out of our cars and looked back to our house and within 20 seconds we saw our house burning. There were flames coming out under the veranda. While we were standing there, another fire spotted about 50 metres down the road so we decided to get out of there and get to Wodonga.

Others decided to stay and defend their homes. One example is Peter Olorenshaw, who lived on a farm (ranch) in Callignee and stayed with his son Tim to try to protect his home. Although this is a long account, the richness of the story as told by Peter draws in the reader:

On our way towards the house Tim and I ran around trying to put out some of the small fires on the front lawn with our boots, but we did not have much success. I also saw that the back lawn was alight. The flames were burning to a height of 1.5–2 metres, which really shocked me, because there was almost nothing there to burn. It seemed that the fire was just using the few shards of grass as a wick to ignite eucalyptus fuel that was blowing through.

It was about then that I was hit by a front of radiant heat. I was on the concrete driveway on the eastern side of the house and when the heat hit I fell to the ground and literally cowered on my knees. It felt like someone had left a fan-forced oven on high for hours and then opened the door suddenly. The heat was incredibly fierce and I suffered minor burns to my ears and neck, despite wearing a hat and a collared shirt. I kept trying to change positions to use different parts of my arms to shield myself.

At this stage, I did not know where Tim was. I yelled out to him to take cover under the carport, although I wasn't sure if that would be effective because of the high velocity of the wind.

When I could stand, I raced to the veranda to get under the roofline of the house, which I thought would be a barrier against the heat. ... Tim had taken refuge under the carport and when I reached the veranda he came to join me. It was intensely hot, probably between 300–400 degrees radiant heat, and we decided that our last stand would be in the house, trying to protect that. We retreated inside the house, where we had already prepared by filling sinks with water and putting towels in to soak. ...

It was very dark outside by now from the smoke but there was an eerie glow from the fire. Tim and I patrolled the house, waiting for the fire to run through. We intended to wait for the fire front to pass and then go outside and put out whatever fires we could. I expected the flames to lick at the sides of the windows, giving us time to put them out with towels and buckets.

What actually happened was that the fire storm impacted dramatically on the west side of the house. The windows blew in with tremendous force and the house essentially imploded. Tim and I were hiding behind a wall in the hallway at the time but I could see into one of the bedrooms. I saw the fire impinge so suddenly that it immediately filled the whole room. Very shortly thereafter the flames entered, [and] the varnished surfaces of the built-in ward-robes and the paint on the walls caught alight.

The atmosphere in the house became intensely acrid and it felt like my lungs were shutting down. One minute I was breathing and the next minute I physically couldn't inhale. ...

We wet our hats and exited the house on the east side, through a sliding door that led to a small concrete paved area. When we got outside, the smoke was incredibly dense. We were carrying four wet towels each and we were trying to breathe through those.

I knew we would be protected from the radiant heat by the house for a little while, until the house actually lit up entirely inside. My aim was to reach our final point of respite behind our 10,000 gallon concrete water tank; however, it was not yet safe to move across the yard to the tank. The radiant heat would have been fatal and the small amount of grassed area was on fire between us and the tank.

Tim and I threw our towels over us and moved quickly across to the tank. We crouched down on the northeast side of the tank, facing into the tank to try and protect our faces from the heat. We had with us our towels, two plastic water bottles and a red dolphin lantern torch and a fluoro camping lantern. At that stage we couldn't move to the southwest side of the tank (which would have given better shelter from the burning home) because there was a cedar cubby house on that side that was well alight. ...

We stayed on the northeast face of the tank until the southern end of the house lit up. The radiant heat now intensified to the point where it began melting both the torch and the water bottle by my right foot. Tim and I were still huddled under our wet towels and I was telling Tim to breathe through the towels, to cup his hands over his nose and breathe through them.

There was fire and devastation all around us and it was clear to me that we could not stay where we were. It crossed my mind at that point that we might be in serious trouble! ... I said to Tim that we had to move around to the other side of the tank. ... Even with some shelter, I couldn't believe how hot it was. We couldn't put our hands from under the towels without the heat impacting on the skin. The ground under our feet was also extremely hot, which I realised later was because we were actually standing on burning embers that were covered by ash.

The wind was still very strong at this stage and with the heat and the wind our towels dried out after about 20 minutes. The towels were our main protection against the smoke and heat, so I knew that we had to wet them down again quickly. Access to the water was on the other side of the tank. Visibility was almost zero now, but I grabbed seven of the towels (leaving Tim with one) and started to head around the tank to wet them. As soon as I stood up, however, I nearly collapsed from lack of oxygen. I hadn't expected the smoke to impinge so markedly on my physiology. I managed to crawl on hands and knees around to the other side of the tank. ... I dunked the towels in the water and crawled back to Tim. I was nearly out of energy just from going that short distance. ...

For the next few hours Tim and I took turns crawling and walking around to wet the towels. The temperature of the water increased markedly over that time. I would estimate that after about an hour the temperature of the water was similar to a cup of tea, about 55 or 60 degrees. If you think about the radiant heat required to heat 5,000 gallons of water up from 4 to 60 degrees in one hour, you can get some idea of how fierce the heat was. We were hot, dirty and sweating profusely and were replenishing our bodies from the single water bottle that we had left, from the hot tank water.

During our time huddled behind the tank, the smoke would sometimes partially clear and we could see some of what was happening with the fire. I could see the remains of Tim's car, just a shell by now. When I inspected the car after the fire, I could see that the glass had melted across the dashboard. I was told that the temperature in the centre of the firestorm must have been somewhere around 1500 or 2000 degrees Celsius in order to melt that glass. Later I inspected other vehicles on various properties and observed the same effect on the glassed areas. ...

By around 8.30pm (that is my best estimate) we could tell that the main fire had moved on. I could not really see how far and in which direction the fire had gone and the air was still extremely acrid, but it seemed safe enough to come out from behind the tank and have a look at the house area.

We wandered around the home farm area of the property, an area of about three-quarters of an acre. There was nothing left. The house was gone and the machinery shed was just a pile of burning metal lying on the ground. There were still spot fires burning all around. I said to Tim that there was nothing we could do now and that we should rest and conserve our strength. ...

As night set in, it was still extremely hot and unpleasant but nothing like we had experienced at the peak of the fire. We rested fitfully on the ground by the tank, and by about 2am the south westerly wind had become really quite cold. We were wet through because of sheltering under the towels and the wind cooled us further.

I actually thought that Tim had gone into shock because he began shaking like a leaf, but he said that he wasn't shocked, just freezing cold. Ironically, he said that he was going to go and sit by the fires to warm up. I actually agreed with him because I was also freezing, so we went down to near where the shed had been and stripped to our underwear. We hung our clothes on the remains of burnt plants and everything dried in about 20 minutes because of the intensity of the heat that was still emanating from the burning wood pile that was by the shed.

After we had dried and dressed, we decided that before doing anything else we should wait for first light and then properly assess the situation. We had suffered substantial smoke inhalation and were both extremely traumatised by the situation.

James Cowdery of South Morang also remained at his property and clearly recalled the moment the fire hit:

Only a few seconds from that first ember I looked around and it seemed to me that everywhere I looked, everything was glowing fire red. No more than five seconds later it seemed as if an incendiary device had ignited and everything around me burst into flames. I did not see a fire front or smoke coming through, just a number of explosions. ... The heat from the flames was intense. ... I fled into the house through the back door and ran down the spiral staircase and climbed into the drain under my house.

. The drain was about one metre wide and the height of a normal room, so a person could easily stand between the wall of the downstairs design office area and the rock face. ... The smoke became almost black and I was having trouble breathing, so I lay down and breathed through the aggregate in the drain. ... I tried to stand at one point but there was not enough oxygen and I couldn't breathe while standing. The sound of the fire outside was just like a jet engine, as if you were standing there when a plane was taking off. Whilst I was under the house, I could see flames shooting through vents in the brick-work of the wall of the main house. ... It was obvious to me then that the house was going to burn down. ...

I took out my mobile phone and rang my children. I contacted my daughter Nina and informed her of my circumstances so the family would know where to find me should I not survive the fires. ... Nina said she would ring me every 10 minutes, which she did.

I think I was probably under the house for about twenty to thirty minutes. I knew that I had to get out because the house was burning and it might fall on me. ... I had left the laundry door open when I had run into the house. I looked out through the flames and could see the ramp outside that appeared intact, so I held my breath and ran through the flaming laundry doorway along the ramp back to the fire-pump that was still running. ... I ran straight into the pump, knocked my glasses off, and I stayed in the water there for a while, whilst the pumps sprayed water all over me. ... I thought I should turn the pump off, as at the time I was concerned that it was a waste of water. I tried to get to it but ... the radiant heat was too intense. ...

I then ran to the back fence of the property and scaled the fence to a vacant block adjacent to my property. The grass was all burnt but there were no trees on that block so I was able to stand there for a moment and look around. I saw that my house was engulfed in flames and there was no hope of saving it. The houses surrounding my property were timber houses, and my house was the only brick one. Of the seven houses I could see, some were still in flames and others had burnt out completely.

I walked down the fence line to Grandview Crescent and stood next to the road watching the houses burn and I also saw the gas tanks blow up one by one. I could see a body against the fence and another body down in a drain culvert, it was obvious that they were dead and there was nothing I could do. I then started walking towards Bald Spur Road, along Grandview Crescent. It was a horrible feeling because I felt like the only person alive at that point.

I walked past the house that belonged to my neighbour Richard Zann and his family. I saw that there were five cars there, including a car that I recognised as belonging to Karma Hastwell, an elderly neighbour who Richard had known for a long time. I later discovered that Richard, his wife Eileen, and their daughter Eva, who lived with them, had perished in the house along with Karma. Richard's son was overseas at the time but his car was in the driveway. Richard worked with the zoological department of LaTrobe University and had expertise in bird life.

Patricia Easterbrook of Mudgegona and her husband decided to stay. She recounted her interactions with neighbors:

We knew that 7 February was going to be a really bad day. ... It was hot and horrible and starting to get windy. ... Some time later we heard mention of fires in the area and we were particularly surprised to hear Mudgegonga mentioned by name in the context of an ember alert. It is such a small place that it is unusual to hear it referred to on the radio. By the time the message came on the radio we could already see the glow from the fires over the hills towards Beechworth. ... After I heard the ember alert I rang our neighbours, John and Sue Wilson.

John and Sue had lived next door to us for nearly 20 years. Their house was due west of ours, about 150m away. Their block was just a large house block without any additional land. The block was carved out of the larger surrounding property belonging to Sue's uncle. The Wilsons had trees right along the south side of the block, about 20m from the house. On the west side of the house there was also a large row of conifers which were destroyed in the fire.

John and Sue have two daughters, Grace and Samantha, neither of whom were living at home at the time of the February fires. Samantha had just moved to Sydney to study and Grace was living in Myrtleford. We had never discussed fire plans in detail with John and Sue, so I don't know whether their plan was to stay and defend. However, I know that in the 2003 fires they didn't leave because at one point during the afternoon of those fires, Sue rang Lindsay when she saw the smoke and seemed quite panicky. Her husband John wasn't home at the time and she wasn't sure what she should do.

When I called the Wilsons after hearing the first radio warning about Mudgegonga, the phone was engaged. I presumed that someone else had heard the ember alert and was on the phone to them.

At around 8:30pm, we were sitting outside under the large oak tree. We have a battery-powered radio and had taken that out with us so we could listen to updates. The radio was still repeating the Mudgegonga ember alert from before. By this stage it was dark outside and there was a huge red glow from the fires to the west.

I decided to give John and Sue another ring. This time Sue answered and said "Oh hi Pat, how are you going?" She was always a lovely, bubbly and happy person. I said "I'm good Sue, but I'm just ringing to see if you guys are okay. Do you need a hand? Do you want us to come down and help?"

Sue said "What are you talking about?" I told her that there had been an ember alert for Mudgegonga on the radio and that it sounded pretty serious. She said that she didn't know anything about it, they were just sitting inside watching something on television. I suggested that she put ABC radio on but Sue said they couldn't get the ABC.

Sue said she would put John on, so I spoke to John and said that I thought it was very serious. I said that the radio had been talking about an ember alert for an hour or two by now. John said "Thanks for letting us know. That's terrific, I'll get it all organised now." That was the last time I spoke with either John or Sue. ...

At around 10pm, when we were again sitting under the oak tree, I recall that I was becoming very alarmed. I remember that I said to Lindsay "I don't want to die." He said that he didn't want to die either and he asked me if I wanted to leave. I said I thought it was too late because everything I have ever heard says that you have to go early. I felt that with the sky getting redder and redder it was too late. ...

Because the sprinklers [on the roof] were going and we had already done all our preparation, there was nothing to do except wait for the fire to come. It was one of those things where you almost just want it to happen so that you can deal with it and then get on with your life. We could see the fire getting closer and closer all the time, the sky getting much redder and the hills sort of lighting up in all directions. There was a bright orangey glow on both sides of the valley looking from our house to the northwest and west and eventually it spread around to the southwest as well. ...

Soon after that, while we were outside waiting for the fire, I heard an unbelievable roar. It was like nothing I had ever heard before and I remember saying to Lindsay "What the hell is that?" He said "That's the fire" and "Get inside." So we raced inside and then suddenly things were just exploding everywhere. ...

I had known the fire was getting close but nothing prepared me for the way things exploded like fireballs everywhere, all around us.

When the firestorm hit we were both inside. I remember standing by the sofa, holding on to it for support and feeling like I was going to throw up. ... I was frozen there for a while, I'm not sure how long, but then suddenly I saw embers coming in under the front door and that kicked me into action. ... Out of the windows, I could see that everything around the house was blazing. ... The fire "front" never really seemed to pass. The fire just raged and roared around the house for those whole 2 hours. The ute [pickup truck], the barbecue, the tool shed, the hay shed, the tractor—everything was just burning. The trees were burning and the wind just kept roaring through. Fortunately, the house itself never caught alight. The sprinklers [on the roof] had been going for hours and everything was fairly well drenched so that must have helped save the house.

When the firestorm finally started to die down, and I thought. "This is it, it's stopping," I looked at the clock and it was 2:10am. I couldn't believe it had been over 2 hours. If anyone had asked me before I looked at the clock, I would have said that it has been a really horrible ten or fifteen minutes. I think we just got through it on adrenalin. ...

The first glimmer of light in the morning showed the angle of the Wilsons' roofline and I thought it looked normal. This made me think that their house was fine because the roof was still there. However, as it got lighter we realised exactly what we were looking at. John and Sue's house was a horrible mess, with parts of it still smouldering and things around the house still on fire. There was nothing much left of the brick house and the colourbond roof was twisted and collapsed. There were only a few bits and pieces of brick left standing. ...

Some time after that first visit [with police], we saw a number of police cars coming and going from the Wilsons' and then one of the policemen came up and told us that they had found bodies in the house. I was just stunned. I had been so sure they had left.

Some lamented the overexcitement exhibited by local firefighting groups in encouraging people to stay and defend their homes. For example, Joan Davey of Kinglake was devastated by the loss of her son and daughter-in-law and felt it was directly the result of faulty thinking about the leave or stay and defend policy. She stated,

We believe that our family developed false confidence in their ability to survive and fight a bushfire. ... We will always lament [that] this Fireguard Group led to a change in [our son's and daughter-in-law's] attitude from leaving early to staying and protecting their home, with the mantra of the [fire association] that "People save Houses and Houses save People." This surely would not have applied to their circumstances of a timber home, on a ridge, next to a major forest area. ... I trust that mandatory evacuation will be a means of saving lives, although it may be difficult in areas with one road system, but this should be explored. My fear is that no one was game to take the initiative to evacuate.

A Community Affected by the Black Saturday Bushfire Disaster

After the Black Saturday bushfires, which burned for a month, businesses and municipal services in the communities affected by the fire were almost entirely incapacitated. As Graeme Brown, one of the founders of the Marysville and Triangle Development Group (MATDG), a venture that helped victims of the disaster, explained,

Most commercial buildings in Marysville were destroyed by the bushfire and the business owners had no infrastructure that would allow them to keep a revenue stream coming in while they recovered, let alone enable them to redirect resources.

Similarly, other Marysville residents explained that life after the fire was

like living in oblivion. ... It's just rubble, like a bomb site. ... For the first few days, generators were the only power source, water was scarce and there was no access to newspapers, radios or televisions. ... [Residents] had to drive two kilometres out of town to get mobile phone reception. (Cooper 2009)

Community members experienced varying degrees of loss. First, many community members lost their homes and therefore lacked immediate shelter in the ongoing danger, as well as losing the resources in their homes, including clothing. For example, Jacqueline Hainsworth described the destruction of housing in the aftermath of the fire:

There were no houses along Pine Ridge Road that survived the fire. The only building that was still standing was this horrible old fibro shed across the road. His wife had been asking him for years to get rid of it, but it's still there. There are no houses left, not one, out of the 32 houses that used to be in our street. There were burnt-out cars everywhere along the street.

Exposure to the elements after losing their homes increased residents' risk of further devastation and emotional anguish over what had been lost inside their homes, and increased uncertainty about the future. Michelle Buntine reflected on this anxiety, exacerbation, and uncertainty over the future when responding to insurance companies:

I remember someone different from the insurance company ringing me every week saying they were still waiting on an asset list. I remember saying to them, I don't own a computer, I don't own a pen and paper, I am in emergency accommodation, I don't have the time, my brain is not right to sit down and actually write that list for you. I also didn't want to face it—I didn't want to sit down and remember what I had lost and I didn't have the energy to do it.

Second, the Black Saturday bushfires caused physical hardships and health-related issues, which were exacerbated by the destruction of resources for healing these wounds. Mary Kenealy, an elderly resident, recalled the following:

There was only one wheelchair at the relief centre, which I used. To treat me, they had to put a canula in my hand and attach me to a drip. When they put the canula in, there was no stand to hang the drip onto so I had to sit up holding the drip above my head to keep it running into my hand. I was appalled that a designated relief centre like that did not have better emergency medical equipment and supplies. No one returned for hours to check on how I was, and a large blood clot developed in the back of my hand. When someone eventually got back to me, they had great difficulty removing the canula, and I had severe bruising for many days.

Health-related issues were not restricted to the period immediately following the disaster. For example, Ron Sorraghan described the lingering health problems he endured associated with the fire:

For the first two months after the fire, we worked like crazy to get back on the property, but after that we were physically and mentally exhausted—we literally fell over and got sick. In the 12 months since the fire, Anne and I have needed to have five general anesthetics each for various health problems—I had a melanoma that the doctors put down to the stress of the fire.

Third, because of the damaged vehicles, roads, and infrastructure required for normal transportation, people felt unable to escape. Therefore, they were forced to deal with persistent threats from a precarious environment, such as ongoing fires; emotional trauma from living in a disaster zone; and continued reminders of the loss of property, human life, and animal life. Doug Walter pointedly explained the feelings of being cut off and to a certain extent forgotten:

People who stayed and defended their properties were not only cut off by the roadblocks but were largely overlooked by everyone in the immediate response phase. Neither has the Council accepted their lack of capacity to manage the crisis. They rejected offers of help in the early days after the fire when help was most needed and have, as a result been seriously found wanting. I believe that was a serious mistake. ... It took a very long time for services to come to us ... it took over two weeks for them to come to us and we could not get to Alexandra where resources had been made available.

Fourth, local residents suffered great uncertainty and mental anguish in the aftermath of the Black Saturday disaster. They faced uncertainty concerning the outcome of others' physical well-being and the extent of damage to their property as well as anguish over their inability to communicate with family members, friends, and authorities to indicate their status and obtain updates on the extent of the devastation. Adding to the shock and anguish was the loss of life of close neighbors, family members, and friends. Tomi-Anne Collins explained how a disaster can trigger shock that can negatively affect one's ability to make good decisions about what to do next:

After the fire, I was in so much shock I didn't know what to do. I didn't know whether our house had been destroyed but I knew that we couldn't go back to St Andrews. I've never been a recipient of charity and felt very uncomfortable at the recovery centre; I didn't know what to do with myself.

Communication was also difficult because telephone service, both mobile and landline, was dysfunctional, and other means of communication with the outside world were difficult if not impossible to effect. Ed Cherry described his worry about his daughter's worry this way:

Shortly after we realised that we had lost the water tank, Diana called our daughter Sarah on the telephone but the call cut out just after Diana had told her that we were surrounded by fire and that we were running out of water (we couldn't communicate with anyone from that point onwards). Sarah must have been terribly worried during that time.

Fifth, there were inadequate human resources to fight ongoing fires, manage road closures, and attend to medical needs. This caused local residents great concern, as indicated by Graeme Brown:

What some people might call the "immediate aftermath" of Black Saturday went on and on for weeks. People had died or were missing, others like us had lost their homes, fires continued to burn, many services, including Victoria Police and the CFA, seemed overwhelmed, and everything was chaos.

Graeme's point is well illustrated by Samantha Siddle, who said:

It wasn't until nearly the end of that week that David had asked the driver of one of the CFA trucks to come to our home to put out a troublesome tree that had continued to burn. This was the first time since I had made my call to triple-zero that I had sighted a CFA truck on my property. Not one truck came to see if David needed any assistance or for that matter whether I [had] made it out of the house safely. Basically, we were simply overlooked. I am extremely disappointed that no-one responded to my call, especially given that after the initial fire was sent out on the pagers, my call was next in line but that didn't seem to make any difference whatsoever. About 10 or 12 days after the fire, I had to request the CFA to come out to my property again to put out a tree that had reignited. ... [This] experience tells me that if David or myself are not there to save our home, nobody else will.

Sixth, Black Saturday led to the loss of livestock, animal feed, fencing to contain animals, and other equipment critical to reducing additional losses. Pat Easterbrook described her feelings over the loss of livestock:

At some time on Sunday, Lindsay went across to a neighbouring farm belonging to a man in his 80s named Clarry. He went to see if there was anything that Clarry needed help with. Clarry had 43 cattle that needed to be shot and he wasn't coping well because he had never had to do anything like that. Lindsay, Clarry, and Danny, another neighbour, went and shot some of the cattle. We also had to shoot four of ours. The rest of our little herd had died immediately in the fire. The sound of the shots was just awful, especially as the rest of the valley was so quiet and looked like the end of the world had come.

The inability to contain livestock and provide animals with feed and water exacerbated the losses from the firestorm. Moreover, there was considerable uncertainty over the financing for the rebuilding of infrastructure, including fences, barns, and other structures critical to minimizing further losses. Robin McDonald explained that "one of the most difficult decisions after the fires was working out what to do with our herd. We had little for the cattle to eat and, with no fences, we had no way of keeping them in." Philip Szepe explained how potential solutions to this problem were largely thwarted:

The difficulties that we encountered with getting feed and fuel through the roadblocks were problems we faced every day. ... We eventually found that the best way to get through the roadblocks was to bypass the formal channels of control. ... Getting our supplies, for our farm, on and off the mountain became extremely frustrating. What I found most difficult to deal with in the aftermath of the bushfires were the restrictive and inflexible measures that were introduced by the government during the recovery process. Although we had the means and the resources to move forward, we were denied the ability to do so because of overly restrictive regulations and obstructions.

Seventh, local residents lost their income sources with the loss of business buildings, products, and customers owing to the area's devastation and faced both short-term (immediate livelihood) and long-term (retirement) economic setbacks. These economic losses created considerable financial uncertainty and anxiety. For example, Robin McDonald's ranching business faced devastation in the aftermath of the disaster:

We considered various options [for the business]. At a local meeting shortly after the fires, [the government] advised people that we would have to sell or slaughter our cattle. However, these were not viable options. Selling was not really available because after such a long drought and then the fires, no one had enough grass to feed their own cattle, let alone buying another herd of nearly 300. We couldn't bring ourselves to slaughter the cattle for a number of reasons. The farm is our livelihood and if we slaughtered the herd we would have no income. We have put many years into developing a quality breeding herd, selecting their genetics and spending thousands of dollars on getting good bulls and so on. Also, the female cattle were on the point of calving.

Finally, various combinations of eliminated resources, such as loss of a home plus loss of economic livelihood, caused distress, anxiety, confusion, and other emotions associated with the trauma, loss, injury, and hardships created by the fires. Both Joan Davey and another victim described the impact of the trauma on their health. Joan Davey said,

Late Sunday night I became ill because of the stress of being at the Whittlesea Relief Centre; seeing and hearing the trauma of the various stories of both survival and loss, grown men crying, and my family was still lost. I was transported to Epping Hospital by ambulance.

Another victim said,

[After the fires] it was like living under lockdown for three months—the area was declared a crime scene. Living in the destruction, often seeing body bags on the street. You would see guys in white suits—nothing was hidden. It was surreal. This was happening but it was hard to absorb. Nothing was covered up, it was all in your face. It was like living in a science fiction movie. Lives have changed forever. (Borrell, Vella, and Lane 2011: 64)

The Black Saturday bushfires disaster was one of the worst in Australia's history. It generated an array of losses that had far-reaching consequences for communities, organizations, and individuals. In digging beneath the statistics of loss, we see the complexity involved in various responses to the disaster and the considerable variety in how individuals experienced and responded to the crisis. This observation is acknowledged in prominent research on responses to crises (e.g., Bonanno 2004) and suggests overly generalized crisis responses should be avoided and more space provided for ad hoc solutions to an unfolding situation. Furthermore, even those experiencing a similar loss, such as the loss of a home, may respond differently, depending on a variety of factors (Bonanno et al. 2010). Therefore, effective attempts to alleviate suffering will likely be highly customized and informed by specific needs, which is why victims themselves are often the most capable of providing effective compassionate relief to fellow victims (Drabek and McEntire 2003).

Practical Implications

In this book we eschew the usual research caution of not extending beyond well-confirmed data to formulate opinions about crisis responses and describe some practical implications. We hope our research findings prove useful to community, organizational, and individual decision making, as well as to government policymakers. We want to start by discussing the "leave early or stay and defend" advice provided to residents in Australia in preparation for a bushfire.

The worst of all options is to leave the property late; however, in a disaster, it may be difficult to determine what is late because of breakdowns in communication and general uncertainty. In retrospect, we know what late looks like—people trapped in cars on impassable roads who are hit by a disaster that injures or kills them, for example. However, the disaster will likely unfold in an unpredictable manner, which makes it difficult to judge the right time to leave. Therefore, "early" should likely be the soonest individuals hear severe warnings of a potential disaster.

In light of the general uncertainty surrounding a disaster, including where it will strike and how severely, we suggest that the best option is to leave early. We are not sure why government policymakers and others are reluctant to focus on this as the best option—certainly better than the stay and defend option, which probably should be restated as the "stay and try to defend with the possibility of dying" option. We realize that this is a strong statement, but we also believe that the stay and defend option is deceptive because it assumes some sort of success despite the high uncertainty of the situation. That is, "defend" in this context refers not so much to the positive outcome of having success-fully defended one's house and property but to the process of defend-ing one's house and property, which may or may not have a positive outcome. To understand this future, individuals confronted with criti-cal decision making in a fire situation need to consider the payoff of the potential outcomes and the probability of each of these outcomes occurring (assuming specific actions are taken) to make an informed decision. There are four potential outcomes: (1) you leave early, and the house is not destroyed; (2) you leave early, and the house is destroyed; (3) you stay and defend and successfully save the house; and (4) you stay and defend but do not save the house, and there is additionally a high likelihood you will be severely injured or lose your life. The cost of the leave early strategy is the potential loss of one's house and other property. This is a significant outcome, exacting a financial and emotional toll on the family. However, the loss of prop-erty is a less severe consequence than the cost of being wrong when choosing the stay and defend strategy: in addition to a potential loss of property, defenders could lose their lives. Family and friends could lose loved ones, which would generate considerable grief, as well as economic hardship. The long-term losses to the community deprived of its members may well exceed the long-term losses associated with destroyed property.

Challenges with the Stay and Defend Decision-Making Process

If a person can guarantee with high certainty that he or she will be able to successfully defend the home, then defense might make sense. However, there are flaws in this decision-making process. First, a disas-ter situation cannot be known with certainty. How could a person possibly know the force and fury of a natural disaster? Disasters are unique and unpredictable, few people have experience with disasters, and the constellation of factors that contributes to a crisis event rarely repeats in exactly the same way. Thus there is considerable uncertainty about the defend strategy that has to do with the nature of the disaster itself.

Second, the stay and defend decision is exacerbated by overconfidence. Overconfidence and its corollary, a belief that success will follow if only we try hard enough, can be useful in certain circumstances but are detrimental when assessing strategies that have life-and-death consequences. In such a situation the individual is competing against nature. Natural forces can be so powerful that it is not humanly possible to defend against them. Individuals must recognize that humans have a tendency to overestimate their own capabilities and underestimate those of their opponents, which leads to flawed thinking.

Finally, people generally do not want to withdraw and leave because they interpret doing so as representing a lack of commitment to their family and community, as well as a sign of cowardice and unwillingness to fight for what is important. We think that the opposite is true. To one's family and community, the loss of a house is bad, but the loss of a family member is far worse. Houses can eventually be replaced; loved ones cannot. Rather than representing cowardice and weakness, then, leaving early is a courageous decision because it puts family well-being above personal ego. Again, personal ego and machoism can be highly beneficial in some instances, but in the context of a disaster, they could lead to a wrong decision, with devastating consequences.

Throughout this book, we suggest an alternative way to fight for the community that does not involve risking the high costs of a failed stay and *try* to defend strategy. While we will explore these alternatives in detail throughout the book, at this stage, we advise individuals in disaster zones to leave early as part of a strategic withdrawal, returning only when it is safe to do so and they are ready to bounce back into action to help alleviate victims' suffering and their devastated community. Although the rest of the book focuses on how spontaneous venturing can help alleviate suffering in the aftermath of a disaster, the purpose of this chapter was to highlight the suffering arising from the choice of fire strategy in an attempt to inform strategic decision making in the future to reduce the level of suffering caused by a natural disaster and thus reduce the demand for spontaneous venturing.

Our practical implications may be summarized as follows:

1. Disasters are often powerful, unique, and unpredictable.
2. Those facing a potential disaster should leave early.
3. Individuals should not try to defend in the face of a disaster.
4. Life is worth more than property.
5. People should not overestimate their abilities to succeed (which is tough to do).
6. People should not underestimate the (possible) strength of what they are defending against.
7. Leaving early as a temporary move is part of a sequential strategy in the aftermath of the disaster (a topic developed further in the book).

In the following chapters, we explore what we have learned from our research on individual and community responses to disasters as part of the sequential strategy response to disaster. In addition to the Black Saturday bushfires, we explore a disaster response in Haiti, a less developed country. By examining the disaster response in two different settings, we sought to understand how individuals might respond in a context in which disaster is an added stressor to an already very difficult environment for aid and self-aid.

2   Limitations of the Command-and-Control Disaster Response

Command and control systems are uniquely compromised in ... disasters because of the massive disruption of communications, transportation, and financial systems; the scarcity of resources; the inability to deploy first responders into the severe damage zone; and ethical dilemmas for triaging patients. ... [However, disaster experts] noted the command and control framework ... should be retained. It affords sufficient flexibility and adaptability to be used. The establishment of command and control starts with developing specific plans and policies ahead of time, ensuring clarity in roles and responsibilities, and planning for complex commands throughout the affected region. To facilitate the transfer of command and control ... to an outlying community, documents should be in place in advance of [a disaster].

—Davis, Reeve, and Altevogt (2013: 45)

In chapter 1, we highlighted the potential devastation disasters can cause and presented our recommendation that those in the path of an impending disaster should heed early warnings to leave. We also highlighted that heeding early warnings to leave is the first step in a strategic response to a disaster. However, before we offer new insights into disaster responses, it is important to review current knowledge and debates on the topic. To a large extent, knowledge of disaster responses is connected to the command-and-control system—the process by which an emergency manager exerts command and control over a disaster response and recovery operation. This chapter introduces the command-and-control system, explains how it works, and details its expected benefits. We then discuss differences of opinion on the effectiveness of this approach and review how other forms of organizing relate to command-and-control initiatives.

Command and Control

The government and other organizations dedicated to disaster response are typically managed by a command-and-control system. The command-and-control system dominates because the responsible government departments—such as the Department of Homeland Security, the National Guard, and so on—are often staffed by ex-military personnel (e.g., firefighters, police officers, and other first responders), especially in leadership positions (Marcum, Bevc, and Butts 2012). This command-and-control management system is based on a bureaucratic model that has four primary features (see Schneider 1992):

1. The command-and-control system requires clearly defined objectives, namely, preventing disasters from occurring in the first place, preparing communities for potential disasters, providing relief from the suffering caused by disasters, and facilitating recovery.
2. The command-and-control system requires a formal structure to coordinate the various actors under its umbrella. For example, a formal structure identifies roles and responsibilities for the local, state, and federal government bodies and a basis for centralized decision making. It provides stability to the organization's operations.
3. The command-and-control system requires a division of labor. Again, if we take the government response as an example, different levels of government have different responsibilities for disaster management. Local government is the first (of the government levels) to respond to the disaster, by linking victims to government resources (Rossi, Wright, and Weber-Burdin 1982). The state government is the linchpin between the local and federal governments (Mushkatel and Weschler 1985), and the federal government provides guidance, coordination, and resources to the lower levels of government.
If each level of government performs its duties and executes its responsibilities, then this division of labor (given clear objectives and formal structure) is expected to provide an efficient disaster response (Schneider 1992).
4. These policies and procedures provide direction on how each actor in the system can best carry out the tasks necessary for an effective response. These policies and procedures are eventually embedded in routines that can be quickly activated to provide speedy and efficient action consistent with the policies and procedures. "There is

considerable pressure on those within the system to abide by these standard routines" (Schneider 1992: 136).

A command-and-control system is reflected in the National Incident Management System (NIMS) in the United States for organizing in the aftermath of a disaster by coordinating the many different levels of government to ensure a unified approach that delivers an efficient and effective disaster response (Anderson, Compton, and Mason 2004). The idea is that this system provides a chain of command in which the upper levels make decisions that are passed "down the chain," based on information that has been passed "up the chain" from those closer to the field (Marcum, Bevc, and Butts 2012).

Despite its widespread use and a strong belief that it should work, there is considerable evidence that the command-and-control system has substantial limitations (Dynes 2003; Neal and Phillips 1995). Although proponents of the command-and-control system acknowledge instances of the system's ineffectiveness, they largely remain committed to it.

First, the command-and-control model assumes that "individuals and private organizations are often unable to cope with the stresses and strains of events like hurricanes, earthquakes, and floods. ... [Therefore] people turn naturally to government for assistance" (Schneider 1992: 135). Communities in the wake of a disaster are seen as helpless victims dependent on government assistance, especially when the disaster is widespread and an organized response requires collaboration. Waugh and Streib (2006) explain that after experiencing coordination problems in the early 1970s, disaster responders began implementing a command-and-control model. Waugh and Streib (2006: 134) note the following:

When events get larger and involve more participants, a unified command is created. Unified command usually means more sharing of information and coordination of effort, but participation in decision making is limited in large emergency response operations. There are practical limits to participation, particularly when quick decisions are needed, but there are also limits imposed by culture and convention. Noncollegial professions typically do not find open communication and participation comfortable. Public health professionals, for example, generally expect open discussion of issues before decisions.

As time has progressed, the "coordinative role ... in large intergovernmental, intersectoral, and multiorganizational" operations has become increasingly important in guiding the command-and-control approach to disaster response (Waugh and Streib 2006: 135).

Second, the command-and-control system assumes that for "the majority of disasters that occur in the US, the relief effort proceeds smoothly, and government operations are perceived to be successful" (Schneider 1992: 137). However, proponents of the command-and-control system acknowledge that while sometimes the response is not perceived to be effective, they argue that such a perception is largely based on the tendency of mass media to blame government for program failures rather than because "real" issues exist with the response (Schneider 2014).

Finally, over and above the media supposedly creating an inaccurate account of the command-and-control response, proponents of this system also attribute the perceived failures of disaster response to the human behavior of those in the disaster zone:

To the extent that disruptions occur they are expected to be temporary and manageable. It is believed that government officials have anticipated and prepared for all possible contingencies; standard operating procedures have been designed accordingly. The problem is that the public's response to any specific disaster is unpredictable. Some emergent norms are highly consistent with previously existing behavior patterns and routines (e.g., orderly evacuations, voluntary relief efforts, etc.). In such cases, the government response can work the way it was intended. In other situations, the emergent norms conflict with the usual social environments. This conflict may take many different forms, from vocal public dissatisfaction, to violence, and social unrest. This creates patterns of interaction that are unanticipated by the government response system. Hence, no specific contingencies exist for dealing with them. When this occurs the gap between governmental planning and human behavior is particularly wide, and the response process will probably be viewed as a failure. (Schneider 1992: 138)

Based on the assumptions that the mass media "almost always blame the government" (where the mass media reporting is believed to represent a simplistic, incomplete, and inaccurate view) and that human behavior in disaster zones is erratic, Schneider (1992: 143) reiterates the following:

Success and failure is almost entirely a matter of public perception than objective reality. Private Citizens cannot be expected to comprehend fully the difficulties and complexities involved in any recovery effort. At the same time, people are naturally absorbed with their own personal problems caused by the disaster. Consequently, individual citizens are likely to view anything short of immediate, direct, comprehensive help as failure. When one takes a broader perspective, virtually all of the governmental relief efforts are successful. Not surprisingly the [emphasis is on] ... the overriding importance of maintaining standard operating procedures and the pre-established division of labor. Departures from bureaucratic statutes and guidelines no matter how well intentioned inevitably have an adverse effect on the response process.

Hang On: Sometimes Perceptions Are Based on Reality, Not Irrationality

Up to this point, we have avoided criticizing the limitations of the command-and-control model. While we certainly acknowledge the importance of broad coordination of disaster mitigation, preparedness, and response from large institutions, it is equally important to state that disaster scenarios are difficult—if not impossible—to fully antici-pate and control (Drabek and McEntire 2003; Waugh and Streib 2006). The command-and-control approach dominates the rescue and recov-ery landscape, despite the evidence that it is ineffective in a natural disaster environment. We offer this book as a corrective to what we see as an imbalance in the literature on disaster recovery, in the hope that our perspective might bring attention to other means of responding beyond the typical command-and-control schema. However, we first want to explain the command-and-control system and the degree to which it is embedded in government and nongovernment organiza-tional responses to crises and to highlight the lengths to which its defenders will go to protect and perpetuate it. For these reasons, we have held back our perspective, which is the primary topic of this book.

In this part of the discussion, however, we take on some of the defenses of the command-and-control system and offer a different per-spective. The following accounts offer two simple examples of inef-fectual disaster response under the command-and-control system:

Example 1: In the Texas Hill Country response [1978 flash flood], for example, one county sheriff recounted the intense frustration he felt while standing outside his cruiser that was parked at a ravaging river bank. He had no way to communicate with a pilot in a helicopter that was hovering over a victim hidden from view by tree branches. A communication chain linked him to a dispatcher who, in turn, could reach a state agency that could relay messages to the federal military base that had radio contact with the pilot. This chain was activated minimally, however, when used episodically, these chains reflected the consequences of distortion typically found in such multi-person relays. (Drabek 1985: 88)

Example 2: [After the Black Saturday bushfire had passed] we sat out for 24 hours, no one came. ... I need medication for my cardiomyopathy and we really needed to be rescued. We didn't get rescued until the Arthurs Creek brigade Captain came with two response units on Sunday at about 5.30pm. ... Nobody could come through because it had been declared a crime scene and when the Captain came he said, "Nancy, who else is there? Where are you?," because they were used to just going in and seeing destruction, dead bodies mainly, at the end of each drive. He said "I'm overriding it completely [the rule precluding entry into the crime scene area] because I care more about the living than I am concerned about the dead at this time." So that was just absolutely mind boggling to me—to call it a crime scene and then close it off and leave people in there. We kept trying to make the point to the police that they would have more dead bodies if they didn't go in and get people out and he said he was being met with fairly rigid responses. (Geoffrey Mortimer)

As these accounts illustrate, disasters lead to widespread uncertainty, challenges, and nuanced needs that are nearly impossible to centrally manage. With these examples in mind, we return to our response to defenders of the command-and-control system.

First, a defense of the command-and-control system is that "when one takes a broader perspective virtually all of the government relief efforts are successful" (Schneider 1992: 142). With that logic, under what conditions could a command-and-control response to a disaster ever be considered inadequate or ineffective? Changing the criteria for effectiveness or making them so broad that they become meaningless is dangerous for those in harm's way and forestalls a deeper understanding of the disaster response process. It is important to think about the level of analysis when testing the effectiveness of any model, but that does not mean that other levels of analysis are not important. Therefore, it is important to keep sight of the fact that the outcome of a disaster response is highly consequential at the individual and community levels. Individual people are killed and physically and emotionally scarred, and communities also face physical, psychological, and emotional problems, many of which can be exacerbated rather than alleviated by a centralized, noncustomized response (Bonanno et al. 2010; Jensen and Waugh 2014). Furthermore, categorizing disaster response as a success rather than a failure dichotomizes a critically important outcome. Because of the consequential nature of the disaster response outcome, disaster responses are better characterized as falling on a curve from more successful to less successful, rather than evaluated according to a paradigm biased toward success. The use of a continuous variable for the assessment of disaster response effectiveness allows recognition that the response always has room for improvement, which in turn provides both motivation and information for learning. There is little to learn when a disaster response is categorized as a "success," especially in light of the dominant attribution error of assigning success to internal causes, such as the actor's thinking, capabilities, and actions (Jellison and Green 1981).

Second, the conclusion that most disaster responses are successes results in a doubling down on—or perhaps an increased commitment to—the existing command-and-control system. Moreover, such a conclusion rests on several assumptions that are not necessarily operative: that responders to a disaster actually use the command-and-control system; that those using the system all use it in the same way; that the system is effective regardless of the severity, speed of onset, or scope of a disaster; and that "to use the system will lead to the correction of common response shortcomings" (Jensen and Waugh 2014: 5). For example, Schneider (1992: 141) concludes that "departures from bureaucratic statuses and guidelines no matter how well intentioned, inevitably have an adverse effect on the response process." Maybe these deviations affect the "rational" process, but being enamored of the process means the outcome gets short shrift. If in the Texas Hill Country example above the sheriff had circumvented the formal chain of communication to somehow contact the helicopter pilot directly and rescued the drowning man and saved his life, this behavior might have resulted in a saved life that otherwise would have been lost. Perhaps circumventing the system or using the system in a different way than it was designed to be used may have led to other negative outcomes, but we cannot conclude that this process is an unambiguous success if a man dies. Contrary to what is argued from a command-and-control perspective, a well-intentioned departure from the schema may very well be the key to an effective disaster response. This position is reflected in the entrepreneurial actions of those local to the disaster zone, as we report throughout the book.

Third, because "individual citizens are likely to view anything short of immediate, direct, comprehensive help as failure" (Schneider 1992: 143), disaster response should be evaluated on the extent to which help is immediate, direct, and comprehensive. If the disaster response is slow, indirect, and insufficiently customized, then the implications can be more serious than simply criticism from the mass media: some people may die, and others may experience prolonged suffering. These losses are experienced at a personal level and are hugely consequential.

Any aggregation of outcomes to offer a broader perspective on disaster response should not lose sight of these hugely consequential outcomes at the individual level of analysis.

Fourth, to attribute the cause of bad outcomes to victims' "public dissatisfaction, to violence, and social unrest ... [that] creates patterns of interaction that are unanticipated" and obstruct the command-and-control process is likely to reflect rationalization through reverse causality. That is, rather than the collapse of sense-making obstructing a potentially effective process, it is likely the inefficacy of the process that leads to a collapse in sense-making (Weick 1993). Moreover, how effective can a control system be that is designed to help individuals facing a disaster if it is ill suited to dealing with the unanticipated human behavior triggered in those circumstances?

Fifth, proponents of the command-and-control schema require that the conditions in the aftermath of a disaster be largely known for the process to be effective at providing immediate relief and achieving long-term recovery. The assumptions of stability and relative certainty are critical for bureaucratic systems, which operate according to a series of complex rules, procedures, and routines (Brown and Eisenhardt 1997). However, conditions in the aftermath of a disaster, even if we exclude variances in human behavior, are rarely so orderly. In the aftermath of a natural disaster, the environment is highly uncertain, highly dynamic, and often highly complex (Aldrich 2012; Shepherd and Williams 2014; Williams and Shepherd 2016a). In fact, the most common definitions of a crisis describe it as unanticipated, infrequent, and novel (Pearson and Clair 1998; Williams et al. 2017), which suggests it is difficult to completely prepare or plan for such an event.

In such highly uncertain, dynamic, and complex environments, we expect that organizations that are bureaucratic—that is, those with clearly defined objectives, formal structures, divisions of labor, and sets of policies and procedures—will fail to adapt (Brown and Eisenhardt 1997). In a rare admission of the limitations of the command-and-control system, its proponents nonetheless still seem committed to the system, even though such commitments do not appear to address the fundamental issue. Specifically, Schneider (1992: 143) has stated the following:

Finally, it may also be necessary to change certain aspects of the bureaucratic structure itself; it may be useful to develop special standard operating procedures that are to be used in unusually severe disaster situations. In such cases, the federal government should take an earlier and more commanding role in the response effort.

However, the critical lifesaving questions relate to what these special standard operating procedures actually are: what is their content, where did they come from, how do they work, and why does the system fail to operationalize them? From this admission of the fallibility of the command-and-control system, we might be getting somewhere—at least a hint of the benefits of a dynamic capability, which itself is a step away from command and control.

Finally, to assume that "people are naturally absorbed with their own personal problems caused by the disaster" leads to the conclusion that "individuals and private organizations are often unable to cope with the stress and strains of events like hurricanes, earthquakes, and floods [such that] people turn naturally to government for assistance" (Schneider 1992: 143). However, there is ample evidence that this assumption is false (see Drabek and McEntire 2003 for a review). Many people are resilient in the face of potentially traumatic events (Bonanno et al. 2006, 2007), and, as we explain throughout the book, victims are well positioned and strongly motivated to help others who are also suffering. Therefore the assumption of victims' self-interested behavior runs counter to substantial evidence that people are not helpless, are prosocially motivated, and do act to help others (Comfort 2007; Drabek and McEntire 2003; Shepherd and Williams 2014; Williams and Shepherd 2016a, 2016b). Indeed, Comfort (2007: 191) noted that "there were extraordinary acts of courage and generosity by individuals and groups during this massive event [Hurricane Katrina in 2005], but the capacity to harness those individual actions into a coherent response and recovery was missing."

In sum, despite the long-held faith in the command-and-control system, its widespread use, and attempts by proponents to dismiss its limitations, there is considerable evidence of its ineffectiveness (Anderson, Compton, and Mason, 2004; Comfort 2007; Dynes 2003; Marcum, Bevc, and Butts 2012; Neal and Phillips 1995; Takeda and Helms 2006a, 2006b). Furthermore, the world is quite different than it was in the early 1970s when the command-and-control system was developed. Disaster responses now involve

myriad organizations of multiple types with a range of individuals within them responding to different hazards, operating in different geographic areas, with different values, cultures, priorities, and resources in situations where emergent groups and volunteers will likely emerge and converge to render assistance. ... [Disaster] response is a complex issue that defies easy, blanket solutions; and, important policy and program decisions ... ought not to be made within closed management systems. (Jensen and Waugh 2014: 14)

Indeed, after analyzing the use of command-and-control schemas in the disaster response to both the 2004 Indian Ocean tsunami and New Orleans after the 2005 Hurricane Katrina, Takeda and Helms (2006b) concluded that "the very nature of a catastrophe requires a very different management mindset" than that offered by the command-and-control system.

Detailed Limitations of the Command-and-Control Response

In a study of six major disasters over a two-year span, Drabek (1985) found four consistent problems with the command-and-control system for disaster response. The first relates to localism. Not surprisingly, the first to respond to a disaster are those closest to the disaster zone. However, owing to the heterogeneity of the responding local residents and the complexity and uncertainty of the situation, there is a lack of standardization. The combination of heterogeneity and lack of standardization leads to fragmentation—schisms and disjunctures—in the command-and-control system.

Second, disasters create substantial obstacles to communication, especially across agencies, which severely hampers the transmittal of information up and down the chain of command. These communication problems are caused by the large volume of diverse and largely unrefined information and the limited information-processing capacity available to make sense of this input. For the same reason, little information is able to go down the chain from the top (Drabek 1984) and out to those outside the immediate system, including victims. For example, as people input information into the command-and-control system, they generally request certain information in return, yet the system is often unable to comply with these requests because it becomes overwhelmed. This has the effect of slowing the disaster response (Takeda and Helms 2006b). Moreover, the disaster itself can directly affect physical and social structures (Marcum, Bevc, and Butts 2012; Takeda and Helms 2006b), which further exacerbates problems of communication and coordination—the critical elements of a command-and-control system.

Third, even data that are processed are unlikely to "fit with [the] current paradigms [because of the uniqueness of each disaster, thus] providing data the system has not addressed before" (Takeda and Helms 2006b: 400), and without a mechanism to change (e.g., people are told to follow the standard operating procedures [Schneider 1992]), a disconnect develops between what response is needed and what is delivered (Jensen and Waugh 2014).

Fourth, in light of the complexity and uncertainty surrounding the situation in the aftermath of a disaster and the impossibility of the system "knowing all," collecting, assimilating, and acting on information from outside the command-and-control system become critical for an effective disaster response. However, the command-and-control system tends to ignore relevant outside information (Takeda and Helms 2006b), especially in the immediate disaster response, when that information would be most useful. It seems that by acquiring a deep understanding of plans and the overall system, people develop a strong belief in the viability of these plans and assumptions, which is consistent with the planning fallacy (Buehler, Griffin, and Ross 1994; Kahneman and Lovallo 1993). Indeed, building on evidence from Hurricane Katrina, Takeda and Helms (2006b: 404) found that not only were those who were part of the command-and-control system "reluctant to analyze outside information, but [they also had a] disdain for accepting assistance from actors outside of the system and an aversion to using activities which are not already part of the system even when critical to saving lives." Such individuals fail to learn about the conditions on the ground, or their learning is substantially obstructed because they ignore or discount relevant information generated from outside the system.

Finally, in an environment of high uncertainty, it is likely that some actions will fail to proceed as anticipated or will not deliver expected results, but so long as these actions lead to learning, which in turn can inform subsequent actions, progress can be made toward a more effective disaster response. However, the rational perspective underlying the command-and-control system leads to the strong belief that it represents the optimal response and requires that those in the system persist with its standard operating procedures (e.g., Schneider 1992). Indeed, those within the command-and-control system have a strong loyalty toward the way things should be done and band together to commit to the system. However, when the command-and-control system is not providing an effective disaster response, it appears that those in the system double down—they escalate their commitment to a losing course of action (Takeda and Helms 2006b)—which can have a devastating impact on those in the disaster zone.

In our own analysis of the Black Saturday bushfires in Victoria, Australia, and the 2010 Haiti earthquake and tsunami swarm, we found evidence that the command-and-control system does not provide a path to clear success in responding to disaster. Although we highlight limitations with the command-and-control system, we laud the motives and abilities of those working in the system: we have a great deal of respect for those who work in dedicated disaster response organizations. However, the command-and-control system is not a panacea for disaster response shortcomings. Though it can do some things well, the command-and-control approach often stumbles when it comes to the rapid delivery of customized solutions to local suffering. Thus it is important to look at other means of disaster response that might be more effective than and complement what the command-and-control system is good at, the accumulation of compassionate responses that are broad in scope and large in scale. By compassion we refer to "(1) noticing or attending to another's suffering, (2) feelings that are other-regarding and resemble empathic concern, and (3) responses aimed at easing the suffering" (Lilius, Worline, et al. 2011: 874; see also Clark 1997; Dutton et al. 2006). We return to other options later. First we look again at the Black Saturday disaster to further explore the limitations to outsiders' compassionate responses in a command-and-control situation and the ways in which those limitations contributed to persistent suffering in the aftermath of the disaster.

Obstacles to Nonlocal Delivery of Compassionate Resources in Command and Control

After the Black Saturday fires devastated local resources, a major dilemma emerged: how to organize to enable *the speedy delivery* of resources in the form of *customized products and services* that would alleviate victims' suffering. Several victims mentioned that outsiders who were trying to help after the disaster were often "lost in the local environment" (Doug Walter), did not know who needed help or from whom to get information (Michelle Buntine), and sometimes offered resources or assistance that, while appreciated, did not address victims' current needs (Graeme Brown; see also Austin 2009; Kissane 2009; Mann 2009).

Obstacles to Speedy Delivery of Compassionate Resources in Command and Control

Speed of delivery entails the "timely availability and delivery of resources to those who are suffering" (Dutton et al. 2006: 72). The speedy delivery of compassionate resources after a disaster is imperative to alleviate individuals' current suffering, lessen the chance of additional suffering, and help individuals begin the recovery process. In the case of the Black Saturday bushfires, our analyses revealed several issues obstructing the speedy delivery of nonlocal compassionate resources to victims.

First, outsiders had difficulty navigating the local social and physical environments as a result of their inability to identify legitimate local leadership groups, thus delaying the delivery of goods. For instance, as Caldwell (2009) noted in a news article,

There are issues because there are the two systems [local and nonlocal]. If you bring vehicles from the metropolitan area up into a fire zone, and they don't have the rural communications, they can't communicate with the police communications area facility out at Wangaratta [the local fire area].

Similarly, in a report describing what transpired after Black Saturday, the Boston Consulting Group (2009) stated that nonlocal responders "have far too often delayed recovery, strained local morale, and wasted opportunities for developing local initiatives, by a reluctance and tardiness to engage with locals via its [impromptu] leadership group. [Outside resource providers] were puzzlingly slow to become engaged with the local community." Likewise, several informants (e.g., Graeme Brown, Lachlan Fraser, Doug Walter) attributed outsiders' reluctance to recognize local groups (thus contributing to their lack of speed) to "power and politics" issues as external providers were averse to surrendering decision-making authority to local responders out of fear of losing power and control.

Second, a speedy compassionate response was also delayed by individuals' excessive adherence to existing bureaucratic processes, and specifically their inability to formulate and rapidly implement innovative solutions to address critical needs. Several victims (e.g., Rhonda Abotomey, Graeme Brown, Philip Szepe, Ann Leadbeater) were frustrated by outside responders' (particularly government entities') overdependence on complex procedures in an almost entirely novel situation that demanded new and creative solutions to mount a quick response to individuals' needs (Austin 2009; Kissane 2009; Mann 2009). One local resident, Graeme Brown, noted the following:

The key problem with the recovery effort ... appears to be that many of the people trying to help us are not able to work in a flexible way. ... It seems as though the rest of the world is being normal and that it has a conventional way of doing things—people are trying to use those conventional means to address an unconventional set of circumstances. It's as though nothing can be done to help us unless the bureaucratic system has the appropriate method or policy in place.

That is, nonlocal responders followed complex rules and regulations rather than enacting simpler rules that would provide flexible yet rational opportunity capture (see Bingham and Eisenhardt 2011; Eisenhardt and Sull 2001). Indeed, local residents expressed frustration with the rigidity of the command-and-control system. As Philip Szepe explained:

Most difficult to deal with in the aftermath of the bushfires were the restrictive and inflexible measures by the government during the recovery process. Although we had the means [human workforce] and the [logistical] resources to move forward, we were denied the ability to do so because of overly restrictive regulations and obstructions.

Local residents believed that both the plan itself and the execution of the plan were faulty:

The Government's emergency response plan was unclear about which authorities had responsibility for issuing warnings and advising people to evacuate. And anyway, the commissioners report that the plan was not followed. (Austin 2009)

Finally, the delivery of outside resources was impeded by damaged and broken infrastructure. The fires had destroyed buildings, disabled communication infrastructure, and blocked roads, creating significant obstacles both to communication between local and nonlocal people and to transportation (i.e., relief delivery mechanisms). As a result, local residents' and responders' requests for resources were frequently outdated when received by responders acting within the command-and-control system (Teague, McLeod, and Pascoe 2010), and efforts to deliver resources were often obstructed by roadblocks, crime scene investigations, and the like, leading to delayed and often incorrect resource deliveries.

For example, Penny Jewell explained that roadblocks were set up, blocking access to certain escape routes. She reported, "We had the radio and television on, but the information wasn't focusing on the [fire affecting our immediate area]. We were having trouble getting local information, and I think a lot of the information that was coming through wasn't accurate." Similarly, Joan Davey explained that for many homes in her area, there was only single-road access. This made it very difficult when those roads were shut down and all means of accessing accurate and reliable information were lost. Another witness, Vicki Ruhr, explained her experience this way:

> I got out of my car [at a roadblock]. … I asked [the people at the block] if they knew what was going on. Everyone looked a little stunned and they shook their heads. … I began asking questions whilst pulling out my mobile phone so that I could call triple zero [emergency response; same as 911 in the United States]. The call did not get through. I was surprised by that and I then became quite worried after I only heard a recorded message. The message said something about "currently experiencing a large number of calls" with an instruction to "call back later." After that failed phone call, I remember noticing that the weather was deteriorating: the wind was increasing and there was a large amount of debris and dust blowing in the air. … [I found Mr. Hendrie, the fire captain]. Mr Hendrie was very pale, and he had beads of sweat running down his face. His eyes were wide and he appeared quite terrified. He did not speak directly to me or any of the other residents but I clearly remember thinking that if our [fire] Captain looked like that, then something really, really bad must have been happening. I thought that he was displaying signs of shock, and he was obviously having difficulty keeping himself together. My instincts told me I wouldn't get any helpful information from him.

Obstacles to Customization of Nonlocal Compassionate Responses in Command and Control

Customization is the "efficient patterning and shaping of resources to meet the particular needs of those who are suffering" (Dutton et al. 2006: 73). In the disaster context, customization refers to delivering appropriate items in the correct quantity and at the right time. Several local residents described how needs for food and shelter, equipment, insurance and legal support, and many other forms of assistance evolved on an almost daily basis, and how suffering would go unattended unless responders were able to alter their actions fluidly in response to changing needs. As an example, Graham Linklater initially requested help with fencing, which was a critical need as he had no means to contain his livestock. After receiving no response, he organized fencing himself. Four months after he fixed the fences, supplies did arrive, leading Linklater to say, "We did have to foot the bill ourselves for rebuilding the fences … [but] on the bright side though, I have enough material for ordinary fence maintenance for the next 10 years."

Therefore, despite the availability of resources from nonlocal people and agencies, substantial barriers prevented those resources from reaching victims to alleviate their suffering and render timely aid. Because of these barriers, many donated items were wasted:

Hundreds of thousands of dollars' worth of clothes, toys, whitegoods and furniture, donated for bushfire victims after Black Saturday languish[ed] in a disused dairy nearly two months on because a bureaucratic hold-up means there's no place from which to distribute them. ... It's been a bloody nightmare. I don't blame the individuals, it's just the system. It is so frustrating when you want to do something to help on the ground, you are blocked at every turn. (Doherty 2009b)

Tons of other items, such as food and clothing, rotted or were destroyed in storage as a result of lack of protection from the elements and rodent infestations, while still other donations simply sat unused because they did not match victims' needs, including hundreds of donated blankets (Wilkinson 2009).

We found three primary obstacles to customization that caused waste and failure to alleviate suffering. First, there was often a mis-match between what nonlocal people and agencies gave and what local residents needed. For example, Graeme Brown explained that what the town really needed was "white goods," such as refrigerators and microwaves, but all he received was an abundance of blankets, which he did not need (Wilkinson 2009). People who needed financial advice were offered counseling:

We had a case manager come to talk to us and she said: "You just don't fit in anywhere [in the relief system]. You're going to go broke." And we said, "Thanks very much!" And she said, "We can offer you counseling [for going broke]!" (Marilyn Mason, cited in Kissane 2009)

Second, there was a lack of appropriate local logistical knowledge. Graeme Linklater shared this belief:

Local knowledge and local resources were not utilised as well as they should have been to fight [ongoing] fires. For example, we have milk tankers that can hold 28,000 or 40,000 litres of water which could have been deployed to safe areas and used to fill the fire trucks. This would have allowed the fire trucks to fill up more quickly and ensure that water got to where it was needed.

Graeme Brown reinforced the notion that the nonlocal approach to distributing resources was not customized to the situation victims faced and thus worsened their suffering. He reported, "We don't want to sound ungrateful ... but when we needed it [goods, food, aid] after losing absolutely everything, things were still being organized. And to get down to Melbourne was just one more hurdle we couldn't face" (Wilkinson 2009).

Finally, nonlocal solutions derived from a command-and-control construct did not adequately consider the area's specific conditions as outsiders lacked even a general understanding of the local geography and the implications it had for delivering resources. Robin McDonald explained, for instance, that outside responses were "managed from a distance, and local information and local knowledge often seem[ed] to be disregarded." Other local residents reported that their towns were simply "forgotten" as nonlocals did not even know of some towns' existence, let alone their specific needs (e.g., Graeme Brown, Jim Kennedy; Ross 2009). For example, it was reported that "when someone [a local resident] struck out for Healesville to ask when the relief effort might reach their town, they were told [by authorities], 'But there's nobody in Narbethong'"—a place where 150 people were struggling to survive (Doherty 2009b). Because of outsiders' lack of local geographic knowledge, those needing aid felt that nonlocal responders failed to effectively meet their urgent needs after the fires (Marr 2009; see also Austin 2009; Kissane 2009; Mann 2009).

Moreover, not only was there evidence of the limitations of the command-and-control system to deliver needed resources to victims of the disaster, but in some instances the command-and-control system created obstacles to victims helping themselves. Graeme Brown recounted a number of stories

of local people offering their help and being turned away or ignored. For example, when roads and tracks needed to be cleared of trees and debris, local people I know from the forestry industry offered their time, expertise and equipment to do the job [but were turned away]. ... These local people know that country like the backs of their hands, knew how to clear timber and who had the specialist equipment that was needed.

After identifying the limitations of the command-and-control system, we came to a similar conclusion as did Takeda and Helms (2006b: 405), who, after analyzing the command-and-control response to the tsunami in 2004 and Hurricane Katrina in 2005, concluded that "the very nature of a catastrophe requires a very different management mindset."

Based on the above, we—along with others—conclude that the command-and-control system is not the solution to all the challenges

of alleviating postdisaster suffering and that a different mental disposition is required for thinking about disaster response. A hint about what
that disposition should involve can be seen the actions taken in the
voids created by the ineffectual responses of the command-and-control
system. We start with the recognition that in the hours following a
disaster, there is a "complex array of organizational demands that
constitute[s] a unique managerial problem" (Drabek 1985: 85): there is
high uncertainty as the aftermath reveals problems and issues that
were unexpected—and perhaps largely inconceivable prior to the
disaster. Things are no longer normal: they deviate substantially from
routine patterns of events and interactions, thus making current routines ill suited. How does one deal with the unexpected and the
unpredictable?

Beyond Command and Control: Self-Organizing Emergent Response Groups

An effective disaster response needs to be flexible in responding to a
dynamic, complex, and uncertain environment. This flexibility in disaster response can take a number of different forms.

Recognition of the novelty of the situation and the lack of fit to existing plans, structures, and routines often results in the formulation of
new responses to reflect the changing environment (Marcum, Bevc, and
Butts 2012; Mendonca, Beroggi, and Wallace 2001; Webb 2004). New
response structures developed after the fact have been referred to as
ad hoc control structures. These ad hoc structures are a "form of collective improvisation in which simultaneous adjustments by multiple
actors within a heterogeneous environment converge to a solution that
is beyond the capability of any one action to completely anticipate or
determine" (Marcum, Bevc, and Butts 2012: 519).

Because the environment in the aftermath of a disaster is highly
dynamic, the disaster response also needs to be fluid with respect
to decision making, establishing priorities, developing innovative
response structures, and designing processes (Takeda and Helms 2006a,
2006b). Improvising (Shepherd and Williams 2014; Wachtendorf 2004),
self-organizing (Comfort 1985), and boundary spanning (Mulford 1984;
Uhr, Johansson, and Fredholm 2008) are all important characteristics of
a fluid response.

The novelty of the situation, the dynamical environment, and the
need to respond urgently to victims' needs mean that ad hoc emergent

response groups tend to form (Drabek and McEntire 2003; Kreps and Bosworth 1993; McEntire 2007; Quarantelli 1988, 1996; Uhr, Johansson, and Fredholm 2008). Emergent response groups are impromptu teams that come into existence to provide relief in the aftermath of a disaster; that is, they are groups with "no pre-existing structures such as group membership, tasks, roles or expertise that can be specified ex ante" (Majchrzak, Jarvenpaa, and Hollingshead 2007: 147; see also Drabek and McEntire 2003; Tierney, Lindell, and Perry 2001; Tierney and Trainor 2004). These groups are characterized by a sense of urgency, which provides motivation to act quickly to help victims of the disaster. In addition, emergent response groups are characterized by constantly changing task definitions and task assignments, multiple (and some-times conflicting) purposes, and the use of nonroutine resources, arrangements, and capabilities (Bigley and Roberts 2001; Drabek and McEntire 2003; Tierney, Lindell, and Perry 2001), and they typically operate "outside formal authority, structures and response plans" (Maj-chrzak, Jarvenpaa, and Hollingshead 2007: 150). Their members often do not know each other at the time of group formation (and may not interact after the disaster response) and the group is heterogeneous with respect to the skills, knowledge, and motivation of the members. Also, because of the element of high volition or volunteership, group membership is often fleeting; indeed, these groups are sometimes described as "swarms" (Majchrzak, Jarvenpaa, and Hollingshead. 2007). These attributes of emergent response groups provide the flex-ibility, tools, and resources to adapt in ways that enable them to help victims in the chaos created by a disaster. They learn, innovate, and adapt and thus are highly effective at disaster response. Indeed, Maj-chrzak, and colleagues (2007: 180) make the following important obser-vation about these groups:

Whereas emergency response groups were initially viewed by federal agencies as an aberration that needed to be stopped, recent disaster research concludes that such groups are not aberrations at all, but can be observed in all large-scale disasters; that emergent behavior cannot be stopped; and the emergent activity fills a void that cannot be filled by command and control approaches to disaster response.

After scrutinizing the importance of disaster response, the limita-tions of the command-and-control system, and the existence of ad hoc, self-organizing emergent response groups, we decided to gain a deeper understanding of disaster response by examining the response behav-iors of such groups. The rest of this book describes our journey, the insights generated by the journey, and the implications these insights have for practitioners and scholars.

Practical Implications of Response Choice

The command-and-control system breaks down in the very environment in which is it meant to operate. Why does disaster management rely so much on the command-and-control system? Because it is what people know and what they can control. However, as we highlighted in this chapter, there is a host of reasons why disaster responses should not rely on command and control. Indeed, relying on the command-and-control system for a disaster response can represent commitment to a losing course of action that can potentially do more harm than good. A command-and-control schema should be used for what it is good at, such as efficient operations in a stable, predictable environment, which is more often the case for aspects of disaster response that occur at some distance from the disaster site rather than on-site. However, a command-and-control system should not be relied on for mounting an effective response in the uncertain aftermath of a disaster, and when the system fails to achieve an effective disaster response, those who are part of the system should not be judged negatively. In that case it is the system, not the people working in it, that is flawed.

An effective response is far more organic than an established command-and-control structure. Response groups may spontaneously emerge and improvise to find solutions to unanticipated problems that arise in the uncertainty of a disaster's aftermath. It is easier to talk of implications when individuals assume they know what they are dealing with, namely, a certain or predictable environment, which is not typical of a disaster. Individuals need to free themselves and others of the shackles of command and control and of previous routines, affiliations, and expectations so that everyone is prepared to "go with the flow."

Go with the flow when people's lives are at stake? This approach is difficult to imagine but can be critical. By going with the flow, we mean engaging fully in the present as it unfolds dynamically, addressing problems as they arise, making use of the resources at hand in novel combinations, forming teams and relationships with others engaged in related activities or on the scene, thinking creatively, and improvising, which fuses design and action. This approach will likely entail ignoring or even working counter to the command-and-control system. Even as we recognize that the command-and-control model can handle well some important tasks that require order, it is also important to realize that people will break rules to help others. Insofar as rules are created for known situations, but there is considerable uncertainty in the aftermath of a disaster, it is reasonable to assess current action according to present conditions, whether or not that approach follows rules, to help others.

Following are some guidelines for those who participate in the command-and-control system of disaster response:

1. Do not assume people will follow rules because in many instances they will not follow the rules as they seek to address immediate needs.
2. Give people flexibility in how they respond and adapt.
3. Apply command-and-control techniques differentially: use them in some instances and for some tasks but not for others (which is antithetical to the system).
4. Do not assume that the system is right and people are fallible. It is most likely the other way around.
5. Work in a supporting role, not a controlling or constraining role, with response groups that emerge ad hoc around a disaster: facilitate their creation, give them freedom to operate, and provide them with the resources they ask for.
6. Do not be concerned with how to justify decisions to support such ad hoc emergent response groups or how you will be evaluated in the future by people with 20/20 hindsight.
7. Do not consider deviating from the command-and-control model to be wrong. Indeed, lack of deviation is likely to be a surer indication of an ineffective response.
8. When assessing responding organizations, consider the uncertainty in their decisions and actions in the context of the moment in which they occurred, rather than the certainty that magically appears after the fact.
9. Recognize that errors will inevitably occur, and that there are errors of omission and errors of commission. What are the errors of acting versus not acting, respectively? More specifically, what are the errors from flexibly responding versus the errors from following the command-and-control system?
10. Have faith in the emergent potential of individual knowledgeable actors. None of the decisions in the aftermath of a disaster are easy, especially because of the uncertainty that swaths a dynamic situation. Faith that people will do their best under trying circumstances, that

local residents will spontaneously form response teams, and that local residents are highly motivated and capable of helping others (and not focused on self-interest) afford the flexibility needed to mount an effective response. Having faith involves taking a risk and is not easily defended after the fact, but mustering the courage to do so is likely to lead to the sort of effective emergent response needed in the aftermath of a disaster.

3 Spontaneous Venturing to Organize Compassion in the Aftermath of a Disaster

On Black Saturday there were three towns that were absolutely smashed. Kinglake, Marysville and Flowerdale. Two hundred and twenty-four homes were lost in Flowerdale. Thirteen people died. [I'm here to tell you] about a community [member] who said "we've got a problem and we've got to solve it ourselves." What frustrates me in life ... is that as soon as something goes wrong, [people say,] "they've got to fix it. ..." We've got to own our outcomes and when something's important to us, we've got to do something about it because when there is no "they," you are the "they." We are the "they." We've got to say, "What are we going to do about this?," because when you're faced with that and that's what's left of your town, and there's no one else. ... In Flowerdale, there was no "they." There was no one else. It was just the locals.

—Responder to Black Saturday bushfires (quoted in Williams 2010)

Many events can lead to human suffering. Natural disasters, though they often surprise those affected, occur somewhere in the world on a regular basis, often leading to suffering for many. For example, the 2011 annual report of the International Federation of Red Cross and Red Crescent Societies reported 406 natural disasters (excluding wars, conflict-related famines, technological disasters, diseases, and epidemics) worldwide in 2010 alone (Armstrong et al. 2011). All told, these natural disasters generated more than $123 billion in damages, killed over 300 million people, and displaced or otherwise negatively affected an additional 300 million people. Although 2010 was an outlier with respect to the number of people affected, these devastating events consistently cause substantial suffering (Armstrong et al. 2011).[1]

Apart from the direct damage caused by a disaster, additional problems often stem from the organizational response to the emergency (Dynes 1974). There are well-known examples of established organizations failing to effectively help disaster victims. In 2005 the U.S. Federal Emergency Management Agency (FEMA) and other government agencies mounted an ineffective response to Hurricane Katrina (Sobel and Leeson 2006), nongovernmental organizations (NGOs) delayed in helping victims of the 2010 Haiti earthquake (Zanotti 2010), and various international organizations, including the United Nations, have stumbled in attempts to effectively address disasters, including the 2008 Nargis cyclone in Myanmar and the 2008 earthquake in Sichuan province, China (Kapucu 2011). The evidence suggests that established disaster response organizations are not sufficiently effective at quickly alleviating the suffering of all disaster victims (e.g., Schneider 1992; Van Wart and Kapucu 2011; Zanotti 2010).

Though organizational theory scholars studying this phenomenon usually begin with the existence of an organization, then turn to theorizing about the extent (and mechanisms) of alleviating suffering, focusing instead on the exercise of compassion to alleviate suffering suggests that other approaches to disaster response are available. Compassion may be conceptualized as "(1) noticing or attending to another's suffering, (2) feelings that are other-regarding and resemble empathic concern, and (3) responses aimed at easing the suffering" (Lilius, Worline, et al. 2011: 874; see also Clark 1997; Dutton et al. 2006). To successfully address the needs of the suffering in a disaster response scenario, compassion needs to be organized to "extract, generate, and coordinate resources—e.g., social support, food, shelter—but [also to] ... calibrat[e] the response to individuals' unique needs" (Dutton et al. 2006: 61). Even here, some organizations are able and inclined to harness their normal structures in response to members' pain (Dutton et al. 2006), whereas others are less able or less inclined to do so (Delbecq 2010; Hazen 2003, 2008; Kanov et al. 2004). But what happens when established organizations' ability to obtain, create, and organize resources is itself significantly weakened?

The literature on disaster response shows that the effectiveness of established organizations' responses to a disaster is often limited and that entrepreneurial disaster response groups appear to emerge and provide responses when established organizations do not or cannot (see Drabek 1986; Drabek and McEntire 2003; Stallings and Quarantelli 1985; see also chapter 2). By exploring the relatively uncharted world of new ventures that come into existence to alleviate victim suffering after natural disasters, we hope to improve compassion organizing processes to lessen suffering after natural disasters.

Drawing on our earlier research (Shepherd and Williams 2014), in this chapter we sketch out a theory of organizing compassion through spontaneous venturing—that is, the spontaneous creation of new ventures—in response to a disaster. Here the difference between volunteering and entrepreneurial venturing should be noted. Volunteering involves offering one's services free of charge to an entity, a venture or a firm, that organizes a response. Entrepreneurial venturing entails the organizing of resources, including volunteers, to pursue a potential opportunity, which in this case is the opportunity to alleviate suffering in the aftermath of a natural disaster. By combining evidence from the disaster response to the Black Saturday bushfires with theories of compassion, organizing, and motivation, we hope to generate insights into how organizing through spontaneous venturing can alleviate suffering. By *spontaneous venturing*, we mean the rapid emergence of a de novo or de alio new venture. In the context of a natural disaster for which outside resources are abundant yet established organizations are insufficiently effective at organizing compassion, spontaneous venturing is an effective means of customizing abundant resources, that is, customizing the large scale and scope of resources provided from sources unaffected by the natural disaster and delivering those resources quickly to alleviate suffering. This form of compassion organizing is effective because it is quick and highly customized to victims' needs.

This sketch of a theory suggests three new insights.

First, while aid organizations such as the Red Cross already exist to alleviate individuals' suffering, and some are able to adapt their standard structures and routines to help during disasters, there are still times when these organizations are unable to fully alleviate suffering using their normal structures and routines. At such times the primary source of compassionate response resources to alleviate suffering (Frost et al. 2006) may come from outside the disaster area in the form of entrepreneurial ventures. Looking at such alternative approaches enables us to explore individuals' suffering (and the alleviation thereof) beyond prevailing organizational boundaries, specifically the ways in which local individuals who are affected by the disaster facilitate compassion organizing to meet community members' needs. Furthermore, while the extant research on compassion has highlighted how those who are more fortunate often provide resources to those who are less fortunate (Dutton et al. 2006; Lilius, Kanov, et al. 2011), we investigate a self-organizing aspect to compassion—that is, when locals who are themselves suffering organize compassion to meet community members' as well as their own postdisaster needs.

Second, victims' suffering can serve as a signal for entrepreneurial opportunity, as the prompt for the prosocial motivation of spontaneous entrepreneurs, and as an expression of the empathy of the broader community, which becomes a source of resources. Though the formation of temporary groups has been studied in a variety of contexts, including filmmaking (Bechky 2006; Goodman and Goodman 1976), firefighting (Bigley and Roberts 2001; Weick 1993; Weick and Roberts 1993), and education (Miles 1964, 1977), and though this literature has highlighted the value of temporary organizations (Bigley and Roberts 2001; Faulkner and Anderson 1987) and the ways knowledge (Hale, Dulek, and Hale 2005; Majchrzak, Jarvenpaa, and Hollingshead 2007) and actions (Bechky 2006) are coordinated within these temporary organizations, there is only a limited understanding of the emotions that motivate such ventures' creation and termination. We investigate the compassionate creation of temporary organizations by exploring victims' suffering as the signal of an entrepreneurial opportunity, the prosocial motivation of spontaneous entrepreneurs, and the empathy of the broader community as a source of resources.

The third insight is that unlike many new ventures, which are most interested in achieving economic profits (Barney 1991; Shane and Venkataraman 2000), the entrepreneurial process for organizing altruistic resources to deliver products and services to alleviate suffering from a natural disaster has economic sustainability as a utilitarian need, not a goal: the ventures must be sustainable to continue to deliver the noneconomic benefits (Bansal 2005; Patzelt and Shepherd 2011). Even though these organizations are a critical mechanism for alleviating suffering and the claim that the creation of new ventures is a central issue for the field of entrepreneurship research (Gartner 1985), organization and entrepreneurship scholars have not sufficiently explored the spontaneous creation of new ventures.

These three insights—spontaneous entrepreneurial aid may come from ad hoc, informal groups outside a disaster area, victims' suffering may prompt such an entrepreneurial compassionate response, and entrepreneurial groups need to have a reasonable economic footing to be able to deliver aid—are the main points of our book. In this chapter we first explore the relevant theoretical contexts of organizing compassion, disaster response, and organizational emergence, then consider evidence from the Black Saturday bushfires disaster to present the spontaneous venturing model of disaster response.

Theoretical Background

Organizing Compassion

Taking a positive psychology perspective, previous scholars (Cameron and Caza 2004) have investigated and elucidated the ways compassion can be organized to lessen individuals' suffering after adverse experiences (e.g., Dutton 2003; Dutton et al. 2006; Kanov et al. 2004; Lilius et al. 2008). This suffering, which can result from a variety of experiences, including disasters, personal tragedies, mistakes, or work-related events (Frost 2003), entails "the experience of pain or loss that evokes a form of anguish that threatens an individual's sense of meaning about his or her personal existence" (Dutton et al. 2006: 60). To help individuals overcome this suffering, organizations can engage in compassion organizing—"a collective response to a particular incident of human suffering that entails the coordination of individual compassion in a particular organizational context" and involves adapting the organization's everyday work structures and routines to help alleviate suffering (Dutton et al. 2006: 62). Compassion organizing is enacted when the organization recognizes members affected by painful or traumatic events (e.g., the loss of a team member's home to fire), which generally stems from existing relationships or connections; feels the grief of the affected team members (e.g., feels sadness for the loss of property resulting from the fire); and responds to painful events using existing structures (e.g., newsletters, meetings) to organize relief efforts (e.g., extracting, generating, coordinating, and calibrating resources to meet the sufferers' needs) (Dutton et al. 2006; Kanov et al. 2004; Lilius, Worline, et al. 2011).

Recent research on compassion organizing has focused on how unaffected organizational members organize to help affected members recover from traumatic or painful events (Dutton, Workman, and Hardin 2014; Dutton et al. 2006; Frost et al. 2006; Worline and Dutton 2017). This compassion organizing helps those suffering organizational members heal from, learn from, and adapt to the adversity facing them (Dutton et al. 2002; Powley and Piderit 2008). As the suffering organizational members benefit from the compassion organizing, it appears that the organization benefits also. Organizing compassion to help organizational members positively influences the view that individuals have of their co-workers and organization (Lilius et al. 2008), promotes organizational resilience (Powley 2009), and enhances firm productivity (Lilius, Worline, et al. 2011).

Although research has shown a number of benefits of compassion organizing, it is not necessarily an easy or emotionally comfortable task. Indeed, it appears that because compassion organizing is effortful and potentially draining, people may be less willing to respond to the subsequent suffering of a colleague (Figley 2002; Frost 2003; Jacobson 2006; Lilius, Worline, et al. 2011). Furthermore, organizations vary in how they respond to suffering *within* the organization (see Dutton, Workman, and Hardin 2014; Kanov, Powley, and Walshe 2017 for review). While some organize compassion to alleviate member suffering (Dutton et al. 2006; Kanov et al. 2004; Lilius, Worline, et al. 2011), other organizations respond with indifference or avoidance (Delbecq 2010; Hazen 2003, 2008), either because organizational members are unsure how to provide for victims' physical or emotional needs (Bento 1994; Charles-Edwards 2000; Hazen 2003) or because strict organizational policies (e.g., overadherence to mechanistic goals, time-off policies, privacy concerns) discourage compassionate responses (Hazen 2003; Stein and Winokuer 1989). These insights into the organizing and potential limits of compassion are of particular relevance to our consideration of the phenomenon of spontaneous entrepreneurship, in which we explore compassion organizing in the aftermath of a major crisis that affects not only many organizational members but also many organizations. Specifically, we extend compassion organizing theory beyond intraorganizational motivations to the creation of new ventures that organize compassion for individuals and communities outside their organizational boundaries.

Disaster Response   There are two primary research themes in the disaster response literature. The first emphasizes command and control (Siegel 1985), which involves "clearly defined objectives, a division of labor, a formal structure, and a set of policies and procedures" (Schneider 1992: 138) for coordinating individuals and organizations in response to a disaster (Anderson, Compton, and Mason 2005; Department of Homeland Security 2004; Majchrzak, Jarvenpaa, and Hollingshead 2007). Research in this stream has emphasized the importance of planning (Lagadec 1996; Peek and Mileti 2002; Quarantelli 1988) and efficiency (Comfort, Ko, and Zagorecki 2004; Kelly 1995) and highlights the many benefits provided by the planned activities of disaster response organizations, including governments, the Red Cross, and other organizations that plan for and respond to disasters. However, responding to a disaster is difficult under command and control: there is considerable uncertainty about the damage and suffering caused by the disaster; there are obstacles to traditional means of communication; and differences across organizations' missions, procedures, and routines make coordination difficult (Auf der Heide 1989; Drabek 2005). These challenges have been found to lead to interorganizational conflict and task interference. Vital tasks remain undetected, ignored, or unassigned; inefficiencies arise as multiple actors perform the same task; and there is underutilization of human resources (Marcum, Bevc, and Butts 2012; Webb 2004).

As the limitations of command and control for specific disaster responses have become better recognized (Drabek 1987; Drabek and McEntire 2002, 2003; Kiefer and Montjoy 2006; Neal and Phillips 1995; Quarantelli 1986; Wenger 1992), some scholars have emphasized the need for better planning (Mileti 1989) or restructuring (Britton 1989) to improve the process (i.e., solutions within the command-and-control approach). However, even with improvements in the command-and-control system, there are still gaps between the organized response and the ability to address victims' needs, leading other scholars to explore the phenomenon of emergent behaviors by collectives in response to disasters, especially when established organizations are ineffective or slow in responding (Drabek and McEntire 2002; Marcum, Bevc, and Butts 2012), which is more likely for large disasters (Drabek and McEntire 2002, 2003).

This stream of research on emergent collective behavior to disasters represents a sociological perspective (Drabek and McEntire 2003; Marcum, Bevc, and Butts 2012). It acknowledges the phenomenon that individuals and organizations "converge" at the site of a disaster to help those affected by the disaster (Quarantelli 1986; Waugh and Streib 2006), focuses on disasters as unique social problems (Kreps and Drabek 1996; Quarantelli 1996), and investigates the nature of the social structures created to address these social problems (Kreps and Drabek 1996; Marcum, Bevc, and Butts 2012)—problems that are unlikely to be solved using current approaches or by the government (Bryson, Crosby, and Stone 2006; Roberts, Bea, and Bartles 2001). These emergent response groups often involve the people, organizations, and communities most affected by the disaster (Stephens 1997; Wenger, Quarantelli, and Dynes 1987), who cease current operations to focus their attention, efforts, and resources on completing tasks made salient by the disaster (Auf der Heide 1989). Emergent response groups have been described as having no preexisting structures (e.g., previous group membership, tasks, roles, or expertise) and as using both nonroutine resources and activities to respond to the nonroutine circumstances disasters create (Drabek and McEntire 2003; Kreps 1990; Majchrzak, Jarvenpaa, and Hollingshead 2007; Tierney, Lindell, and Perry 2001). These groups appear spontaneously after a disaster (Dynes, Quarantelli, and Kreps 1981; Neal and Phillips 1995), involve collaborative coordination (Stallings and Quarantelli 1985; Voorhees 2008; Waugh and Streib 2006), and are flexible and innovative (Neal and Phillips 1995; Tierney and Trainor 2004). Furthermore, through action, they build trust (Bryson, Crosby, and Stone 2006, Majchrzak, Jarvenpaaa, and Hollingshead 2007), legitimacy (Laufer 2007; Voorhees 2008), and knowledge (Drabek 1987; Majchrzak, Jarvenpaa, and Hollingshead 2007). Indeed, these emergent groups can be considered a "new" form of collaboration across individuals, organizations, and sectors for the purpose of facilitating coordination and resource management in response to a disaster (Bryson, Crosby, and Stone 2006; Marcum, Bevc, and Butts 2012). That is, they are distinct from established disaster response groups such as police forces, firefighters, and film crews (Bechky 2006; Bechky and Okhuysen 2011; Bigley and Roberts 2001).

Although this stream of research has acknowledged the importance of emergent groups in response to disasters and details the social structure of these groups (Drabek 1987; Drabek and McEntire 2003), "much remains to be learned about the internal dynamics of these emergent response groups" (Majchrzak, Jarvenpaa, and Hollingshead 2007: 147) from management and organization theory perspectives (Voorhees 2008). Although Majchrzak and co-workers (2007) made an important step in this direction by investigating the transactive memory system of emergent response groups to explain how expertise within a group is coordinated, there is still much to learn about how this behavior emerges to alleviate the large-scale suffering caused by a disaster (Enander 2010).

Organizational Emergence   New venture creation, including the various concepts associated with organizational emergence, is perhaps the most fundamental concept associated with entrepreneurship (Gartner 1985; Katz and Gartner 1988; Shane and Venkataraman 2000). Entrepreneurship scholars seek to understand how and for what purposes new ventures emerge, including the sociological, psychological, and economic factors that influence decisions to act on opportunities (McMullen and Shepherd 2006; Shane and Venkataraman 2000). Understanding these concepts influences other important entrepreneurship concepts, such as firm success (Gartner 1988; Shane and Venkataraman 2000), growth strategies (Wright et al. 2000), and causes of failure (Cardon, Stevens, and Potter 2011; Shepherd, Douglas, and Shanley 2000). Similarly, new ventures have an impact on society by creating jobs, improving economies, and facilitating innovation (Aldrich and Ruef 2006; Delacroix and Solt 1988; Sørensen 2007). However, many ventures fail before taking hold (Brush, Manolova, and Edelman 2008; Gimeno et al. 1997), resulting in a number of outcomes—both positive and negative (Shepherd 2003; Ucbasaran et al. 2013)—for both individuals and society.

Given the impact new venture formation has on individuals and society, many researchers urge an increased focus on the factors influencing firm emergence (Aldrich 1979; Gartner 1985; Katz and Gartner 1988; Reynolds and Miller 1992; Yang and Aldrich 2012). Scholars argue that the most opportune (and empirically challenging) time to learn about founders and the processes of organizational emergence is during the very early stages of venture emergence (Aldrich and Ruef 2006; Katz and Gartner 1988; Yang and Aldrich 2012), before other stakeholders begin to take on significant roles. During the earliest stages of organizational founding, there is extensive heterogeneity in founder routines (Katz and Gartner 1988), approaches to resources (Barney and Arikan 2001; Ireland, Hitt, and Sirmon 2003), perceptions of the environment (Gartner 1985; Katz and Gartner 1988), and creative actions to keep the emerging organization "alive" that are overlooked "if researchers do not begin studying them in the months immediately following their initiation" (Yang and Aldrich 2012: 479; see also Aldrich and Ruef 2006).

Indeed, there is a gap in our understanding of how decision makers manage the extreme uncertainty associated with new venture creation, what forms of value they generate, and what variables influence decisions to act, as well as subsequent choices pertaining to resource acquisition, firm objectives, and venture growth.

Spontaneous Venturing as Compassion Organizing in the Aftermath of a Natural Disaster

Figure 3.1 illustrates our spontaneous venturing model to alleviate suffering after a natural disaster (building on Shepherd and Williams 2014). The figure recognizes the large amount and wide variety of resources generated by outsiders in response to a disaster through the

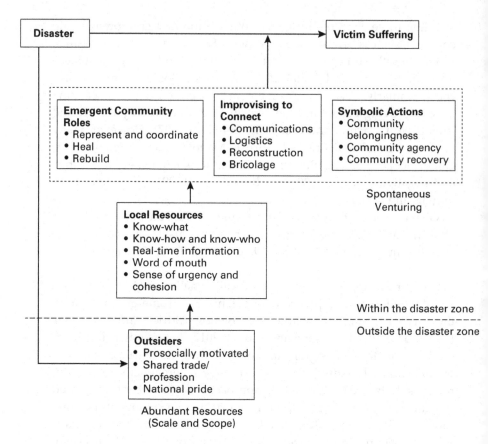

Figure 3.1
Spontaneous Venturing in the Aftermath of a Disaster to Alleviate Suffering
Source: Shepherd and Williams (2014).

mechanisms of prosocial motivation, affinity through shared trade or
professional careers, and national pride. Although these compassionate
resources are large in scale and broad in scope, they need to be customized and quickly delivered to victims by those in the disaster zone.
While numerous physical resources are depleted by a disaster, many
nonphysical resources remain (and are even enhanced), including local
knowledge (i.e., know-what, know-how, and know-who of the geographic region), local means of communication, and a strong sense of
cohesion—all stemming from the identity derived from being local.
These resources help explain spontaneous venturing to alleviate suffering through newly created ventures' (1) performance of emergent
community roles through representing and coordinating the commu-

nity, healing the community, or rebuilding the community; (2) improvisation to make connections in terms of communications, logistics, reconstruction, and bricolage; and (3) undertaking of symbolic actions to communicate community belongingness, agency, and recovery. In the discussions that follow, we detail the nature of our model. In appendix 3.A we describe the spontaneous ventures referred to in this chapter.

Broader Community as a Source of Compassionate Resources
Although the Black Saturday bushfires caused considerable destruction in the disaster zone, they also unlocked numerous resources on a large scale. The spontaneous entrepreneurs recognized, or came to realize, that their local communities were nested within larger communities. When these nested communities were devastated and fighting for their survival, figuratively and literally, members of the broader community were highly prosocially motivated—that is, they wanted to put forth effort out of their desire to assist others (Batson 1998; De Dreu 2006; Grant 2008; Grant and Berry 2011; Grant and Sumanth 2009)—for a number of reasons.

First, some members of the broader community felt a personal connection to the devastation. Kate Harland, a registered nurse from Melbourne who volunteered to help victims, described her experience:

I watched the news on television, and on Sunday, I listened to the radio, and I couldn't believe what had happened. I thought, "This is dreadful," but after the initial shock, I wasn't thinking of doing anything. Then I heard that Brian Naylor had died, and his was a face I knew; I had grown up with his face on TV as a child, and all of a sudden, he was not there. This made me think that this was actually real; this was actually happening.

The following morning, she drove to a relief center and provided medical aid for more than a week. Kate was one of hundreds of volunteers who were motivated by a personal connection to either the victims or the communities devastated by the fires.

Second, members of the broader community often shared a common trade or profession with the fire victims and thus felt a desire to help a fellow member of their trade community because of direct alignment of needs with available skills and resources. For example, farmers from all over Australia sent supplies, materials, and offers to assist animals for fellow farmers (Judith Clements, Karleen Elledge). Similarly, members of the broader hotel community and affiliated associations shipped materials and collected donations for affected hotel owners (James Kennedy).

Third, many donors and volunteers were highly motivated to help because of national pride and sympathy for victims. This motivation is perhaps best captured by a revised version of Bruce Woodley's famous 1987 song "I Am Australian," which was performed two weeks after Black Saturday during a national memorial service and became a theme song for the relief effort. In introducing his song, Bruce Woodley explained to the audience of victims that this was a song of "hope and comfort for your weary hearts and for you to know that Australia is with you." An excerpt of the lyrics reads:

From the ashes of despair our towns will rise again!
We mourn your loss, we will rebuild. We are Australian!
We are one, but we are many
And from all the lands on earth we come
We share a dream and sing with one voice:
I am, you are, we are Australian!
We are one, we are many, we are Australian!

Finally, members of both the national and international community were motivated by a sense of altruism and sympathy for victims after viewing the extent of the devastation as portrayed in the media and by celebrities and response organizations (e.g., the Red Cross) and the Australian government. On realizing the incredible degree of devastation, individuals, organizations, and governments sought means to provide support.

The Importance of Local Nonphysical Resources

The extensive involvement of and response from the broader community created an abundance of resources. In the context of a resource-poor local environment but an abundance of resources offered by people and organizations outside the local community, a significant issue developed: how to efficiently coordinate people and activities to quickly deliver the resources as customized products and services to ease victims' suffering. Spontaneous venturing offered a solution to this problem. This began with the recognition that though physical resources in the disaster zone had been destroyed, nonphysical resources had not, and so could provide the basis for spontaneous venturing.

Spontaneous Venturing Based on Local Know-what   Actions were taken by local residents. Through the engagement of local actors, the spontaneous venturing processes were initiated and managed by individuals who were themselves victims, which facilitated the organizing of compassion. As victims themselves, members of the spontaneous ventures had deeper insight into what other (nonmember) victims were thinking and feeling, which translated directly into the customized development and rapid deployment of relief efforts that met local needs. Because needs were urgent, relief organizers had to "get it right" fast and early to be effective. Graeme Brown described how only by living through an event can one really understand the needs of others. Graeme's sentiment was captured in the following news interview:

Graeme Brown, who lost his home, says the main problem is the emotional legacy of the tragedy and the personal trauma suffered by so many. "People haven't just lost their houses, they've lost their whole lives—where they went to school, where they grew up, where they shopped. ... It's all gone and people are really struggling with that." [For this reason] Mr. Brown leads the Marysville [and] Triangle [Development] Group (MATDG), set up to ensure a community voice in the recovery process. (McKenzie 2009)

For victims like Graeme Brown, the suffering brought an acute understanding of how to organize an effort that addressed the various physical and emotional needs of those in the community. As a victim, Brown and other founding members of MATDG were able to offer a rapid and customized response to bushfires. Brown explained that immediately following the fires,

MATDG organised community meetings at the Marysville Golf Club, which helped us to get an idea of who needed help and exactly what it was that they needed. This led to the development of the temporary residential village in Marysville ... logistics—erecting marquees, distributing community notices, etc.—behind many of the funerals and memorial services which were held ... [and offering] counselling rooms in Taggerty where people could come and have a coffee and chat to a professional counsellor in private or just chat with other members of the community.

As victims, members of MATDG knew exactly what members of their community needed, therefore enabling a customized solution that could be delivered quickly (e.g., communication, memorial services, temporary housing) and could direct outside resources (e.g., placing counselors in the small community of Taggerty based on need).

Indeed, by being local, members of the spontaneous ventures knew the people who were victims, which gave them insights into what these victims had lost, what they were thinking, how they were feeling, and what they needed to help alleviate their suffering. Karleen Elledge became the point of contact for locals, gathering knowledge pertaining to victim needs that was then translated into the customized bundling and delivery of goods. She described the experience this way:

After a few days, we also started getting phone calls from people who needed help. Baw Shire Council started calling us every hour on the hour to give us a list of people needing help. The Victorian Farmers Federation, the Livestock Exchange, the Salvation Army, and Cardinia Shire Council were also sending people to us. Calls for help just started coming from everywhere. Because my phone was going mad, I arranged for my phone to be diverted to other phones. Cardinia Shire Council supplied us with disaster plan phones and an internet connection, and we ended up having seven full-time volunteers working at the Bayles CFA [Country Fire Authority] station on administrative jobs, including answering the diverted calls.

Spontaneous Venturing Based on Local Know-how and Know-who
By being local, members of the spontaneous ventures knew which local people could help get things done. That is, they knew who had the skills to complete specific tasks. The fires burned areas that were rural and often difficult to navigate, making it challenging for outsiders to even understand where community members were, let alone how to rapidly deliver goods and services to address specific needs. To make matters worse, the landscape had been severely altered, which some-times made it difficult even for local residents to recognize what remained of their community. One victim, Jacqueline Hainsworth, explained it this way:

When we got there, we found pretty much nothing. The whole street was rubble; it was just a moonscape. I'd driven that road for 10 years, but as we were driving up, I didn't know where I was. There were no landmarks because the houses and trees had all burned. At first, I couldn't work out which house was ours; they all looked the same.

Members of spontaneous ventures utilized local knowledge to over-come these obstacles, enabling the speedy customized delivery of criti-cal resources to local victims. One spontaneous venture member, Anne Leadbetter, described the volunteers she utilized this way:

Volunteers ... were predominantly local people, some of whom had actu-ally lost their own homes, who were well known to the community, and who had good local knowledge as well as the ability to communicate effec-tively with the very traumatised people who surged through the doors. As well, the volunteer staff acted as the link with the key agencies that arrived to help and provided relevant local knowledge. This local knowledge was particularly important when working with agencies as local volunteers had local geographic knowledge (as well as knowledge of people and community connections). The geographic knowledge was vital as the maps in the Shire office were not entirely accurate for the whole of the Kinglake Ranges—I suspect there are very few maps in existence which are accurate for our area. Also, many roads have locally used names but have totally different "formal" names. For example, the Whittlesea-Kinglake Road is called Main Road by locals, the Heidelberg-Kinglake Road is referred to as the St. Andrews Road or Hurstbridge Road, and the Kinglake-Healesville Road is referred to as the Mt. Slide Road.

Local volunteers were critical to the success of this venture through providing the locally specific information needed to navigate routes, access affected areas, rescue victims, and render other needed services. Without this customized local knowledge, the delivery and deployment of outside resources would have been delayed, furthering victim suffering.

James Kennedy, another spontaneous venture member, turned to local residents with specific skill sets to coordinate recovery efforts and maintain the operations of his venture. He noted:

It became obvious to us very early that we needed somebody to coordinate the comings and goings at the hotel and to deal with the situation. We asked Joanne Kasch to coordinate the operations of what quickly became an unofficial relief centre. The place was in disarray, and we were struggling to cope with the situation. Over the coming weeks, Joanne did an outstanding job in assisting us with the maintenance of the hotel—cleaning sheets, etc.— coordinating the delivery of supplies and donations and liaising with all of the suppliers who helped us.

Kennedy was able to rapidly access the local human capital needed to run the operation. His knowledge of victims' needs as well as the customized skill set required to accomplish the venture's mission furthered the relief of victim suffering.

As another example, the MATDG venture was able to connect individuals in the community to rapidly address an incredible variety of needs that only local residents were capable of both understanding and fulfilling. Bruce Ackerman, a local plumber and member of the MATDG venture, proved to have the local skills needed to rapidly deliver customized solutions both in the immediate and the long term. A reporter explained his interview with Bruce:

For eight days after the fire, Ackerman told me, he had helped the police as they searched for bodies in collapsed houses. During a fire, he explained, people usually take shelter in the bathroom: "And who would know where the bathroom is? The plumber." Thirty-nine people in Marysville lost their

lives; Ackerman's neighbors Liz Fiske and her son were among the dead. ...
While we drove around the town, Ackerman's phone rang constantly. It sometimes seemed that there was little in the town that he wasn't doing. He had
helped reinstate water service, refilling the depleted reservoir. He was head of
a committee to establish a temporary village nearby to house residents who
were rebuilding their homes. That morning, he had dug a grave. (Kenneally
2009: 56)

Sometimes spontaneous entrepreneurial actions were not so much
the result of entrepreneurs' know-how as the result of tapping into
others' know-how and connections:

I learnt that the essential element of sustainable recovery is to find and engage
with the strengths and networks that existed in a community before the disaster. Every community has something that works for them and that they value.
It is worth taking the time to identify and connect with those networks and to
build on the pre-existing strengths wherever possible, and that is what we tried
to do in those first weeks. It's hard to imagine how you would facilitate recovery without understanding what was valued before. To do otherwise runs the
risk of defining the community by its emergency rather than by the great things
that usually happen there. (Anne Leadbeater)

Spontaneous Venturing Based on Real-Time Information   Because
of the prominent role she played in her local community, shortly after
the fire, Karleen Elledge began receiving calls from neighbors needing
assistance and later from organizations that recognized she was a legitimate contact to supply important resources to relieve others' suffering.
In turn, Karleen's knowledge of the local community enabled her to
coordinate the prompt acquisition, bundling, and delivery of resources
that were highly customized to victims' specific needs. Karleen then
shared this knowledge with outside volunteers by giving them customized "delivery sheets" for needy individuals. She explained that "volunteer drivers were given delivery sheets and would drive through the
yard and stop at the various stations, picking up what they needed to
deliver." Furthermore, Karleen's knowledge of local needs allowed her
to customize delivery by directly matching donors with victims, which
she accomplished by "arranging for a donation to be picked up and
taken straight to a farmer," for example (Karleen Elledge). This process
not only allowed for accuracy in meeting specific needs but also created
a fluid logistical flow, ensuring goods were delivered rapidly. The
victims greatly appreciated this personalized attention as each had
specific needs many outsiders would not necessarily understand. One
victim, Michelle Buntine, explained as follows:

Karleen arranged for teams to go out to our property and help. They helped us clean up the wire off the ground and what was left of the old fence posts. Karleen also sent a team of women out to look under the roof of my house and go through the rubble. At the time, I didn't want to know about it; I just wanted to get rid of it. I thought that if it was out of my sight, then it would be out of my mind. I am grateful that they went through the rubble because now I have a crate of things that they salvaged. No one else would know what they were, but I know that a certain blob was that ornament and that another blob was my jewellery. What Karleen provided was really practical. When you haven't lost any family members or your pets but you have lost your house, it is practical assistance that you need most. I think the assistance provided by Karleen is why our community is so far ahead compared to other communities that are rebuilding. It has been very effective. It was due to Karleen. She has her own cleaning business, which she shut down while she was doing this.

As locals, spontaneous entrepreneurs had real-time information, which enabled them to adapt responses to be more effective at alleviating suffering. Anne Leadbeater explained:

Listening to the community and tailoring our information to the questions asked also meant that the complexity of the information kept pace with the recovery. For example, on the first day, we were talking about water and fuel. By the ninth day, we were talking about Worksafe and tax issues for small business.

One spontaneous entrepreneur, Vicki Ruhr, noted that being a local meant that she was a good "ear," and as a result, she was the source of information about how other locals were doing in the aftermath of the disaster:

I have also worked with a lot of people in the community who are involved in health and well-being. Since the fires, I have continued to work alongside health care professional and psychologists in Kinglake to assist people in dealing with the physical and psychological impacts of the bushfires. From carrying out this work, I have realised that full recovery for the people in our community will take a very long time. Our community is pretty stuffed. ... Since moving to Eltham, I have had a lot of people from the Kinglake community come to see me, seeking support and assistance in the recovery process, including friends, associates, and people who knew me as someone who was quite involved in the Kinglake community prior to the fire. These people have either not had case workers or have not had satisfactory experiences with the case workers who were appointed to them. In addition to listening to them, I have passed on a lot of information to people about how to go about claiming insurance, rebuilding, and making claims with the compensation fund. I have been able to be a sort of referral service for information and a point of contact for people in the community.

Spontaneous Venturing Based on Local Word-of-Mouth By being local, members of the spontaneous ventures who started something that was valued found that word of mouth about their actions snowballed rapidly through the local network because it came from a trusted source—a fellow local resident. Furthermore, because of their credibility in the local network, members of spontaneous ventures also caught the attention of nonlocal donors looking for the most useful places to invest their time and money to support the relief effort. What made members of spontaneous ventures so helpful was their knowledge of how to deliver goods rapidly to affected areas and where the greatest need was in order to communicate and target locally customized needs. This was the case for Karleen Elledge and was a primary reason she was able to bundle goods customized to specific needs while providing speedy delivery despite the difficult environment:

On 8 February 2009, I went to the general store in Bayles to get a few things, and some people came up to me and asked what had happened and how they could help. When I returned home, Mick and I decided that we would try and get together some hay and fencing gear for some of the local farmers in Labertouche and surrounding areas. We made up a flyer, with my mobile phone number printed on it, asking people to donate spare feed or fencing materials and took that down to the general store. I also e-mailed a copy of the flyer to a business associate. ... My e-mail went through the Shire and it just kept rolling—it even ended up overseas in places as far away as America. By 10 February 2009, my phone was going nuts—hundreds of people were offering to make donations. At that time, we started transforming the Bayles CFA station into a relief centre. ... What started off as a simple flyer just took on a life of its own, and it snowballed into something huge, which I never anticipated.

For this venture, the snowball effect of the venture allowed for an even more efficient (in customization and delivery time) alleviation of victim suffering by enabling the coordination of donors' and deliverers' efforts as they addressed specific local needs.

Another example demonstrating word of mouth about spontaneous ventures' action *and* value snowballing is the MATDG venture. As one of their initiatives, MATDG members utilized a local golf club that had been damaged as a community gathering point. Immediately after the fire, community members were drawn to the golf club for meetings, communication updates, and support in planning next steps. This early sentiment was captured in a news report:

It (the Marysville Golf Club) survived a firestorm that annihilated almost everything else in its path. And now, by default, the Marysville golf and bowls club commands a new status in the community. "Fortuitously or otherwise, the golf club is one of the only facilities left standing in the district," club president (and MATDG member) Doug Walter told a public meeting (of 300 locals) at the clubhouse last night. "I want to tell you tonight that this will be the new hub of the community," he declared to loud applause. "Bugger golf, to hell with bowls. No longer will this club be dedicated to golf, but to the community." (Ricketson 2009)

MATDG's local presence allowed the venture to draw in community members; listen to their needs; and deliver key services, such as communications, shelter, and emotional support in the immediate aftermath of the bushfire. In the early days following the fire,

[The club was] integral in keeping the community together since Black Saturday, and all major community meetings and government services have been delivered from the clubhouse. Club president Doug Walter said it really was the "guts of the town," and he was looking forward to the golf club providing more sporting opportunities to the community, as well as performing arts and accommodation. (Pattison-Sowden 2009)

As with the Bayles Relief Centre directed by Karleen Elledge, MATDG's work at the Marysville Golf Club rapidly snowballed, first through the community and later by coming to national and international attention as a project addressing the evolving needs of the community by transitioning from emergency response to rebuilding. On one occasion, MATDG was approached by Australia's wealthiest miner, Andrew Forrest, the actor Russell Crowe, and the golfer and golf course designer Greg Norman with donations of both time and money to rebuild the course and set the community back on the path to "normal." Doug Walter explained it this way:

They asked me what the club needs, and Greg Norman said "How would you like a Greg Norman golf course (valued at $2 million just for the design)?" in that American accent of his. I said, "Shucks, yes please!" We want to attract people to the area, give them somewhere to stay, something to do, and go into town to buy meals—it really is a catalyst project to get the district going again. (Pattison-Sowden 2009)

He later added, "Crikey! This is going to give people a serious boost" (Rintoul 2009).

A final example of how word of mouth about spontaneous venturing efforts snowballed rapidly is the Gold Coast Getaway, a venture created to give people a therapeutic vacation (i.e., taking a holiday to relax, receive counseling from psychologists, and listen to inspiring stories from motivational speakers). Bruce Morrow began simply

wondering how he could help the fire-ravaged community of Marysville even after losing "all 12 of our buildings, including the family
home and the partly renovated bed and breakfast cottage" (Bruce
Morrow). Again, like the other ventures, his actions started locally and
eventually garnered the attention and donations of nonlocal people
and organizations. He explained it this way:

> It started with a few phone calls to local companies to see if they could assist,
> and it's ballooned out to what we think will be a full-blown adventure the
> children will never forget. We've been fortunate enough to receive some huge
> contributions from Australian companies who have made this trip possible.
> You can really see the spirit of Australia coming together for these kids. It's
> going to be an amazing experience. (Lewis 2009)

As a local resident, Bruce was able to recognize the unique needs in
the community, gather resources, and rapidly deliver services that
addressed those needs.

Indeed, word-of-mouth spread not only among the victims but also
to outsiders, such as Judith Clements, who wanted to help:

> We started off with local farmers. … We thought that we would cover the
> Whittlesea, Upper Plenty, Humevale, Strathewen, Kinglake, and Kinglake West
> areas, but we ended up covering a much larger area (as the effort grew); we
> also got feed to Flowerdale, Strath Creek, Glenburn, and the Yarra Valley.
> Transport companies got involved, and we were getting phone offers of assis-
> tance from all over Victoria, little towns between Ceduna and Port Augusta in
> South Australia, and Toowoomba and Charlton in Queensland.

Spontaneous Venturing Based on "Being Local" By being local,
members of the spontaneous ventures were able to communicate with
victims, especially because, as we found, victims are often inclined not
to listen to nonlocals. Communicating with those affected by the fires
played a large role in developing customized solutions for victims and
in delivering those solutions when and where victims needed them
most. For example, one victim explained the following:

> If this ever happens again, the community has to make decisions. People
> outside just don't get it. Everyone had networks going; we were doing a good
> job. Then the department came and started making it harder. This caused more
> suffering. You have to allow the people in the local community to step up and
> take on leadership roles. … Natural leaders should be employed. They already
> know the people in the community. They're already doing it. (Borrell, Vella,
> and Lane 2011: 72)

Local leaders were effective because they understood local needs, conducted customized relief efforts that efficiently met those needs, and understood how to communicate with victims to assess ongoing needs. As suggested by Graeme Brown, they understood the terrain and were therefore able to act quickly and precisely in addressing victim suffering. In contrast, support programs engineered by nonlocal groups were viewed as overly generalized, alien, time-consuming, and not fit for the particular needs of the various communities affected by the fires, and in some cases they were seen as exacerbating the problem. The benefit of local community leaders, according to Graeme Brown, is that they have

extremely effective and reliable communication skills; the ability to move through the "red tape of government" to get things done in accordance with the needs of the community; and the ability to strengthen and enable all people involved in the recovery process at all levels of government, industry. ... As a person affected by the bushfires, it seems as though the rest of the world is being normal and it has a conventional [non-locally focused] way of doing things.

Spontaneous Venturing Generating a Sense of Urgency and Cohesion As local residents themselves, members of the spontaneous ventures were closest to victim needs and thus generated action and urgency among other local residents, as well as among willing outside donors looking to help. With resources coming in from a variety of sources and victims urgently needing resources to address needs, spontaneous venture members were able to rapidly receive, bundle, and deliver resources. Judith Clements explained her experience:

As the enormity of the disaster became clear, the next day we began to think about the recovery. My father and I were discussing how farming communities often rally to get fodder and assistance to farmers affected by fire or other disasters and thought that we'd better get the process going. It started off quite simply: I called a few farmers to see what was required and found out that about 10 of the 30 [farmers] were affected significantly. As I realised over the next hours just how enormous the need was, I asked Peter Towt, a neighbouring farmer, to get involved because I knew that I couldn't handle it on my own. From that point on, what we thought was going to be a few days of coordinating fodder assistance turned into six weeks of full-time work. We worked fairly closely with the DPI—they had imposed a four-week time limit on the emergency assistance, but we kept it going for another couple of weeks because, in many cases, it was days and weeks before people began to emerge to seek assistance. ... Our role was to organise the distribution. ... We couldn't keep up with calls that were coming in directly. We were calling on friends to help and even agricultural machinery dealers donated tractors for unloading and loading fodder [to handle the calls]. ... We were getting a lot of calls directly and decided to send vehicles directly into the areas to save duplication of handling—because unloading and reloading a semi-trailer takes a lot of effort. ... We made sure that we had a volunteer to escort trucks through the road blocks so that we could distribute the fodder directly instead of unloading it onto one of our own vehicles.

As members of the local community, Judith and her colleagues were able to (1) start a recovery effort in the immediate aftermath of the fire that was customized to local needs and (2) ensure the effort was as efficient and as speedy as possible, going so far as to connect donors directly with victims. This unique ability to both understand specific local needs and coordinate access to the external resource-rich environment was critical for the venture's success in alleviating suffering.

As another example, the re-Growth Pods venture generated an incredible sense of urgency regarding the housing crisis that victims experienced following the disaster. With fires continuing to threaten their properties, those affected were faced with the choice of either abandoning their homes or finding a way to live on their properties without guarantees of key resources, including shelter, food, water, and communication with the outside world (Doug Walter, Juliet Moore). One person who chose to stay explained the situation this way: "In the first week after the fire, there was nothing; we had to do it all ourselves. We couldn't get out, and if you got out, you couldn't get back in again" (Ross 2009). While temporary government housing solutions took six to eight months to come to fruition, re-Growth Pods, prefabricated shelters that can be delivered quickly to disaster zones and used as long-term housing, more rapidly met the needs of victims. Juliet Moore noted, "The re-Growth Pod was delivered to the property of my neighbours, Jacqueline Marchant and Stoney Black, just before Easter. It had taken six weeks from concept to getting it on site." While this delivery was incredibly rapid, the pod could have been delivered even more rapidly had it not been for outside obstacles, as Juliet explained:

We did have all sorts of issues getting [the pod] on site, and this made me aware of what issues everyone faced. We weren't supposed to put it on the site until the site was cleared although we weren't obstructing the block [i.e., land] at all. We also had to wait to get clearance from the coroner. Then there was dealing with council in regard to what we need in the way of permits.

Despite these obstacles, re-Growth Pods was able to generate a sense of urgency to deliver critical services months ahead of other attempts to provide a housing solution.

As soon as Juliet Moore came up with an idea that could relieve others' suffering, she acted, realizing the needs people faced while trying to stay on their property to consider their rebuilding options. She described it this way:

I took two big A1 boards with the designs up to the Kinglake relief centre, and I started to talk to people about it. I also had a film production company contact who wanted to make a documentary of the pod concept. The whole thing sort of grew from there. ... I wasn't aware of any real opposition to what we were doing because, at that point, there weren't really any formalised solutions. ... I don't think anyone has fully grasped the extent of what it means to rebuild this community.

Local Emergent Actions

In the context of the bushfires, local ventures relied heavily on local nonphysical resources as well as on residual local and newly acquired external physical resources to enable local emergent actions that could overcome the numerous impediments to compassion organizing for the alleviation of suffering. These local emergent actions included creating emergent community roles, improvising locally to connect, and introducing symbolic actions of community.

Creating Emergent Community Roles

Overcoming impediments to collecting and delivering outside resources to relieve victim suffering required venturing to create and fill new community roles. Our findings indicate that three emergent roles that combined behaviors, tasks, and desired outcomes were created for compassion organizing that did not exist in the local communities before the fires: community representative, community healer, and community rebuilder.

Spontaneous Venturing to Represent or Coordinate the Community

MATDG members expressed the need to "have a community group to represent and work for the communities" (Judith Frazer-Jans), and the venture created a new role to meet this need. According to MATDG documents, the specific roles of this new venture included "(1) [providing] consultation and communication, (2) [providing] initiative(s) from the community not above it, (3) aim[ing] for 'better' rather than for 'replacement,' and (4) build[ing] confidence and hence build[ing] [community] aspirations" (MATDG meeting notes). This community group "worked very well" (Boston Consulting Group 2009; Judith Frazer-Jans), successfully connecting locals and coordinating action not only to understand specific needs but also to identify and obtain tailored resources that could address those needs in the most efficient manner. For example, Graeme Brown noted the following:

Since the bushfires, I have been actively involved in the Marysville and Triangle Development Group (which is known as MATDG or "Mat Dog"). I was a founding member of the group, and I am currently its president. ... MATDG was never intended to be a decision-making body—its purpose has always been to draw the community together and to be a voice for the community ... as the community reference committee.

In the same way, other local residents served as representatives for smaller communities (Karleen Elledge, Jim Kennedy), frequently functioning as coordinators connecting community members to resources and delivering customized supplies and services. Karleen Elledge, for instance, held a prominent role in her community before the bushfires (she owned a local maid service and served on the local rural firefighting brigade), which enabled her to build trust with community members. As a result, after the fires, she received calls from local people for assistance, and later, larger organizations began contacting her to supply important resources because they recognized her as a legitimate referee in her community. In addition, Karleen's localized knowledge enabled her to quickly acquire, bundle, and distribute important resources that were highly customized to victim needs. Karleen was then able to transfer this knowledge to outside volunteers through a customized resource distribution process, which included providing volunteers with personalized "delivery sheets" for individuals needing help, matching donors and victims directly, and "arranging for a donation to be picked up [from the supplier] and taken straight to a farmer" (Karleen Elledge). This process made the acquisition and delivery of important resources both fast and customized.

In addition, it appeared important that these leadership roles emerged from within the local community rather than outside it:

If this ever happens again, the community has to make decisions. People outside just don't get it. Everyone had networks going; we were doing a good job. Then the department came and started making it harder. This caused more suffering. You have to allow the people in the local community to step up and take on leadership roles. ... Natural leaders should be employed. They already know the people in the community. They're already doing it. (Borrell, Vella, and Lane 2011: 72)

Spontaneous Venturing to Heal a Community In addition to their coordination roles, many local venture members also served as community healers (Karleen Elledge, Judith Clements, Jim Kennedy, Bruce Morrow). As described above, people who started ventures to relieve suffering harnessed their local networks to rapidly connect with victims, ascertain their specific circumstances and needs, and deploy customized solutions. Specifically, the community healers alleviated suffering by helping victims heal from physical injury (Lachlan Fraser), emotional trauma (Bruce Morrow, Jim Kennedy), and grief over property damage and loss (Karlee Elledge, Judith Clements). For example, soon after the fires, Judith Clements realized that lost fencing put an overwhelming "burden on farmers" in her community and immediately took action by starting a venture that organized fencing for those who most needed it. While Judith helped farmers overcome obvious physical needs, she also enabled victims to begin healing because subsequent crises, such as inability to hold or care for livestock, were prevented.

Bruce Morrow—another local resident who was initially called Black Saturday's "biggest loser" because of his loss of twelve properties, including his home—became a community healer in his area. "After recognising many in the community needed to 'get away'" to begin healing from the devastation, Bruce came up with idea of providing community members therapeutic holidays to Australia's beach communities, getaways that included access to counseling and recreational outings. As he noted, "I wanted to use some of my skills to benefit the community rather than just my immediate family."

Spontaneous Venturing to Rebuild Community Community rebuilders played a critical role in helping victims move past initial survival and toward an envisioned future. For instance, after narrowly escaping his burning home just days earlier, Lachlan Fraser started organizing a venture to establish and run a marathon festival in his community. Lachlan wanted to "bring people back to Marysville. He wanted to be sure the town and surrounding communities got the support they needed to get back on their feet. ... [The marathon was designed] to be here for the long haul, just like those from Marysville and surrounding communities would be as they rebuilt their homes and the community" (Fraser 2009). Lachlan knew that one of the best ways to help residents recover was to reenergize tourism, the primary if not sole local economic stimulus, and he was able to rapidly plan and deploy a solution for doing that, thereby making a substantial contribution to the rebuilding effort.

Improvising Locally to Connect

After the disaster, there was widespread disruption of individuals' daily lives and of existing community routines, communication channels, delivery modes, and other infrastructure elements. As a result, new ventures had to quickly develop novel solutions to connect people with the resources they needed. According to one community member, Doug Walter, "Most of the rapid [and customized] responses [came] from ... the community itself." Four themes emerged during our research related to local ventures' improvisation after the bushfires to facilitate compassion organizing: communication methods, logistics, community reconstruction strategies, and bricolage.

Spontaneous Ventures Improvised to Develop Communication Methods After many traditional communication channels were destroyed, venturing locals developed new communication methods to connect with neighbors as well as with resource providers and friends and family outside the affected area. Jim Kennedy, for instance, developed several ways to communicate within and outside the disaster area, including a workaround to get phone service:

We found that we could receive limited mobile phone reception near the summit of nearby Mount Gordon, so for about two weeks after 7 February 2009, I went up there every day for about two hours so that I could communicate with the outside world and organise fresh supplies for the hotel.

Even with this plan, however, Jim's calls were often ignored, causing him to improvise again:

Out of desperation, I spoke to my daughter-in-law (who lives in suburban Melbourne) by mobile phone from Mount Gordon about a week after 7 February 2009 and asked her to contact the media to ask them to report that people were in Narbethong and needing help. She did that, and I understand that our situation was reported on ABC radio by Jon Faine and on 3AW by Neil Mitchell. This prompted swift action from the authorities.

Another improvised solution Jim implemented was daily community meetings at his hotel to communicate with local people who had no contact with the outside world owing to roadblocks or downed power lines. The meetings were a key venue for police, government workers, and other knowledgeable authorities to provide local residents with important information after the disaster. Improvised communication means like these helped establish or reestablish connections between people, enabling the community to overcome problems associated with disrupted routines and disabled infrastructure as well as the resulting suffering, which inhibited both speedy and customized resource delivery.

Organizing regular meetings was also important to communicate the nature of the situation and the response. According to Anne Leadbeater:

We settled into a pattern that seemed to be working well. ... [We set up meetings at which] we would begin by asking the CFA to update us on what was happening locally. ... Then it would generally be the police and then DHS, Centrelink, Red Cross, paramedics, DPI, and the RSPCA. In the first few days, we would talk about the continuing fire threat, water deliveries and material aid, counselling, dangerous trees, grants, avoiding asbestos and other hazards— whatever information needed to be conveyed. ... A regular visible presence was incredibly important. People said to me afterwards that this had made such a difference.

Spontaneous Ventures Improvised Logistics   In addition to communication improvisation, members of local ventures also improvised in developing logistical processes to connect the supply of resources with victims' demand. For instance, Karleen Elledge detailed the complicated process her venture triggered to help local farmers refence their properties, which was a critical need for them:

We had 642 volunteers work for us during those three weeks [of refencing]. It was an enormous logistical exercise, but I organized the volunteers a bit like a CFA [rural fire] brigade with "strike teams" and each volunteer designated to a particular team. We had a team sheet, so I knew exactly who was on what team, where they were going, and what they were doing.

Within weeks of the fire, Karleen and her team were able to quickly refence more than seventy properties using this process. Additionally, as this example shows, Karleen was also able to customize her workforce to meet specific refencing needs, pairing volunteers with particular projects based on their skill sets to avoid any additional damage.

Venturing locals also had to improvise in crafting logistics to overcome barriers caused by the command-and-control system set up by outside (i.e., nonlocal) organizations:

The difficulties that we encountered with getting food and fuel through the roadblocks were problems we faced every day. ... We eventually found the best way to get through the roadblocks was to bypass the formal channels of control. (Peter Szepe)

[Our local experts were] going into the bush [to] do the road clearing and access work, but the police turned them away at a roadblock. … [These local residents] just drove around them, rather than argue … mov[ing] through the "red tape of government" to get things done in accordance with the needs of the community. (Graeme Brown)

Spontaneous Ventures Improvised to Develop Community Reconstruction Strategies   Venturing locals also improvised in designing, developing, and executing community reconstruction strategies to keep community members connected to each other and to their land as well as to "build back better." Some locals responded to the aftermath of the fire with linear planning solutions, first developing a plan and then following the plan with action. However, others planned and acted simultaneously, which led to "unconventional means to address an unconventional circumstance" (Graeme Brown). The MATDG group was very agile in the aftermath of the fires, continually and creatively improvising in their use of the club to rebuild and meet community needs. Further, as Juliet Moore recounted, community members realized how important it was for the rebuilding effort to begin internally, and they knew that not only did this effort require action but that they had it in them to rebuild:

I have a lot of admiration for their attitude towards the rebuilding process, which is "If it's going to happen, we've got to do it, because we can't expect someone else to do it, and if we talk about it, it's not going to happen, and if we open it up to community discussion, we'll just get 5,000 opinions and arguments, so we'll just do it."

Spontaneous Ventures Engaged in Bricolage   The above improvisations mainly helped new ventures overcome barriers to compassion organizing aimed at connecting nonlocal resources to local victims; however, venturing locals also engaged in *bricolage* to create new bundles of local resources to alleviate community members' suffering. Bricolage is a resource acquisition approach whereby individuals make "do by applying combinations of the resources at hand [including human resources] to new problems and opportunities" (Baker and Nelson 2005: 333; see also Baker, Miner, and Eesley 2003; Magni et al. 2009) rather than obtaining new resources. While a bricolage strategy can be either planned or improvised (Baker, Miner, and Eesley 2003), a great deal of improvisational bricolage facilitated resource solutions for emergent actors after Black Saturday. Jim Kennedy, for instance, engaged in bricolage by utilizing his hotel staff as well as other resources at his disposal to create new resource combinations for locals, including new roles, new processes, and new "products," all of which were essential to keeping his new "unofficial relief center" running.

Introducing Symbolic Actions of Community
As is the case with most disasters, the Black Saturday bushfires caused a great deal of psychological suffering among local people. In response, many spontaneous ventures took innovative symbolic actions to help victims deal with and overcome their feelings of loneliness, helplessness, uncertainty, and anxiety.

Spontaneous Ventures Communicated Belongingness First, many ventures helped instill a sense of belonging in the community, thus lessening victims' feelings of loneliness. For example, MATDG did so through a public statement: "Don't give up hope—there's a lot of us in the same boat. ... I'm sure we can do it. Stay positive" (Mann 2009; see also Kissane 2009; Perkins 2009).

Spontaneous Ventures Communicated Agency Members of spontaneous ventures also took symbolic actions to communicate community agency, thus lessening feelings of helplessness and indicating to community members that they were capable of regaining control over their lives and dignity. For example, although Lachlan Fraser lost his medical clinic and home in the fires, he still managed to take action to unite his community, which communicated agency: "As an ultra-marathon runner, I determined in that first week that we must have our own marathon in defiance of the calamity that overwhelmed us" (Fraser 2009). Lachlan, the town doctor, experienced some of the most devastating parts of the disaster, including having to identify friends' remains, undergoing surgery and hospitalization to treat a severe injury he sustained while fighting the fires, and coping with the emotions from having lost so much. As he explained to a news reporter, "The only memento [I] found from [my] home is a Swiss cow bell, lying under ash about 10m from where it once hung in the kitchen. ... [Marysville] is this lonely, grey, ash landscape. It's like a nuclear bomb has hit. And this cow bell keeps ringing. It's like *For Whom the Bell Tolls*" (Carlyon 2009). While still suffering himself, however, Lachlan was able to draw on these difficult experiences to promote healing through his new venture. He eventually used the recovered cowbell to begin the first Marysville Marathon (Fraser 2009), an act that symbolized how he and the community were taking back control to overcome the disaster.

Although these communications seemed to create a stark divide between local and nonlocal people, the distinction was important in motivating local residents to act to maintain the notion of community:

In a sense it's an empowering thing to stare into the abyss. Everything else must be bearable because we wore that. ... We [as locals] have to forge a new sense of ourselves. I know that we will be OK. (Kissane 2009)

Spontaneous Ventures Communicated a Positive Vision of the Future Venturing local residents also took symbolic actions to communicate a positive envisioned community future, thereby decreasing anxiety about the current state of suffering. As might be expected after any disaster, the first step to recovery for many community members affected by the fires was dealing with the early traumas associated with the postdisaster environment (Graeme Brown, Ann Leadbeater, Jim Kennedy). Many community members needed strength and support to make sense of what had occurred and begin to move forward. In this context, symbolic actions that emphasized the community's ability to endure (Graeme Brown), survive (Jim Kennedy), and overcome the worst of it (Doug Walter) prepared community members to take subsequent actions to rebuild. For example, after the fires, 150 individuals stranded in Narbethong reached out for help, only to have nonlocal aid organizations respond by saying, "But there's nobody in Narbethong" (Doherty 2009a). To take action and inspire community members, Jim Kennedy converted the Black Spur Inn "into a massive open house and base for relief efforts" (Brumby 2009) and erected a sign outside the inn that read, "Take heart, the sun will still shine tomorrow" (Doherty 2009a). These actions helped decrease some of the community's stress and anxiety as well as reassure locals that they would indeed persevere. Similarly, Graeme Brown communicated his confidence in the community's strength and resilience by taking actions to empower people "to get their lives back on track" (Graeme Brown, cited in Milovanovic 2009).

Spontaneous Ventures Communicated Community Recovery Members of local ventures took symbolic actions to communicate community recovery and show community members they had the strength to rebuild, thereby helping lessen individuals' uncertainty about the future (Mann 2009; Milovanovic 2009; Tomazin 2009). Venturing local residents' symbolic actions were helpful in generating a path forward to rebuild as community members eventually began realizing that the worst was behind them and that they would recover. For example, Juliet Moore quickly recognized an urgent need to provide shelter for people who wished to remain on their property while rebuilding, and she immediately acted to make her idea reality. Moore's idea—the re-Growth Pod—is a prefabricated shelter that can be quickly delivered to a disaster area to provide immediate safe shelter for victims. Individuals can use the pod as longer-term stand-alone housing or they can turn it into the core of a more extensive shelter. As such, the dwelling not only meets immediate shelter needs, it can also serve as a structural foundation for continuing construction and development.

Similarly, others explained that despite the difficulties it faced, the community itself wanted to serve as the epicenter of the recovery, both symbolically and practically. In an interview with a news reporter, Nora Spitzer stated:

This community-recovery message was also targeted at outsiders: The tourists aren't here, and we've had nowhere to operate from. ... But we're determined to rebuild. I do believe Marysville will come back. (Legg 2010)

Similarly, Doug Walters, a local victim-responder, was quoted in a news story as saying:

We want to attract people to the area, give them somewhere to stay, something to do, and go into town to buy meals—it really is a catalyst project to get the district going again. (quoted in Pattison-Sowden 2009)

Duration of Spontaneous Venturing
Temporary organizations can occur within established (i.e., permanent) organizations (e.g., Bakker 2010; Engwall 2003; Sydow and Staber 2002), through joint collaboration among a number of permanent organizations (Kenis, Janowicz-Panjaitan, and Cambre 2009), or without any direct relationship with a parent organization (Lundin and Söderholm 1995). While the length of the operating term of a temporary organization is often known from the beginning (Goodman and Goodman 1976; Grabher 2002a, 2002b; Meyerson, Weick, and Kramer 1996), this may not always be the case. Indeed, with temporary organizations responding to a disaster, little is known ex ante (e.g., Drabek and McEntire 2003; Tierney, Lindell, and Perry 2001; Tierney and

Trainor 2004), for such ventures operate in environments characterized by high uncertainty as well as great urgency and the need to constantly adapt to new information about victim suffering or resource availability (Drabek and McEntire 2003; Majchrzak, Jarvenpaa, and Hollingshead 2007). Without preexisting structures (e.g., teams, tasks, and roles), without knowledge of the extent of victim suffering, and without knowledge of available resources, it is difficult to anticipate the duration (i.e., life span) of such temporary organizations upon creation.

Four of the eight spontaneous ventures we studied in depth no longer exist (they were temporary), and those that remain have a significantly different role in their respective communities than they did immediately after the disaster. Rather than disbanding because of failure—that is, "the termination of an initiative to create organizational value that has fallen short of its goals" (Shepherd, Patzelt, and Wolfe 2011: 1229)—their disbanding was the result of the successful fulfillment of their mission to alleviate suffering during the critical time of supply-demand disequilibrium.

Our comparison of temporary spontaneous ventures with those that persisted revealed four primary themes. First, temporary spontaneous ventures focused *exclusively* on alleviating the suffering of victims. Although persisting spontaneous ventures also started this way, a hybrid business model emerged. The hybrid business model accommodated an economic element to a longer-term social mission. For example, temporary initiatives, including the opening of impromptu relief centers, lasted only a matter of weeks, fulfilling the critical needs of the community until established organizations could "catch up." As Karleen Elledge explained, "After running the relief centre for about three weeks ... I knew that it was our time to pull out. ... We eventually closed down our relief centre and transported our remaining donated supplies" to a new, government-sponsored relief center. In contrast, MATDG continues to operate as it plays a more long-term role in full-scale recovery, and the continuing leadership gap in their community causes an ongoing need. The group continues to be active in facilitating community activities, replanting vegetation, lobbying state and federal governments for funding, communicating community needs, and generating a plan for the rebirth of the community. These are important activities, but not all are now directed toward alleviating victim suffering.

Second, temporary spontaneous ventures focused on alleviating the *most urgent and fundamental* causes of suffering. For example, the

Whittlesea Farm Relief venture delivered feed and water for animals to limit the ongoing damage and loss of life produced by the fires, and the Black Spur Relief Centre provided the sole source of food and water for stranded inhabitants and relief workers. These causes of suffering, while highly damaging, were relatively short-lived because the ventures were so successful. For example, the Whittlesea Farm Relief venture lasted only six weeks because it was so successful at meeting the community's needs.

Third, temporary spontaneous ventures relied on an *exhaustible resource source* from the external environment. For example, Karleen Elledge explained how she had a limited "source" of hours she could commit to the effort:

I closed my cleaning business for about three weeks while I spent all of my time at the relief centre. I hadn't planned on setting up this massive big thing, but it became a massive big thing. Some of my employees were able to continue their regular jobs, but otherwise, they told me that they understood why the business needed to close.[2]

In contrast, persisting spontaneous ventures transitioned to more reliable supply sources. For example, the Marysville Marathon Festival sought long-term sponsorships to underwrite an annual event that could remind the outside community of ongoing needs, procure donations for needy families, and continue to rebuild the culture of the devastated region, which relies heavily on tourism and visitors to sustain the community. Similarly, repurposed networks reverted back to their previous use but with noted changes to be even more effective in the future. For example, the Taggerty Heights "Dad's Army" was determined to be even more effective in the future in preparing to respond to bushfires and support neighbors. Doug Walter described his plans this way:

I believe that our neighbourhood group structure was very successful in a time of emergency. The key to our success was our ability to communicate by radio when all other means of communication had failed and that we were able to work cooperatively. This idea could be expanded throughout Victoria. I have drafted a local area emergency model. ... If another repeater station were built, it would ensure neighbouring groups could communicate with one another to ensure wider cooperation and support. There are now other groups in Murrindindi Shire which are looking to replicate our arrangement.

Finally, temporary spontaneous ventures stepped up to fill in when established organizations were unable to meet victims' needs. When

the local conditions improved, established organizations were sufficiently caught up to efficiently provide the products and services
(mostly services) needed. For example, local relief centers provided
immediate care until state- or federally run relief centers were able to
take over. Because the fire covered such a large region, it simply took
time for government-sponsored responders to reach everyone. Additionally, once roads were reopened, the traditional infrastructure for
feed and hay distribution was once more operable, enabling access to
infrastructure that had been temporarily disabled. In contrast, the persisting spontaneous ventures developed unique products that differen-
tiated them from established organizations and were able to develop
routines for efficient business operations. For example, the re-Growth
Pod provided both immediate relief to fire victims and a longer-term
solution for the unique customer base living in the Bushland (many
individuals build their own homes or add on to existing structures over
time). The short- and long-term value of the venture was described this
way in a news report:

It's a fantastic concept. What more could people ask for? [It is] a simple, quick-
fix building, connected to your existing septic. It's move in, start living straight
away. ... The re-Growth Pod is not a temporary building, and the beauty of it
is that when you are ready to rebuild, you can simply add what you want ...
[as] the pod is made from totally non-combustible materials and would give
protection in a bushfire. (Ross 2009)

Discussion

This chapter has explored how ventures spontaneously formed to alleviate the suffering of victims in the aftermath of a natural disaster,
thereby extending thinking beyond the traditional views of disaster
response, organizing compassion, and organizational emergence. We
found that ventures immediately formed in the aftermath of a natural
disaster to address both temporary and long-term community needs,
providing a spontaneous view of organizational emergence. In this
chapter, we suggested that one reason for the emergence of spontaneous venturing as a means of organizing compassion after a natural
disaster is what could be described as a resource-asymmetry problem:
extreme resource scarcity at the local level coupled with resource abundance (e.g., donors) at the nonlocal level. To adequately address victim
suffering in this environment, disaster responders need to manage the
resource-asymmetry problem, or as Sirmon, Hitt, and Ireland (2007:

274) explain, "Value [in this case, alleviating victim suffering] is created only when resources are evaluated, manipulated, and deployed appropriately within the [organization's] environmental context." In our context, many resources were debilitated and rendered useless at the local level, yet local needs varied and required a customized response. Externally, resources were abundant, including financial donations, human capital, food and clothing donations, animal feed, and more. Donors were diverse and far-reaching, including disaster response organizations such as the Red Cross, state and national governments, the international community, private organizations, and individuals. This diverse set of suppliers provided an opportunity in the form of resources and a challenge in terms of the need to rapidly combine and deliver customized bundles of resources to address specific local needs.

Spontaneous venturing rapidly delivered customized solutions that accommodated local needs due to local positioning in the community and, as a result, addressed the gap created by resource asymmetry in two ways. First, spontaneous ventures used bricolage, or made do with the means and resources at hand (Baker and Nelson 2005; Lévi-Strauss 1966), which included "dependence on pre-existing contact networks as the means at hand," as well as on other skills, tools, and materials that could be rapidly accessed and repurposed to address victim suffering (Lévi-Strauss 1966: 17). Second, spontaneous ventures also engaged in "resource seeking" (Baker, Miner, and Eesley 2003) and sought new resources made available in the resource-abundant external environment, successfully bridging the connection between resource providers and victims. We explore resource seeking and networks in the next chapter.

Interestingly, the findings above lead us to speculate on two additional insights. First, the parochialism of "being local" may have a potential downside: while the literature has attributed blame for continued victim suffering in the aftermath of a disaster to established nonlocal organizations (e.g., Drabek 1985; Schneider 1992; Sobel and Leeson 2006; Stallings and Quarantelli 1985), we found some evidence that even if (or when) established organizations are responsive in their compassion organizing, victims may not be receptive. That is, an emphasis on being local may be a double-edged sword: on the one hand, an emphasis on being local facilitates spontaneous venturing that quickly customizes resource deliver to alleviate suffering, but on the other hand, it may inhibit established nonlocal organizations' delivery of resources at the scale and scope that could help reduce victim suffering. Second, the findings from our studies provide evidence that those who initiate and manage spontaneous ventures—that is, those who alleviate victims' suffering—are also victims, and that the process of organizing compassion for others helps alleviate their own suffering (a relationship developed further in chapter 5). This indicates that there is a basis for self-organizing compassion.

Spontaneous Venturing

In this chapter, we uncovered instances of ventures that immediately formed in the aftermath of a natural disaster (see Shepherd and Williams 2014; Williams and Shepherd 2016a) to address both temporary and long-term community needs by providing a spontaneous view of organizational emergence. This view highlights that the entrepreneurial process may be unplanned, spontaneous, and sometimes temporary but still capable of generating well-being for victims. The major insights concern the conditions and activities that characterize successful responses to suffering after a natural disaster and, more broadly, spontaneous venturing. There are a number of implications for the entrepreneurship and adaptation literatures.

First, we found that under some conditions—namely, in the aftermath of a natural disaster—the entrepreneurial process can be temporally compressed. Rather than organizational emergence taking years (Gartner, Carter, and Reynolds 2010; Lichtenstein, Dooley, and Lumpkin 2006) or months (Carter, Gartner, and Reynolds 1996), we found that ventures formed in hours. We used the term "spontaneous" to capture the speed of formation and to contrast it to the typical venture formation process discussed in the literature (e.g., Gartner 1985; Katz and Gartner 1988; Lichtenstein, Dooley, and Lumpkin 2006). However, even under these extreme conditions, we found evidence of a (time-compressed) process of organizational emergence—one that was inspired, cut corners, and had a singular focus. Over and above time compression in venture formation, we found that many of these ventures were short-lived, lasting only weeks to months. This suggests that a venture does not need to have a long life to have an impact. Indeed, for some spontaneous ventures, the greater their impact, the shorter their life.

Second, entrepreneurial opportunity is typically considered to occur in "situations in which new goods, services, raw materials, markets and organizing methods can be introduced through the formation of new means, ends, or means-ends relationships" (Eckhardt and Shane 2003: 336). Ventures are formed to exploit opportunities (Gartner 1985; Gartner, Carter, and Reynolds 2010). In the context of a disaster, there may be few opportunities for profit (especially for temporary spontaneous ventures), but the lack of profit potential has little or no impact on the motivation behind the entrepreneurial activities of venture formation. For spontaneous venturing in our research context, the nature of the entrepreneurial opportunity and the motivation to act entrepreneurially to form a new venture was different from that documented in the entrepreneurship literature (Baum and Locke 2004; Baum, Locke, and Smith 2001; Shane, Locke, and Collins 2003): the opportunity and the motivation were to alleviate the suffering of victims in the aftermath of a natural disaster. In important ways, we continue the work of scholars of sustainable entrepreneurship (Cohen and Winn 2007; Dean and McMullen 2007), community-based entrepreneurship (Peredo and Chrisman 2006), and social entrepreneurship (Austin, Stevenson, and Wei-Skillern 2006; Peredo and McLean 2006; Weerawardena and Mort 2006) by looking beyond profit as both a defining characteristic of entrepreneurial opportunity and a primary motivator of entrepreneurial action. In this case, rather than entrepreneurial action reducing environmental degradation (Dean and McMullen 2007; York and Venkataraman 2010) or poverty (Zahra et al. 2009) through survival and legitimation (Kuckertz and Wagner 2010; Nicholls 2010; York and Venkataraman 2010), we found that spontaneous entrepreneurship was an important mechanism for alleviating victims' suffering in the aftermath of a natural disaster and, by successfully doing so, led to a limited life span of some of the new ventures. We believe that future research can continue to add to the literature by further exploring noneconomic motives and outcomes of entrepreneurial action, including the temporary delivery of value.

Third, while the organizational slack literature has highlighted the importance of firms' possessing "excess" resources to fund the experimentation necessary for entrepreneurial action (although with diminishing returns) (Bradley, Shepherd, and Wiklund 2011; Cheng and Kesner 1997; George 2005), research on bricolage has highlighted entrepreneurial action arising out of resource scarcity (Baker and Nelson 2005). Although we found that resource scarcity triggered some bricolage, we also found that the extreme resource scarcity of the local environment contrasted with the extreme resource abundance of the broader environment in which it was embedded. The problem and the resulting entrepreneurial opportunity were to mobilize, coordinate, combine, and deliver nonlocal community resources in a way that met local needs. That is, although there is a substantial literature on entrepreneurs raising funds from venture capitalists (Cable and Shane 1997; Zacharakis, Meyer, and DeCastro 1999), business angels (Mason 2007; Mason and Harrison 2000; Maxwell, Jeffrey, and Lévesque 2009; Riding 2008), and public investors (Leleux and Surlemont 2003), we found that in the aftermath of a natural disaster, resources were readily available to spontaneous entrepreneurs (often without their even asking for resources); the key was to organize these resources to overcome bottlenecks to the delivery of products and services that alleviated suffering in the aftermath of the disaster. Therefore, rather than resource scarcity or resource abundance as the driver of entrepreneurial action, we found that the gap between local scarcity and the broader (nonlocal) environment's resource abundance triggered spontaneous entrepreneurship. There is an opportunity for future research to continue to investigate the interplay between opportunities arising from resource-scarce environments nested within resource-abundant environments.

Fourth, prior knowledge is central to explanations of why some individuals identify and pursue specific potential opportunities and others do not (Hayek 1945; McMullen and Shepherd 2006; Shane 2000). For example, Shane (2000: 451) stated that some people recognize opportunities while others do not because "people recognize those opportunities related to information that they already possess" from prior knowledge or experience. Indeed, scholars' emphasis has been on prior knowledge of markets (Shane 2000; Shepherd and DeTienne 2005) or technology (Grégoire, Barr, and Shepherd 2010). In our research, the defining feature of the spontaneous entrepreneurs' knowledge was its localness—a geographic idiosyncrasy—that was critical to the formation of ventures that alleviated victims' suffering after a natural disaster. This suggests that as we begin to explore potential opportunities and outcomes that are noneconomic in nature, we will likely need to expand our investigations of prior knowledge beyond technology and markets, or else take a broader view (perhaps not an economic view) of these concepts. That is, rather than demand (i.e., individuals with the capacity to pay for unsatisfied needs and wants), price, and market share, we could further explore satisfying fundamental needs (regardless of the capacity to pay) and outcomes, such as the alleviation of suffering and the number of people helped or saved.

Finally, there is a substantial literature on adaptation (e.g., Brown and Eisenhardt 1997; Virany, Tushman, and Romanelli 1992), which includes adapting to crises (Bigley and Roberts 2001; Grewal and Tansuhaj 2001; Maitlis and Sonenshein 2010; Pearson and Clair 1998) such as natural disasters (Anderson, Hellriegel, and Slocum 1977; Majchrzak, Jarvenpaa, and Hollingshead 2007). Consistent with the adaptation literature (e.g., Fox-Wolfgramm, Boal, and Hunt 1998; Tushman and Anderson 1986), we found that established organizations had difficulty adapting to the complex and shifting nature of a disaster and its aftermath. Rather than focus on why and how some established organizations adapt more effectively than others, the evidence of response to the Black Saturday disaster pointed us toward a different mode of effective adaptation. By changing the level of analysis of adaptation from the established organization to the local community, we found that rapid and effective adaptation occurred through the spontaneous formation of new ventures. These spontaneous ventures stepped in to fill the gap left by established organizations' ineffective responses. Despite being slow, in many instances the established organizations did eventually adapt and begin to effectively alleviate victims' suffering. When they did catch up, the spontaneous ventures often disbanded (happily disbanded by the founders). Future research needs to further explore the relationship between established organizations' adaptation and spontaneous ventures. Does spontaneous venturing speed established organizations' adaptation by "showing the way" and eventually "handing over the reins," or does it delay adaptation by removing the urgency of adaptation efforts (because suffering is being alleviated by an alternative source)? Perhaps future research can build on the corporate venturing literature (e.g., Covin and Miles 2007; Miles and Covin 2002) to understand how established organizations may create their own new ventures in response to a natural disaster that may facilitate their adaptation and achieve important organizational goals.

Conclusion

In the desperate context of a natural disaster, we found spontaneous venturing was triggered by established organizations' ineffective and slow response to the situation. This spontaneous entrepreneurship was characterized by the rapid formation of new ventures to alleviate suffering in the aftermath of a natural disaster; spontaneous entrepreneurs' (who were also victims) reliance on local knowledge and networks to coordinate, combine, and deliver resources from an abundant broader community to a resource-scarce local community; and the short life of most spontaneous ventures. This chapter acknowledges the importance of spontaneous entrepreneurship in the aftermath of a natural disaster.

Practical Implications

This chapter explored in detail examples of locals organizing to alleviate the suffering of fellow victims after a disaster. In doing so, we developed a theoretical model for how these processes of organizing emerged, as well as how organizations shaped victims' recovery. These findings hold a number of implications for various disaster stakeholders (e.g., government and nongovernment organizations, potential victims of a disaster). Perhaps most important, spontaneous compassionate venturing is inevitable: disasters unleash the compassion in individuals, who are drawn to help one another. Therefore these groups need to be integrated—or in the least acknowledged—in broader approaches to disaster response to maximize the alleviation of suffering.

In addition, spontaneous locally organized groups are often the most likely to be effective: they possess often unique local knowledge that enables rapid customized responses to the most immediate needs facing disaster victims. To ignore or obstruct these groups is devastating to the recovery process and inhibits ongoing efforts to work with locals toward long-term solutions. As such, outside organizations (e.g., nonprofits, government agencies.) should formulate plans for identifying and supporting these types of groups when disasters strike. How can agencies rapidly identify whom to support with resources? For potential victims of disasters, it helps to consider alternative methods for local communication should a disaster strike. Furthermore, as individuals develop personal crisis management plans, they could include the possibility that they may have the skills to organize a structured response should their local area be affected.

The following list summarizes the primary practical implications of the material discussed in this chapter.

1. Disasters can cause a lot of human suffering in varying forms and degrees.

2. Designated disaster response organizations face considerable obstacles to providing effective help.

3. Local people (in the disaster zone) face the loss of many emotional supports and physical resources.

4. Even when the compassionate resources employed are of large scale and scope, they cannot effectively reduce suffering if they are not customized and rapidly delivered to victims.

5. Persons and organizations from outside the disaster area want to help but do not always know how to assist or who needs aid the most. Local residents are the key to effective aid delivery.

6. Local residents should focus on the resources they have, not those they have lost, to spontaneously form ventures to help alleviate the suffering of fellow community members.

7. Local residents understand the importance of their local knowledge, and draw on it. They will know what others in the immediate disaster area are feeling and what they need. Spontaneous ventures should leverage this knowledge of local conditions, of who can get things done and how things are being done when local physical resources are devastated.

8. Spontaneous ventures should seek real-time information from local sources to inform their decisions and action, especially when the environment has changed quickly. This may entail acquiring information through word-of-mouth.

9. Spontaneous ventures should use community members' localness to coordinate other local people, organize those from outside the area to provide needed resources, and create a cohesive response. Indeed, localness may be necessary to overcome obstacles created by the command-and-control system.

10. Local residents should feel able to take action and trust their knowledge of their neighbors, their surroundings, and nontraditional ways of getting things done.

11. Local residents in a disaster area can emphasize the importance of community by representing, coordinating, healing, or rebuilding the community. This will help alleviate some suffering.

12. Local residents should feel free to improvise—that is, to design and act at the same time. Improvising is especially important to enhance communication (for coordination), facilitate logistics (to speed the delivery of customized compassionate resources), and create new bundles of available resources (including remaining local resources) to help alleviate suffering. This response may entail using

resources for purposes not previously envisioned and combining in creative ways resources not previously combined.

13. Local residents in a disaster area can overcome feelings of loneliness by undertaking actions that communicate that the community still exists and that victims still belong to that community.

14. Local residents may also overcome feelings of helplessness by undertaking actions that demonstrate that what the community does now will have a positive impact (on others and the community). Taking small positive steps today can lead to additional resources and positivity in the future.

15. Local residents can overcome anxiety by undertaking actions that communicate a positive vision of the future, such as working to "build back stronger" or "build back better." A disaster, while devastating, can provide the opportunity to rebuild many things in a community so that is even stronger than before.

16. Local residents can overcome uncertainty about the future by undertaking actions showing that the community has the ability and the desire to rebuild. A good way to show this is to actually begin rebuilding, even if it is a symbolic action.

17. Spontaneous compassionate ventures should be assessed according to how well they alleviate suffering. The more successful ventures may disband quickly because the suffering has been alleviated.

18. Perhaps new spontaneous ventures can be repurposed in some way to create a viable commercial business after their initial mission is concluded. Persons involved in such ventures should identify new skills or abilities that emerged through the compassionate venturing process that may be more broadly applied beyond the disaster response.

Appendix 3.A. Spontaneous Ventures Created to Alleviate Suffering

Opportunities to alleviate suffering	Venture founder(s)	Personal losses	Previous job or experience	Spontaneous venture
• Provide immediate and long-term housing solutions to displaced fire victims. • Communicate survivor lists by establishing community-driven websites and speaking directly to media representatives. • Establish regular communications through town meetings and other community-driven communication methods. • Draw on local knowledge and networks to pool, access, and distribute needed resources to affected fire victims. • Establish a rebuilding plan, resources, financing, and other solutions for business owners, providing a "launching pad" for recovery. • Coordinate donations, including raw materials and services, to encourage the rebuilding of businesses. • Provide locally driven psychological support for both the short and the long term. • Provide grief counseling that encompasses both a "loss orientation" and a "restoration orientation." • Engage and draw out community members to identify and address emotional suffering.	Graeme Brown and Judy Frazer-Jans (and others)	• Personal property (home, vehicles, and all possessions) • Business property (medical clinic) • Personal injury requiring hospital stay	• Former shire councilor and mayor, local forestry and tourism (Brown) • Former nurse in charge at a hospital, national defense consultant (Frazer-Jans)	*The Marysville and Triangle Development Group (MATDG)* • The purpose of this group is to reconstruct the Marysville area in terms of population settlement, infrastructure repair and improvement, and business development. • Operations began February 9, 2009, two days after the fire, and are ongoing.

Appendix 3.A. (continued)

Opportunities to alleviate suffering	Venture founder(s)	Personal losses	Previous job or experience	Spontaneous venture
• Coordinate the storing and distribution of food supplies, water, equipment, tools, and other essentials. • Draw on local knowledge and networks to pool, access, and distribute needed resources to affected fire victims. • Use existing equipment and tools for alternative purposes, including clearing roadblocks, fighting remaining fires, and providing for animals. • Utilize local and national networks to obtain feed and fencing materials and distribute them to needy organizations. • Coordinate agistment of animals to locations not affected by the fire, provide medical care to animals, and remove damaged and dangerous materials from properties. • Coordinate donations, including raw materials and services, to encourage the rebuilding of businesses.	Judith Clements	• About 150 acres of farming land were burned, with extensive loss of fencing, native vegetation, and pasture.	• Fifth-generation farmer • Former president of the Victorian Farmers Federation • Member of Whittlesea Agricultural Society	*Whittlesea Farm Relief:* • This group organized the mass identification of supplies (e.g., fodder, fencing materials) and coordinated the distribution to needy farmers. • Operations began February 9, 2009, two days after the fire, and ended roughly six weeks later.

Karleen Elledge	• Coordinate the storing and distribution of food supplies, water, equipment, tools, and other essentials. • Draw on local knowledge and networks to pool, access, and distribute needed resources to affected fire victims. • Use existing equipment and tools for alternative purposes, including clearing roadblocks, fighting remaining fires, and providing for animals. • Utilize local and national networks to obtain feed and fencing materials and distribute them to needy organizations. • Coordinate agistment of animals to locations not affected by the fire, provide medical care to animals, and remove damaged and dangerous materials from properties. • Coordinate donations, including raw materials and services, to encourage the rebuilding of businesses.	• Minor damage to personal property	• Captain of CFA fire brigade (comprising nine members) • Owned and managed a cleaning business (with 14 employees) • Owned a direct-to-the-public cleaning products store	*Bayles Relief Centre* • Started a relief center that provided food, clothing, day-labor support, hay, and animal fodder; coordinated the sorting and distribution of donated items and managed more than 600 volunteers. • Operations began February 8, 2009, one day after the fire, and ended roughly four weeks later; remaining assets were transferred to the Labertouche Relief Centre.

Appendix 3.A. (continued)

Opportunities to alleviate suffering	Venture founder(s)	Personal losses	Previous job or experience	Spontaneous venture
• Coordinate the storing and distribution of food supplies, water, equipment, tools, and other essentials. • Draw on local knowledge and networks to pool, access, and distribute needed resources to affected fire victims. • Utilize local and national networks to obtain feed and fencing materials and distribute them to needy organizations. • Coordinate donations, including raw materials and services, to encourage the rebuilding of businesses • Provide grief counseling that encompasses both a "loss orientation" and a "restoration orientation."	James Kennedy	• Extensive damage to business (his hotel), financial loss from damages and lost profits	• Small-business owner (hotel owner/manager) • Experience with Four Wheel Drive Victoria	*Black Spur Relief Centre* • Provided accommodation, daily meals, water, and emotional support to evacuees, firefighters, and police officers; managed and coordinated the distribution of donated goods, including food, clothing, and bicycles. • Operations began February 8, 2009, one day after the fire, and ended four weeks later.
• Provide immediate and long-term housing solutions to displaced fire victims. • Draw on local knowledge and networks to pool, access, and distribute needed resources to affected fire victims.	Juliet Moore	• Moderate property damage, power disruption	• Partner in an architecture firm	*re-Growth Pods* • Developed the initial design of a cost-effective mobile housing unit that could allow people to return to their homes and begin rebuilding. • Operations began February 14, 2009, seven days after the fire, and are ongoing.

| Doug Walter | • Suffered damage to home and surrounding property as well as destruction to the golf course | • Employee of the Department of Justice, fair trading consultant, vice president of the Marysville Community Golf Club | *Taggerty Heights "Dad's Army"*
 • Converted a previously existing community group (developed to fight fires in their immediate community) to a group focused on obtaining food and resources and continuing to defend at-risk properties.
 • Operations began February 7, 2009, the day of the fire, and are ongoing. |

• Clear roads and utilize alternative routes to rescue individuals and deliver key supplies.

• Use existing equipment and tools for alternative purposes, including clearing roadblocks, fighting remaining fires, and providing for animals.

• Coordinate the storing and distribution of food supplies, water, equipment, tools, and other essentials.

• Establish regular communications through town meetings and other community-driven communication methods.

• Coordinate donations, including raw materials and services, to encourage the rebuilding of businesses

• Provide locally driven psychological support for both the short and the long term.

• Provide grief counseling that encompasses both a "loss orientation" and a "restoration orientation."

• Engage and draw out community members to identify and address emotional suffering.

Appendix 3.A. (continued)

Opportunities to alleviate suffering	Venture founder(s)	Personal losses	Previous job or experience	Spontaneous venture
• Draw on local knowledge and networks to pool, access, and distribute needed resources to affected fire victims. • Establish a rebuilding plan, resources, financing, and other solutions for business owners, providing a "launching pad" for recovery. • Coordinate donations, including raw materials and services, to encourage the rebuilding of businesses.	Lachlan Fraser	• Suffered destruction of home and business and had a personal injury requiring hospitalization and surgery	• Medical doctor and small-business owner • Experience as an ultramarathon runner	*Marysville Marathon Festival* • Organized what became an annual marathon festival to (1) generate solidarity as a community, (2) return tourists to the Marysville community, and (3) raise money for local recovery projects. • Operations began February 14, 2009, and are ongoing.
• Draw on local knowledge and networks to pool, access, and distribute needed resources to affected fire victims. • Provide locally driven psychological support for both the short and long term. • Provide grief counseling that encompasses both a "loss orientation" and a "restoration orientation." • Engage and draw out community members to identify and address emotional suffering.	Bruce Morrow	• Lost his home, all of his family's belongings, and 10 bed and breakfast cottages he owned and operated	• Small business owner and operator	*Gold Coast Getaway:* • Organized a holiday for 50 Marysville victims to Australia's Gold Coast; arranged for donations from corporations, travel groups, and celebrities. • Operations began March 20, 2009, and ended May 11, 2009.

4 Spontaneous Venture Brokering to Alleviate Suffering

I believe our neighbourhood group structure was very successful in a time of emergency. ... The actions of our neighbourhood group in [responding to the disaster] saved our property and lives ... [and] gave us great comfort.

—Doug Walter, local victim-actor, reflecting on Black Saturday

Disasters' utter devastation and frequency have attracted the attention of many socially responsible people and organizations (Shah 2012; USAID 2015) and have inspired scholars to further explore the vital "role and functioning of organizations during adverse natural or social events" (Van der Vegt et al. 2015: 971). Having developed a theory about spontaneous venturing grounded in qualitative data, we now seek to expand that theory to better understand how those engaging in spontaneous venturing manage to access and deploy resources despite experiencing substantial resource loss themselves.[1]

In pursuing this line of inquiry, we build on the entrepreneurship research on new venture resourcing. Disasters are one of many potential environmental jolts of a discontinuous nature (Audia, Locke, and Smith 2000) in that they disrupt resource structures (Wan and Yiu 2009) and have the potential to threaten both existing and emerging firms (Bradley, Aldrich, et al. 2011; Meyer 1982), including, theoretically, spontaneous ventures. However, as discussed in the last, decision makers of established firms as well as new ventures often organize to help others by soliciting and providing cash donations (Madsen and Rodgers 2015; Muller and Kräussl 2011; Oh and Oetzel 2011; Zhang, Rezaee, and Zhu 2010) to alleviate suffering and appear socially responsive (Patten 2008: 599).

While the entrepreneurship and strategy literature has increased our understanding of firms' actions in response to disasters, with few exceptions (Wan and Yiu 2008), it has primarily emphasized corporate giving (as an activity secondary to a firm's primary objectives) by those outside the disaster area as an expression of corporate social responsibility (CSR) and a means of generating intangible firm benefits (Madsen and Rodgers 2015; Muller and Kräussl 2011; Oh and Oetzel 2011; Tilcsik and Marquis 2013). However, as discussed in chapter 3, disasters can generate opportunities for actors within the disaster area to initiate new ventures, de novo and de alio, despite the adverse resource conditions they face. These venturing activities differ from traditional CSR initiatives in two important ways. First, they require more extensive organizing and local engagement than corporate giving campaigns in that they involve the emergence of new organizational structures and routines to address social opportunities as a primary organizational activity. Second, they are often initiated by individual and organizational actors inside the disaster area who may themselves be victims of the disaster. As a result, they are closer to the acute needs in an area yet are also more susceptible to the disaster-caused resource destruction. There is a gap in our understanding of how these new ventures acquire and deploy resources for emergence in such hostile environments, providing a "grand challenge" for researchers to investigate how organizations "shape and mitigate the consequences of disasters" (Van der Vegt et al. 2015: 971). To address this gap, we ask how local new ventures access and manage resources to effectively respond—in terms of scale, speed, and customization—to social problems in the aftermath of a disaster.

A major motivation for our attention to local response came from the experiences of local disaster responders. The types of products and services introduced varied widely; however, each venture shared a commitment to starting an organization as rapidly as possible to address an array of needs. For example, after the Black Saturday disaster devastated the community infrastructure, several women (Jemima Richards, Kate Ridell, Arwyn Taylor) joined together to create an organization that offered social support, counseling, recreational activities, and other services to grieving women. This effort evolved from Jemima's initial work in providing an impromptu relief center. The emergence of this organization and its evolution was described this way:

In the days following Black Saturday, Jemima set up a Private Relief Center on her 50 acre property, on the main road between Kinglake and Kinglake West. Known as 305 (the property number) it serviced hundreds of people daily. Urgently needed goods were dropped and distributed (without the red tape) by an amazing group of up to 30 volunteers who often started at 6am and worked through to 2am the next morning. The site grew to a massive production of 11 shipping containers, internet bus, petrol drum storage, cooked food for the fire affected and hard working volunteers and soooooo much more.

One of those volunteers was Rowena Allen and her partner Kaye Bradshaw. They dropped off pancake mixture to what they thought was the main Kinglake Relief Centre. After realising that 305 was being co-ordinated, organised and run by Jemima, they offered to bring the Uniting Care Cutting Edge Mobile Internet Bus back a few days later and help however was needed. They stayed for the next three months!

305 was a massive and highly successful exercise, but wasn't sustainable. Rowena and Kaye were able to organise for 305, and the Kinglake West Relief Centre to merge and work from the one site at the Uniting Church property in Kinglake West. It was here that the merged relief centers became known as 1050 (the property number on the main road) and was only possible because of the compassion and support of the congregation. 1050 relied on donations and private help to serve meals to approx 300 people every day, offered material aid, essential items and a support network all available to those in need.

After some time, the State Government agreed to fund 1050 and it became the only place where locals could get a nutritious meal, meet others in the same situation in a safe environment and know that those listening really, really understood. Special bonds and friendships formed.

Towards the end of March 2009 when 1050 was winding up, Kate Riddell had a long chat with Rowena Allen running the site. Kate expressed her concerns about the community's future and was looking for a way (especially for the women), to maintain and build upon the friendships, strong bonds and feelings of connectedness that had emerged.

Rowena introduced Jemima and Kate who instantly recognised similar patterns forming in the community, the men and women were handling the trauma of Black Saturday and the aftermath very differently emotionally. Rowena, Kaye, Kate and Jemima organised a small gathering in April with the aim of connecting women in the community and finding out what they needed in order to maintain the inspiring work they were undertaking. It was here that Kate and Jemima met Arwyn and other women who later became members [of the new organization, Firefoxes]. Arwyn, Kate and Jemima after seeing what a huge success the night was, decided to forge ahead together with the group.

The group initially called itself "What Women Want," because this was the question being put to the women each time they meet. From here the answers started flowing ... to be together and have a few laughs ... learning a new skill or a hobby ... guest speakers to educate and inspire ... how to help the children suffering from post-traumatic stress and much more. The continued feedback guides the women's recovery and in turn assists families and the communities to heal, recover and move forward to create a new normal. (Firefoxes.org)

As illustrated in the above example, Black Saturday brought victims together who identified new opportunities to address suffering. These actions evolved from network relationships and a common goal to move the community forward. In explaining why they were capable of addressing local needs, Kate Ridell said:

We talked about what the town needed, what their families needed and also what the women themselves needed. It is just an ordinary group of women who understand each other because people who haven't been through a disaster just don't understand, despite good intentions. ... Women are the pinnacle point in the family so if they fall apart, so does the family. But when we all gathered as a group, the women really opened up in a way they felt they couldn't do around their families and it gave them a chance to communicate openly about "touchy feely" stuff. We want women to band together to learn self-care and strategies to get through disasters.

In this chapter, we build on what was developed in chapter 3 to engage more traditional management theories on the use of networks and resources to help understand spontaneous compassion venturing and its consequences. By extending research on CSR beyond corporate giving to more engaged responses to disasters (i.e., new venture creation), we can gain a deeper understanding of potential solutions to the human problems posed by natural disasters. This research also helps provide empirical evidence that can serve as a vital input for institutional and organizational disaster planning (Jensen and Waugh 2014). In addition, prior research has typically assumed that organizational responses generally involve simply donating money and that these offerings are effective in alleviating suffering (Madsen and Rodgers 2015; Muller and Kräussl 2011). Despite these assumptions, there is strong evidence that this form of helping can be biased toward short-term responses (Thomas and Fritz 2006) and can even be used for other purposes, such as repairing a negative or damaged predisaster reputation of the donating organization—which is not even oriented toward addressing local suffering (Madsen and Rodgers 2015; Muller and Kräussl 2011). In this chapter, we focus on how ventures organize responses after a natural disaster and the effectiveness of these responses.

To address our research question and expand on themes developed in chapter 3, we build on the network social capital (Burt 2005; Nahapiet and Ghoshal 1998), new venture resource mobilization (Sirmon, Hitt, and Ireland 2007; Sonenshein 2014), and compassion organizing (Dutton, Workman, and Hardin 2014; Dutton et al. 2006) literatures. In doing so, we make three primary contributions.

First, organizational research on postdisaster CSR has typically focused on the actions of firms outside the zone of adversity, the ways they identify whom they will help, and the impact of corporate giving on social, reputational, and economic outcomes for their firm (Godfrey 2005; Madsen and Rodgers 2015; Muller and Kräussl 2011; Zhang, Rezaee, and Zhu 2010). The underlying assumptions of this CSR research are that victims are dispossessed of key resources and are in need of outside help, and that the response is effective (Muller and Kräussl 2011; Oh and Oetzel 2011; Tilcsik and Marquis 2013). However, local victims of disasters are often the first to help themselves and others after a disaster (Wenger, Quarantelli, and Dynes 1987), can be innovative in solving problems (Quarantelli 1988), and often create new routines after a major disruption (Auf der Heide 1989). Furthermore, local people are often the most effective in responding to crises because they are positioned to provide a rapid and customized response. Despite this, little has been done to understand other forms and processes of organizational action beyond those associated with CSR. We build on the theory developed in chapter 3 on compassion venturing and empirically find that victims of the Black Saturday bushfires initiated and maintained ventures (de novo and de alio) that alleviated others' suffering. This finding extends our empirical understanding of strategic disaster responses to organizing inside the zone of adversity.

Second, prior research (reviewed in chapters 1 and 2) has suggested that victims face considerable obstacles to self-help after a major loss event primarily because of a loss of resources (e.g., lost property, social outlets, income) or functionality (emotional, physical, or social) (Lilius, Worline, et al. 2011). However, while loss events often generate a number of adverse social and psychological outcomes for victims (Bonanno et al. 2010), victims of such events often retain physical functioning and other key resources, such as social ties and local knowledge (Bonanno et al. 2010; Shepherd and Williams 2014). Recent studies have called for greater exploration of "the structural characteristics of social networks ... [and] the resources embedded and available [in those networks] ... [that] can be accessed and mobilized when actors engage in purposeful action [when responding to disasters]" (Van der Vegt et al. 2015: 973, 975). In particular, there is a need to better understand the "bridges" or "hubs" of network subsystems, the ways they influence capabilities for an adaptive response (in terms of resource access and mobilization), and the effectiveness and efficiency of such a response (Van der Vegt et al. 2015). In short, we know victims retain resources—especially in the form of networks—but we know little about the structure of these networks and the ways in which different network configurations shape organizing processes and outcomes. We theorize and find that actors leverage brokerage relationships within and between communities to pursue opportunities to relieve victim suffering after a disaster, drawing on these "systems" of relationships in different ways to access tools that help ease people's suffering. This work extends research on responses to "ill-structured strategic challenges" (Baer, Dirks, and Nickerson 2013: 198) by exploring structural and behavioral factors that shape the organizing of a response.

Finally, research on one particular type of a social network, network brokerage, has typically explored the benefits of brokerage in terms of opportunity recognition (Bhagavatula et al. 2010; Burt 2005), innovation (Stuart, Ozdemir, and Ding 2007), and uncertainty management (Burt 2000). Brokerage involves an actor, or broker, connecting two otherwise unconnected actors in a resource or transactional exchange. Indeed, brokerage has been equated with entrepreneurial activities, with (new) ventures providing value by bridging "structural holes" within a community (for a review, see Burt 1992, 2005). Despite the extensive literature on brokerage, prior research has not sufficiently considered how different brokerage roles influence resource mobilization approaches—that is, the process for converting a structural capacity for advantage into an actual resource gain. This lack of research is surprising as evidence suggests that the individuals with whom entrepreneurs orchestrate exchanges through brokerage (i.e., actors belonging to similar or different groups) have an impact on exchange outcomes (Gould and Fernandez 1989; Kirkels and Duysters 2010).

Recent research developments on brokerage have shown that "more valuable" research explores not just the presence of brokerage but "how or why ... resources are transformed and combined into new solutions for other actors or subgroups" (Kirkels and Duysters 2010: 376). This research should explore nuance in claims that brokerage is advantageous (Burt 2005) by identifying the contingent value of brokerage as "brokerage structure does not automatically trigger acts of brokerage ... nor does it necessarily realize brokerage benefits" (Shi, Markoczy, and Dess 2009: 1461). We theorize and find that variance in brokerage type influences venture resourcing in the aftermath of a disaster, which in turn influences response effectiveness. This work extends research on network brokerage by clarifying the role of different forms of brokerage for resource mobilization, suggesting that it is not just "greater [stocks] of resources" that enable resilience to external disturbances (Van der Vegt 2015: 973) but that the *type* of stock shapes action, which in turn influences effectiveness. Similarly, our work extends research on CSR responses to disasters by identifying how local ventures draw on social resources to provide effective responses beyond corporate giving campaigns. We discuss the various forms of brokerage below.

Theoretical Development

Victims of disasters often experience extensive loss. However, it could be argued that some resources are potentially strengthened. We believe this to be the case with social resources. As highlighted in chapter 3, we found that local relationships were strengthened as victims banded together under a shared identity and unified cause to address imminent community threats. Building on our observations in that chapter, we now explore in greater detail the nature of the social relationships that are likely to shape spontaneous venturing and—especially—access to resources.

We found many examples of individuals drawing on network relationships while we were compiling the data set for our analysis. For example, one man (Steven) saw his town of Flowerdale burned to the ground—80 percent of the town's homes were destroyed. Rather than focus on temporary shelters, he first organized those around him for the common mission of building the village anew, looking to "reestablish the town as a community" by drawing on "clusters of friends" to create an organization focused on permanent housing, community design, and other resource needs. After organizing the local people, Steven expanded his network scope to include outsiders, beginning first with local and national government figures and eventually garnering the attention of the UK's Prince William, Coldplay's Chris Martin, and many others, who came to Flowerdale to offer support and resources. This example highlights how quickly network relationships coupled with creative action can result in an expanded scope and scale of a response to the natural disaster.

On a smaller scale, another individual (Cindy) launched a collaborative business whereby victims could make and sell artisan goods. In her venture, Cindy drew on her network of local craftspeople to develop an online storefront where victims could sell homemade items, similar to Etsy.com. She thought such a collaborative business might create a space where people could come together to manage their trauma while also helping them move forward on the path to self-reliance. Cindy explained that her venture was "a proactive, productive way of keeping busy that will help in the long-term."

Social Networks: Brokerage Social Capital

Social networks function as catalysts in organizations, specifically during new venture creation (Burt 2005), offering actors structural access to both existing and potential resources (Burt 1992; Nahapiet and Ghoshal 1998). In these social networks, actors can take on structural roles through brokerage (a venture is a broker if it links entities that would be disconnected otherwise; Spiro, Acton, and Butts 2013). Brokerage facilitates the exchange of needed resources (Burt 2000; Gould and Fernandez 1989; Stovel and Shaw 2012), as well as "transactions between other actors lacking access to or trust in one another" (Marsden 1982: 202). Although brokerage is beneficial for almost all venturing activities (Burt 2005), brokers play an especially important role when "the network they belong to is fragmented across different affiliation groups" (Lissoni 2010: 846). For instance, actors may belong to the same organization but work in different functional areas within the organization, such as finance, marketing, or human resources (Kelley, Peters and O'Connor 2009). Likewise, city or community members often belong to different groups based on their religious affiliation, neighborhood, and other interest, which can have an impact on the brokerage roles these individuals take on (Gould and Fernandez 1989; Stovel and Shaw 2012). As such, the meaning of a particular exchange may be very different depending on the subgroups involved in the interaction (e.g., finance to finance versus finance to human resources versus marketing to finance) (Kirkels and Duysters 2010; Lissoni 2010). To explore this issue more deeply, we determined the subgroup affiliations of the spontaneous ventures founded after the Black Saturday bushfires by associating them with distinct nonoverlapping community affiliations identified by the actors themselves (Gould and Fernandez 1989; Spiro, Acton, and Butts 2013). In this setting, brokers facilitated resource deployment within and between communities to alleviate suffering.

Resource Mobilization

Resources allow individuals or firms to creatively pursue opportunities (Katila and Shane 2005; Sonenshein 2014) and ultimately gain a sustainable advantage. Furthermore, in the context of extreme resource loss, having access to the appropriate type of resources at the right time can literally make the difference between life and death. However, both generally speaking and in the specific context of a natural disaster, individuals who organize for new venture creation are typically in a disadvantaged position with respect to resources (Stinchcombe 1965; Villanueva, Van de Ven, and Sapienza 2012). As such, they often have to engage in a variety of activities to obtain and mobilize the resources they need to establish and grow the new venture (Jarillo 1989; Newbert 2007; Newbert and Tornikoski 2011).

There are two main resource mobilization activities: *resource bundling*, whereby entrepreneurs generate new solutions by combining existing resources in novel ways (Baker and Nelson 2005; Powell and Baker 2011), and *resource search*, which often involves looking for financial support, for example (Villanueva, Van de Ven, and Sapienza 2012). As illustrated in the Firefoxes example above, bundling might include gathering local resources (human and tangible resources) and then redeploying or comingling them for alternative purposes. Similarly, in the Flowerdale example above, Steven engaged in resource bundling initially, but also found ways to attract the attention of outsiders, who provided resources, legitimacy, and needed attention that led to the donation of additional resources.

New ventures frequently undertake both resource bundling and resource search, even engaging in both activities simultaneously (Baker and Aldrich 2000; Baker, Miner, and Eesley 2003). In this chapter, we explore how different configurations of network relationships and resource mobilization approaches shape the effectiveness of a compassionate venturing response. Specifically, we suspect that in the disaster context, brokerage relationships affect the ways ventures mobilize resources in response to victim needs (beyond focusing on donations as in CSR). Figure 4.1 illustrates our brokerage model of postdisaster venturing. The figure highlights the possible structural network roles—bonding brokerage or bridging brokerage—ventures may play, as well as the ways these roles influence the effectiveness of ventures' responses (i.e., magnitude, delivery speed, and customization) through resource mobilization activities, including resource bundling and resource search. In the discussion that follows, we offer a more detailed explanation of the concepts mentioned above and consider how they influence the effectiveness of a response. However, we begin by exploring what it means to respond effectively to a disaster.

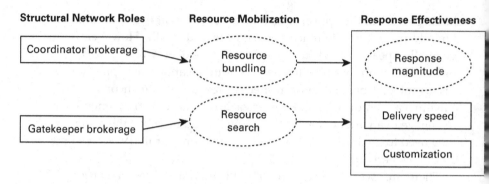

Figure 4.1
Brokerage Model of Postdisaster Venturing
Source: Williams and Shepherd (in press).

Compassion Venturing: The Effectiveness of Responses in the Aftermath of a Disaster

Compassion involves sensitivity to others' pain (Lilius, Worline, et al. 2011) and entails "a sustained and practical determination to do whatever is possible and necessary to help alleviate [victims'] suffering" (Rinpoche 1992: 187). After a disaster, doing "whatever is possible and necessary to alleviate suffering" sometimes involves coordinating resources and creating new organizational structures (Drabek and McEntire 2003); that is, it involves organizing compassionate new ventures (Shepherd and Williams 2014; see chapter 2). Often these new ventures are organized by the disaster victims themselves (for a review, see Drabek 1987; Drabek and McEntire 2003). We found many examples of victims noticing the suffering of *other* victims in a wide-ranging scope of needs. For example, one person (Monty) recognized that many of the victims had domestic animals or herds that were in need of care because the fires had burned more than 450,000 hectares of land. Monty organized to identify and document horses, cattle, and other animals that could then be transported to farmers outside the fire area until local residents could get back on their feet. Similarly, Cris started a "Men's Shed," a local center for "nurturing mateship and creating feelings of belonging" for men. Cris recognized that men and women were grieving in different ways and therefore needed alternative ways to express and manage grief. Cris organized a number of people in his network, including local health care providers, craftsmen, tool providers, and school administrators, to provide training, therapy, and equipment, all with the goal of "addressing men's physical, emotional, and social health." Cris managed this activity despite experiencing his own family home's destruction as he and his family, who had narrowly escaped death, continued to deal with their own grief. As Cris's wife, Vicki, explained in a statement to the Bushfire Commission:

On that day [Black Saturday], our house and most of our possessions were destroyed by the bushfires after we tried to defend the house. We also lost all of our pets except the dear old family dog. ... I experience a wide-range of human emotion on a daily basis. I am exhausted, I feel despair and dismay every day and I have immense trouble thinking about the future. ... I hear my friend, Suzanne, who perished in the fires. I hear her voice and I hear her screams—often.

Vicki went on to state: "I am now a bushfire-affected person, labelled as a 'victim' or 'survivor.' I like to think of myself as simply one of the lucky ones and somebody who lived to tell the tale." This comment illustrates why victims of the disaster were so capable of understanding and addressing the needs of the other local residents: they were themselves experiencing the consequences of the disasters directly.

Compassion Venturing and Value Creation

For all types of ventures (Austin, Stevenson, and Wei-Skillern 2006; Dean and McMullen 2006), it is necessary to discuss how value is created and what form that value takes. The idea of measuring how effective an organizational response is in alleviating others' suffering, though seemingly obvious, is essentially absent from the management literature. That literature deals more with how firms' actions to help others benefit or hurt the helping firm, not how firms' actions affect the victims themselves (Madsen and Rodgers 2015; Muller and Kräussl 2011; Oh and Oetzel 2011; Tilcsik and Marquis 2013). The emerging literature on compassion organizing (see Dutton, Workman, and Hardin 2014; Shepherd and Williams 2014; Williams and Shepherd 2016a; Worline and Dutton 2017 for review) suggests that *response effectiveness* after a negative event is reflected in the degree to which actors successfully alleviate victim suffering. Response effectiveness is determined by four factors, scope, scale, delivery speed, and customization (Dutton et al. 2002), with scope and scale often being combined to reflect response magnitude (Bansal 2003; Dutton et al. 2006; Normann 1977). These four factors share commonalities with findings from the CSR literature on the ways corporations generate attention for their philanthropic activities (Madsen and Rodgers 2015). While we explored these concepts to some degree in chapter 3, we now seek to empirically measure and test these concepts using a larger data set.

Response magnitude—that is, the extent and breadth of actions (Dutton et al. 2006; Lilius, Kanov, et al. 2011), refers to both the scale (i.e., total quantity or volume of resources contributed to alleviate victim suffering) and scope (i.e., the extent or variety of resources contributed to ease suffering) (Dutton et al. 2002) of the response. *Delivery speed* involves "the timely availability and delivery of resources to those who are suffering" (Dutton et al. 2006: 72; see also Dutton et al. 2002; Lilius, Kanov, et al. 2011). After a natural disaster, numerous physical (e.g., blocked roads, disabled infrastructure, disrupted communication lines) and psychological (e.g., grief, posttraumatic stress disorder) challenges arise. Some people are in a better position to cope with and overcome these challenges and are able to rapidly harness their existing resources and resource mobilization approaches to deploy novel solutions in the disaster-stricken environment. Finally, *customization*, which referring to the "efficient patterning and shaping of resources to meet the particular needs of those who are suffering" (Dutton et al. 2006: 74), emphasizes the need to deliver the proper amounts of resources when and where they are needed most, which in turn influences how effective a venture is at alleviating suffering after a disaster. We next theorize how brokerage and resource mobilization affect ventures' response effectiveness.

Brokerage Roles: Structural Sources for Resource Access to Alleviate Suffering

As discussed in previous chapters, disasters destroy or damage many resources and affect both victims and the larger community (Bonanno et al. 2007, 2010). However, unlike other types of capital that can be lost or harmed, social relationships are a resource that can be "renewed and enhanced during the emergency period" (Dynes 2005: 7). Generally speaking, venture creation entails pursuing opportunities "without regard to resources [the venture] currently control[s]" (Stevenson and Jarillo 1990), a fundamentally different approach from that of traditional CSR donation campaigns. In compassion venturing after a disaster, ventures must face uncertainty associated with resource access, partnerships, and other factors influencing their survival (Hite and Hesterly 2001; Stevenson and Jarillo 1990). Social networks allow these firms to take advantage of their relationships with others—that is, social capital—to fill gaps in their social structures to obtain and effectively distribute critical resources (Burt 1992, 2005). Specifically, brokerage connects actors who would remain unconnected otherwise, thus providing access to valued resources (e.g., information, physical resources, trust), where the broker connects previously unconnected people (Burt 2000). In relation to the creations of new ventures, brokers draw on their network position to "transfer trust and commitment from pre-existing relationships to newly formed ones" (Kelley, Peters, and O'Connor 2009: 223; see also Uzzi 1996).

To gain a deeper understanding of brokerage's influence on organizing, we need to analyze structural variation in brokerage roles and the ways in which this variation affects subsequent outcomes (Gould and Fernandez 1989; Stovel and Shaw 2012). Brokerage roles come in a variety of forms and can include serving as a gatekeeper for a specific group and influencing access to that group; acting as a go-between for two separate groups; or taking on a combinatorial role within a group, helping to connect group members and their different skills (Gould and Fernandez 1989; Stuart, Ozedemit, and Ding 2007). The root of brokerage theory is that actors' subgroup affiliations influence how those actors perceive and react to opportunities (Gould and Fernandez 1989; Kelley, Peters, and O'Connor 2009; Kirkels and Duysters 2010).

Gould and Fernandez (1989) outlined five types of broker roles based on individuals' subgroup affiliation (see figure 4.2),[2] with each role type having an associated structural information flow and group orientation. Importantly, this classification stresses "the limits [and bounded benefits] of a broker's capacity to effectively facilitate interaction" (Stovel and Shaw 2012: 142). The five types of broker roles are coordinator, gatekeeper, itinerant (consultant), representative, and liaison brokerage (see figure 4.2).

Our goal is to understand how individuals within the Black Saturday disaster area drew on their networks with both others in the disaster zone and individuals outside the area to organize resources to relieve victim suffering. For example, *itinerant* (consulting) brokers may organize a group to which they do not belong, such as when a government agency comes into a disaster area and organizes various groups of locals. *Representative* brokers come from and remain in groups outside the disaster area, brokering resources between their group on the outside and disaster-stricken groups on the inside. Finally, *liaison* brokers are those who link members of different groups when all three parties involved come from different groups. Again, these types of brokerage are not the focus of this chapter.

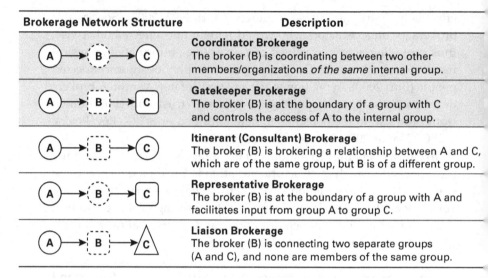

Brokerage Network Structure	Description
	Coordinator Brokerage The broker (B) is coordinating between two other members/organizations *of the same* internal group.
	Gatekeeper Brokerage The broker (B) is at the boundary of a group with C and controls the access of A to the internal group.
	Itinerant (Consultant) Brokerage The broker (B) is brokering a relationship between A and C, which are of the same group, but B is of a different group.
	Representative Brokerage The broker (B) is at the boundary of a group with A and facilitates input from group A to group C.
	Liaison Brokerage The broker (B) is connecting two separate groups (A and C), and none are members of the same group.

Figure 4.2
Gould and Fernandez's Brokerage Roles
Source: Williams and Shepherd (in press).

Instead, our goal is to understand the brokerage relationships revealed through exchanges between disaster-stricken venture creators and other actors, including suppliers, collaborators, supporters, and customers (similar to Fernandez and Gould 1994; Lissoni 2010). For this reason, while investigating each of these brokerage roles is expected to be valuable, we concentrate on the coordinator and gatekeeper brokerage roles (see figure 4.2) while controlling for the other three roles. The *within-group* coordinator role indicates heightened interaction between members of a group the broker belongs to (Gould and Fernandez 1989; Spiro, Acton, and Butts 2013: 134), whereas the *between-group* gatekeeper role indicates the absorption of outside groups' resources into a broker's existing group or groups (Gould and Fernandez 1989; Kirkels and Duysters 2010; Spiro, Acton, and Butts 2013: 134). Our goal in investigating these two brokerage roles is to understand whether and how ventures' within- and between-group brokerage roles in communities hit by disaster explain variation in their response effectiveness.

Coordinator Brokerage The goal of coordinator brokerage is to increase or enhance interactions between members (e.g., organizations, key leaders, individuals) of the same group to lay the foundation for improved trust, status, and coordination within that group (Kelley, Peters, and O'Connor 2009; Spiro, Acton, and Butts 2013). Further, coordinator brokerage often serves as a form of "informal insurance," providing victims access to established support networks for financial, physical, emotional, and logistical assistance (Beggs, Haines, and Hurlbert 1996; Hurlbert, Haines, and Beggs 2000). As an example of this, one individual (Kerry) recognized that his legal network could help provide urgent legal help for victims. He coordinated with local legal professionals to begin addressing an array of needs ranging from will preparation and submitting insurance requests to handling job loss. Turning to his affiliate group, Kerry was able to quickly identify and activate direct connections to address needs in the community. We propose that coordinator brokerage facilitates resource mobilization— namely, resource bundling—and therefore positively affects response effectiveness for three primary reasons.

First, strong connections within a group that ventures voluntarily identify with likely increase actors' knowledge of existing resources available for bundling or repurposing and engender flexible cooperation from in-group members as they use those resources to achieve compassion-related goals (Lilius, Worline, et al. 2011). Because of their history of cooperative interactions with other network members (and the resulting trust) (Obstfeld 2005), coordinator brokers generally have leverage when it comes to "mobilizing solidarity" (Aldrich 2012: 31) and motivating action (Putnam 2000). Strong group connections likely improve ventures' ability to align their responses to victim needs and to increase the speed of resource transmission to the proper individuals (e.g., resource providers, customers) (Shi, Markoczy, and Dess 2009). In a similar way, as brokers utilize their personal and community knowledge to develop postdisaster solutions, they likely encounter existing resources (e.g., equipment, logistics solutions, labor) that may have gone unnoticed otherwise but can be repurposed (Sonenshein 2014) to alleviate victim suffering.

Second, after a disaster, communication is often disrupted (Drabek 1985), and tasks are generally divided based on jurisdictional boundaries within affected communities (Wenger 1992). Because of this lack of communication and disruption of normal organizational operations (Neal and Phillips 1995), ventures with connections to various local community members are better positioned to develop and cultivate new norms, communication channels, and services to meet unfolding needs (Dynes 2005). Such ventures are more likely to view the disaster-stricken community as a resource in itself—an essential outlook for combining and repurposing resources to alleviate suffering (Mileti 1989). For instance, a new venture established after a disaster might be aware of nontraditional communication methods for sharing key activities (e.g., phone trees, "bush telegraph," community meetings) and organizing the appropriate stakeholders. In short, compassionate ventures that actively organize to alleviate victim suffering after a disaster provide leadership, structure, and some form of stability directly to the affected area, likely enabling resource mobilization that is both flexible and innovative.

Finally, high-profile disasters generally attract a substantial amount of media attention (Wenger, Quarantelli, and Dynes 1987). This media coverage in turn prompts numerous individuals from outside the disaster zone to donate their time, resources, or money to help victims (Quarantelli 1986; Auf der Heide 1989), thereby providing the disaster-stricken community access to unsolicited resources. Because of their strong community ties, coordinating brokers are well positioned to create and improve a group's identity (i.e., the new venture is "doing good" in the community), an identity that is often communicated to outsiders. As such, outsiders are likely to take notice of this coordinator brokerage, enabling the brokers to access and reuse potentially extensive outside resources for local initiatives to alleviate suffering. This view goes against traditional perspectives of coordinator brokers, which view these individuals as lacking "social relays" to connect them to outside resource providers. Rather, for natural disasters, when outsiders are influenced by extensive media attention and are eager to contribute to genuine recovery efforts (Quarantelli 1986; Auf der Heide 1989), coordinator brokerage and its associated resources (i.e., local reputation, knowledge, and coordination capabilities) are likely to be essential for obtaining and bundling resources. Indeed, in our research, we found that after a particularly devastating natural disaster, new venture coordinator brokerage had a positive relationship with ventures' use of resource bundling (Williams and Shepherd in press).[3]

Gatekeeper Brokerage   Gatekeeper brokerage occurs when an actor connects a nongroup member with a member from his or her own group (see figure 4.2) (Gould and Fernandez 1989). Gatekeeper brokers gather information and resources from an outside group and subsequently pass them on to their own group (Hargadon 2002; Stovel and Shaw 2012). For instance, a gatekeeper broker in a community affected by a disaster may harness his or her existing relationships with individuals outside the community (e.g., food suppliers) to devise innovative solutions for bringing in necessary supplies. Additionally, gatekeeper brokers are often given access to novel information from outsiders (Burt 2005) that they then use to aid the disaster-stricken community. For example, one individual (Karl) wanted access to architecture services as so many people needed to rebuild their homes. Specifically, he realized that using architectural expertise could enhance the value and improve the quality of the new homes, an approach known as building back better. He explored his network outside the disaster area, ultimately identifying nineteen architect-designed models that offered a variety of plan types of between two and four bedrooms, a variety of materials and construction types, and a variety of architectural design approaches, all of which could be adapted to suit a range of possible site conditions.

As this discussion suggests, after a disaster, gatekeeper brokerage will likely have an effect on the community's resource mobilization, with local ventures engaging in resource search to help ease victim suffering.

First, a significant benefit of serving as a broker between two groups is access to numerous resources that are unavailable inside one's own group or community (Burt 1997, 2000, 2005). These brokerage connections are likely to be particularly valuable after a disaster as the negative event may have destroyed many of the actors' local resources. Moreover, actors gain additional knowledge and information from their brokerage connections (Hargadon 2002; Powell and Smith-Doerr 1994), which can then be applied in the postdisaster environment. Thus, given their boundary-spanning connections, gatekeeper brokers are uniquely positioned to harness their external connections to obtain new resources to replace those damaged or destroyed in the disaster

Second, gatekeeper brokers frequently develop innovative ideas as they integrate knowledge from one group into another (Burt 2000, 2005). Individuals who have worked with multiple groups in the past are generally better able to identify how an idea or practice from one group can aid another group (Reagans and Zuckerman 2001). This contact with outside knowledge appears to trigger the development of new products, services, or goods to address victims' immediate needs as new ideas frequently arise from applying concepts from one domain to another (Hargadon 2002; Powell and Smith-Doerr 1994). For instance, several compassionate ventures harnessed their external networks to develop innovative customized solutions to help those affected by the Black Saturday bushfires. As gatekeeper brokers generate ideas like these, they likely undertake further resource-seeking activities to implement their ideas within the affected community.

Finally, because of the constraints imposed by the postdisaster environment, gatekeeper brokers likely have to make do with what is available. However, they generally do so by drawing on existing network resources in creative ways (Baker and Nelson 2005: 333) to seek and then to utilize resources to meet their venture objectives. Ventures with access to resources beyond their local network (and outside the disaster area) likely broker more resources through search activities than through bundling activities. Additionally, because of the destruction caused to these ventures' environment, gatekeeper brokers may feel that outside resources are more salient, valuable, and effective than resources closer to home. Looking for and mobilizing these outside resources may take substantial time, however, thereby limiting these actors' ability to conduct other resource mobilization activities. More specifically, after new ventures have identified and obtained external resources through their networks, they have to incorporate those resources into their current operations, leaving little time or energy for other resources activities (e.g., bundling or repurposing local resources). Indeed, in our research, we found that in the aftermath of a devastating natural disaster, gatekeeper brokerage has a positive relationship with resource search (Williams and Shepherd in press).

The Mediating Role of Resource Mobilization and Response Effectiveness

Above, we proposed that new ventures' network structures influence the strategies they use to access resources. However, just because a venture has access to resources does not necessarily mean it also has an advantage; rather, value is generated only when actors "use and alter resources … [and] creatively act on objects … to transform them into something useful" (Sonenshein 2014: 840). Ventures have varying views on how resources can and should potentially be used (Penrose 1959), a fact that has led organizational theory scholars to investigate how actors mobilize (i.e., utilize and adapt) resources instead of simply studying outcomes resulting from diverse resource caches (Baker and Nelson 2005; Sirmon, Hitt, and Ireland 2007; Sonenshein 2014). In the aftermath of a disaster, resource mobilization is essential to effectively alleviating victim suffering. Perhaps given the likelihood of additional physical, financial, and emotional suffering if failure occurs, new ventures operating in disaster areas become very creative and active in both repurposing existing resources and seeking new resources to meet their goals. We expect that variance in ventures' approaches to resource mobilization (i.e., resource bundling and resource search) will affect the response effectiveness of their solutions.

Resource Bundling as a Way to Mediate between Coordinator Brokerage and Response Effectiveness   Resource bundling is one way to translate brokerage connections into response effectiveness because "there is a wide scope for judgment" on how ventures should use resources, and "resources can be viewed as a bundle of possible services" (Penrose 1959: 67). In the disaster context, ventures can generate value by finding creative ways to use existing resources, which in turn enables them to identify potential actionable ideas (Baker and Nelson 2005) and novel solutions for problems (Garud and Karnøe 2003; Sonenshein 2014). As such, for several reasons, we propose that resource bundling likely serves as a mediator between coordinator brokerage and response effectiveness.

First, community routines and infrastructure, including government operations, organizational practices, and emergency response processes, are generally disrupted after disasters (Auf der Heide 1989; Quarantelli 1986). Even with these disruptions, however, many important local resources remain intact, including local knowledge, relationships, equipment, and facilities (Shepherd and Williams 2014). Also, outsiders generally flood disaster-stricken communities with needed resources, which—although helpful—creates a significant challenge for these communities in terms of coordinating and dispersing these resources (Drabek 1985; Wenger, Quarantelli, and Dynes 1987). In this environment, coordinating brokers are likely to play an important role in bundling, combining, and repurposing both existing local resources and unsolicited resources from outside the disaster area to help the community recover. Because of their resourcing practices and relationships within the community, coordinating brokers' postdisaster responses have the potential to be extensive in both scale and scope. This suggestion is especially interesting because in most contexts, resource bundling does not scale extensively (Baker and Aldrich 2000; Baker and Nelson 2005); however, after a disaster, it is critical in meeting victims' needs (Drabek and McEntire 2003).

Second, to bundle resources effectively, an actor must know what resources are available in the community (Baker and Nelson 2005). Because local resources are generally divided among many individuals, knowing what is on hand and ultimately combining existing resources requires the actor to engage with a variety of stakeholders, including other individuals involved in the venture and customers (in this case, victims) (Baker 2007; Garud and Karnøe 2003). This form of bundling usually occurs through interactions between customers or recipients of services and the venture or provider, with the customer providing detailed information regarding his or her needs, which in turn enables the provider to focus on what resources can be used for other ends. Thus, after a disaster, victim-actors who have roles as coordinating brokers in the community and undertake resource bundling activities will likely interact with victims to understand their particular needs and then develop customized solutions to overcome their problems. This customization is especially important in the postdisaster context because failing to develop tailored solutions not only decreases the likelihood that a solution will be effective but can even make victims' problems worse (Currier, Neimeyer, and Burman 2008).

Finally, because disasters frequently affect thousands of people in a short period of time, it becomes especially challenging for the affected community to rapidly coordinate and deploy outside assistance (Auf der Heide 1989; Newbert 2007). As a result, the first people to help in these critical situations are often the individuals directly affected by a disaster themselves (Wenger 1992). In this context, coordinating broker ventures are likely to enable rapid resource delivery by quickly assessing existing resources, communicating with victims to understand their needs, and then combining available resources to begin to meet victim needs (instead of waiting for outside resources) (consistent with Dynes 2005; Quarantelli 1986). Utilizing existing resources in this way can enable an almost instantaneous response to help victims after a disaster, which is also likely to enhance the effectiveness of that response (Dynes 2005; Mileti 1989). Indeed, as one of our studies (Williams and Shepherd in press) shows, after a natural disaster, resource bundling serves as to mediate the relationship between coordinator brokerage and response effectiveness, creating a positive indirect relationship.

Resource Search as a Way to Mediate between Gatekeeper Brokerage and Response Effectiveness   Individuals conduct resource searches to gather additional resources to reach a desired goal—in this case, improving the effectiveness of responses to alleviate victim suffering after a disaster. Unlike in traditional management contexts, resource search in the disaster context is unique: there is an urgent need to gather, coordinate, and deploy resources to aid others. And unlike the traditional resource search, which typically involves gathering and storing resources for future innovation and growth (Katila and Shane 2005), compassionate ventures must quickly seek, procure, and immediately deliver available resources.

We expect that this form of resource search, emphasizing immediate resource deployment and use, mediates the relationship between gatekeeper brokerage and response effectiveness for several reasons. First, a venture can improve its ability to survive and grow by acquiring new resources (Brush, Greene, and Hart 2001; Stinchcombe 1965). Thus, as gatekeeper brokers determine the best way to integrate diverse outside resources into their operations, they are likely to expand both the scale and scope of their responses to meet the goals set forth by their financial donors (Jarillo 1989; Newbert 2007; Newbert and Tornikoski 2013). Additionally, as these ventures advance in their mission to ease suffering, access to outside networks and engagement in resource search activities are likely to positively affect venture growth, which can also improve their response magnitude.

Second, actors who organize in the postdisaster context have to overcome a variety of obstacles to successfully alleviate suffering (Drabek and McEntire 2003). Lack of communication between victims and potential resource providers (Drabek 1985, 2005; Dynes 2005) is one such obstacle—a barrier that makes pairing outside resources with victim needs inside the affected area particularly challenging (Auf der Heide 1989). When this lack of communication persists, responders have no choice but to match outside resources to assumed needs without considering victims' customized needs in terms of resource type, amount, and assortment (Drabek 2005; Dynes 2005). Generalizing resources in this way is necessary to quickly increase the scale of operations when delivering goods or providing services, but this approach typically fails to meet specific local needs (Currier, Neimeyer, and Berman 2008). Thus gatekeeper brokers' engagement in resource search activities likely decreases the customization of their responses.

Finally, acquiring resources in the aftermath of a disaster is generally difficult because vital infrastructure is damaged, including roads and vehicles (Drabek and McEntire 2003; Dynes 2005), and the increased number of emergency responders can significantly affect normal transportation routes (Wenger, Quarantelli, and Dynes 1987). Thus resource search in disaster-stricken areas often involves navigating impaired infrastructure, a task that is fundamentally time-consuming and prone to considerable delays (Drabek 1985, 2005). Such delays affect actors' ability to both collect information regarding victim needs and deploy needed resources to the disaster zone (Drabek 2005; Drabek and McEntire 2003). Because of the challenges gatekeeper brokers face when searching for new resources in the postdisaster context, delivery speed is likely to be reduced. In line with the above logic, we (Williams and Shepherd in press) found that after an extensive natural disaster, resource search mediates the relationship between gatekeeper broker- age and response effectiveness; a positive indirect relationship with response magnitude but negative indirect relationships with delivery speed and customization.

Discussion

Disasters generate extensive social problems on a fairly regular basis, leading to critical economic, social, and environmental issues that imperil people, businesses, and entire communities (Bonanno et al. 2010; Cannon and Schipper 2014). Management scholars have been called on to contribute to the "grand challenge" of investigating the "role and functioning of organizations during adverse natural events" as organizations increasingly encounter "disruptive events from a broad range of threats and hazards" (Van der Vegt et al. 2015: 977). Thus far, the extant entrepreneurship and strategy research has gener- ally focused on activities that are secondary to organizations' main objectives, such as providing corporate donations from outside the disaster zone, and the ways in which these activities affect firm out- comes for the firms themselves (Madsen and Rodgers 2015; Muller and Kräussl 2011; Oh and Oetzel 2011; Tilcsik and Marquis 2013). We sub- stantially extend this CSR research by focusing on organizing to allevi- ate victim suffering as a primary firm activity initiated by victim-actors located within the disaster zone. Building on the literatures on social networks, resource mobilization, and compassion organizing, this chapter provides numerous insights for the literatures on CSR and venture resourcing.

First, we widen CSR research on outsider organizations' corporate giving to include compassionate venturing by local disaster victims and the affect this venturing has on firm value (Madsen and Rodgers

2015; Muller and Kräussl 2011) by investigating the effectiveness of venture creation in the postdisaster context—an action that is likely to be pertinent in the broader context of CSR responses to disasters. More specifically, for us to gain deeper insights into how ventures' efforts to alleviate suffering affect their value, we need to understand how successful these ventures' initiatives actually are (be they in the form of monetary donations or more involved responses like those discussed in this chapter, such as creating de alio new ventures). The data we gathered on venture networks, resourcing, and response effectiveness illustrate that many individuals inside a disaster zone do not lose all their resources after a significant disaster event and that some individuals harness their network ties and diverse resourcing strategies to help ease victim suffering through compassionate venturing. These network connections enable actors to identify and pursue opportunities to help ease suffering that go beyond monetary donations, which in turn shapes the effectiveness of their responses in terms of magnitude, speed, and customization. These findings align with and expand the recent work of Madsen and Rodgers (2015), who argued that CSR efforts attract more attention (and thus increase firm value) when they are genuine, urgent, and enacted. Similarly, we found that new ventures attracted others' attention when they obtained resources and support to ramp up and maintain their venturing efforts.

Our findings suggest that firm actions (beyond corporate giving) in the postdisaster context not only help the afflicted community but also provide value for new ventures in the form of startup resources. These findings create additional opportunities to explore venture engagement in response to disasters and the ways in which this engagement affects associated firm and community outcomes. Does higher engagement—that is, venture creation versus financial donation—increase an existing firm's likelihood of greater long-term performance? In a similar vein, CSR research has investigated how firms' prior reputation influences their participation in CSR activities (Godfrey 2005; Schnietz and Epstein 2005). Future research can build on these studies by exploring how ventures' level of engagement influences their reputation and CSR relationships. For instance, future CSR research can investigate the response effectiveness of venture solutions at multiple levels—magnitude, customization, and speed. Such research is likely to provide interesting insights regarding organizations' CSR activities as well as the value ventures obtain from undertaking these activities. Does a firm generate more value from providing highly customized responses than from merely donating cash? Do rapid, smaller-scale responses provide more value than delayed responses of greater magnitude? Do some ventures—namely, those with an established positive reputation—participate in "more engaged" helping activities compared to others (i.e., those with a negative reputation)?

Second, while previous research has stressed the substantial resource losses experienced by disaster victims (Lilius, Worline, et al. 2011), these individuals are rarely ever completely resourceless or helpless but generally retain a variety of resources (Bonanno et al. 2010). Throughout this chapter, we have explored brokerage—an aspect of ventures' network structures—nad actors' ability to coordinate and deploy resources through brokerage, likely making them more successful in alleviating victim suffering after a disaster than nonvictim outsiders. This finding is an initial response to calls for researchers to gain a deeper understanding of the ways in which various structural characteristics have an impact on ventures' response effectiveness (Van der Vegt et al. 2015), and particularly how structural relationships enable resource mobilization. Further, our finding that gatekeeper and coordinator brokerage facilitate access to different resource types could be a starting point for studying ventures' strategic decision making when facing extreme resource constraints (Baker and Nelson 2005), thus improving our understanding of why some actors decide to pursue opportunities even when they have few resources while others do not (Penrose 1959). Similarly, this work expands research on how ventures respond to poorly structured strategic challenges that are difficult to work through (Baer, Dirks, and Nickerson 2013). This altered view of loss opens further research pathways to better clarify ventures' resource positioning and needs after a significant loss event. In this context, helping disaster victims may entail backing victim-led venturing efforts instead of merely donating money or materials.

These findings could ultimately lead to substantial changes in how CSR-oriented help is provided and for what purpose. After a disaster, numerous actors gather at the devastated area, including corporations, nongovernmental organizations (NGOs), and individuals. Together, these individuals form a "donor community" that puts forth extensive effort and resources to rebuild the impacted area (Becerra, Cavallo, and Noy 2014; Cannon and Schipper 2014; USAID 2014). However, these "helping" efforts often fail to fully meet desired goals (Becerra, Cavallo, and Noy 2014), which leads to waste and further suffering in many cases (Bourguignon and Sundberg 2007; Easterly and Pfutze 2008). As our data revealed, seeking and bringing in outside resources does positively affect response magnitude; however, these activities do not appear to affect response customization or speed, both of which are essential for alleviating suffering after a disaster (Dutton, Workman, and Hardin 2014; Dutton et al. 2006). Rather, our findings suggest that for response efforts to be effective, we must take a more nuanced approach to assessing how victims experience loss after a disaster, highlighting that a true assessment of lost and retained resources should inform the way disaster responders think about victims. We anticipate that this altered perspective could result in more effective assistance and perhaps even increased return on CSR initiatives.

Finally, a large body of research is devoted to investigating the important role brokers play in entrepreneurial processes (for a review, see Burt 2005), including new venture creation (Bhagavatula et al. 2010; Burt 2005). Although this research underscores the benefits of a broker-age position in a network, there is a dearth of studies exploring the subaspects of brokerage and their effect on important outcomes (Gould and Fernandez 1989; Kirkels and Duysters 2010). Our data reveal different broker roles based on the group membership of actors involved in brokerage relationships. We found that these roles help shape the resourcing strategies firms use and thus the effectiveness of their responses to alleviate suffering after disaster. This finding points to the contingent value of brokerage in the postdisaster context, which is consistent with Shi and co-workers' (2009) finding that brokerage does not automatically provide an advantage. As such, future research exploring ventures' responses to disasters could benefit greatly by examining brokerage roles in afflicted communities, as well as how these roles affect CSR initiatives' effectiveness in improving firm value. In addition, research on venturing in different contexts could take a more nuanced view when investigating how actors engage in broker-age and with whom, which will likely enhance our overall understanding of venture resourcing and growth.

Moreover, because of the value of social networks and resource mobilization in disaster contexts, future research could pinpoint pre-emptive measures that disaster-prone communities might implement to improve organizational and community responses in the event of a disaster. Such research aligns with the goals of organizations like the U.S. Agency for International Development, the Red Cross, and the Red Crescent Society (Cannon and Schipper 2014; Shah 2012), which seek to "catalyze sustainable, transformational change" in communities hit by disasters—an objective that necessitates supporting victims who want to be part of the recovery solution (Shah 2012: 7; see also Drabek and McEntire 2003). This support could involve the creation of preemptive networks that could be activated if and when a crisis arose.

Conclusion

Because disasters are complex events, they often generate chaos. However, they also tend to unleash engaged prosocial responses from a variety of actors, including corporations, governments, NGOs, and new ventures. This chapter illustrates that ventures' relief initiatives in response to disasters can go beyond monetary corporate giving campaigns to include compassion venturing, with ventures' brokerage network relationships providing critical structural access to resources that can help ease victim suffering. Our findings also reveal that the effectiveness of ventures' responses—namely, their magnitude, customization, and speed—vary for a variety of reasons. Building on the network and compassion organizing literatures, the findings from this work provide interesting contributions to the literature on CSR. Our results also lead to a practical conclusion for disaster response efforts: even though disaster victims may experience great loss, they are not necessarily helpless after that loss; instead, these insiders play a vital role in alleviating the pain and suffering of a large population after a disaster hits.

Practical Implications

This chapter has highlighted the importance of identifying a broader set of resources when considering options for action after a disaster. Specifically, individuals' network relationships are one of the most readily available resources to motivate rapid, immediate action. We emphasized further that a number of methods for accessing and deploying resources exist, all of which can and should be used synergistically. This means that new outside resources can coexist with local efforts to repurpose and recombine.

Beyond the idea that responders should take a more expansive view of resources, this chapter has further pinpointed the potential value various types of organizations, established or new, can provide. Specifically, we empirically explored the effectiveness of disaster responses by spontaneous ventures and suggested that this same standard be used to assess the effectiveness of other efforts to address victim suffering. What does this mean? When individuals organize an effort to help, especially if they are far outside the disaster area, they need to ask themselves, "Is my effort really helping the local needs in a customized way? Will my efforts reach the victims in a timely manner? Will my efforts be appropriate in scale or scope?" Answering these questions will likely result in fewer actions that hamper relief provision. Those from outside the disaster area should seek to collaborate with those who have established networks within the area. This can be the best way to facilitate ongoing efforts to relieve suffering. As we discuss in later chapters, local residents are often frustrated by outsiders who focus on establishing new organizations or programs instead of first supporting local relief efforts.

The practical implications of chapter 4 are summarized below:

1. Do not assume that all resources are lost in the aftermath of a disaster. Rather, seek to identify those with local network resources who are trying to contribute to the relief effort.
2. Recognize the variety of ways to resource a project or compassionate venture. New resources could be pursued, or existing objects could be repurposed for new actions.
3. Outsiders should consider identifying local projects or initiatives to support rather than launching their own new initiatives. While this will provide a lower profile for the donor, it will likely have a much greater impact in terms of the customization, speed, and magnitude of the response.
4. Local residents should consider what resources they have on hand that can be redeployed immediately as these are just as effective as, if not more effective than, getting the "perfect fit" resource from outside. For example, could buildings, equipment, staff, and other resources be repurposed for disaster relief work?
5. Connections within and between communities are both important; they simply provide different types of benefits. Those with connections to outside community members should look for ways to draw on those connections to facilitate organizing efforts. However, they should do so knowing that such connections will likely offer access to less customized resources. In contrast, those with deep local connections should seek to extract, combine, and use the tacit knowledge of the community to establish whether more effective ways to communicate, transport goods, or perform other functions might exist.

6. NGOs, government agencies, and outside organizations should seek to collaborate with local efforts as they possess the most critical resources (i.e., networks) to identify needs and funnel goods/services to address those needs.

7. "Communities" are not always evident to outsiders. For example, two different villages in an area might be considered one community when they are actually very different from one another. In seeking to engage and collaborate with a community, it is important to learn how members of communities self-identify. Responders should avoid assuming they know a community as this can inhibit the speed and effectiveness of a response if they get it wrong.

5 Self-Help by Spontaneously Venturing to Help Others

For it is in giving that we receive.

—Saint Francis of Assisi

The sole meaning of life is to serve humanity.

—Leo Tolstoy

We make a living by what we get; we make a life by what we give.

—Winston Churchill

Making money is a happiness; making other people happy is a superhappiness.

—Muhammad Yunus

Up to this point in the book, we have primarily focused on how spontaneous venturing benefits the "customers" of the venture. This makes sense as organizational scholarship, especially entrepreneurship research, seeks to explain how organizations create customer and stakeholder value. In fact, one of the main points we have made up to this point is that organizational scholarship holds incredible potential to add to our understanding of organizing to alleviate suffering for victims of a disaster—which is an alternative firm outcome. In the context of this book, the customers are victims of the disaster who are suffering.[1]

This line of inquiry extends the primary objective in entrepreneurship research, which is the study of opportunities for the creation of value (Shane and Venkataraman 2000). While we have focused on the value venturing creates for others, chiefly by alleviating suffering, venturing also creates benefits for entrepreneurs themselves. For the entrepreneur, this value has most frequently been considered in terms of an economic opportunity (Haynie, Shepherd, and McMullen 2009) that leads to more than "average profits" (Fiet 2002: 2; see also Kirzner 1997; Shane 2000). However, a growing stream of research has focused on other elements of value for stakeholders, including the opportunity to mitigate environmental (Cohen and Winn 2007; Dean and McMullen 2007; Patzelt and Shepherd 2011) or social (Austin, Stevenson, and Wei-Skillern 2006; Mair and Marti 2006, 2009) problems.

Though entrepreneurship research has expanded beyond economic value creation for others, we still know very little about the different forms of value, especially noneconomic value, entrepreneurs create for themselves through venturing. This topic is particularly important to explore in the context of this book as it seems to be critical in understanding how compassionate venturing affects the creators of these ventures, especially when entrepreneurs are themselves victims of a potentially traumatic disaster. Could taking action actually make things worse? If compassionate ventures cease operations, does this add insult to injury? In this chapter, we seek to better understand how compassionate venturing may shape the lives of those taking action.

Venturing and the Benefits It Has for the Entrepreneur

Research has found that individuals, through entrepreneurial action, can gain noneconomic benefits, or "psychic income" (Gimeno et al. 1997: 758). Such benefits may include creating a desired identity after a traumatic event (Haynie and Shepherd 2011; Oyserman, Terry, and Bybee 2002; Teal and Carroll 1999) or gaining general satisfaction from the autonomy of self-employment (Evans and Leighton 1989; Smith and Miner 1983). As well, individuals find enjoyment and enhanced self-efficacy in creating innovative solutions in resource-scarce environments. In this context, entrepreneurs often participate in resourceful activities, such as tinkering with existing materials and arranging combinations of resources in such a way as to produce new objects of increasing complexity (Baker and Nelson 2005; Hayward et al. 2010).

Building on this foundational work of entrepreneurial resourcefulness (and its impact on the entrepreneur), recent studies have explored the concept of resilience as patterns of behavior that underlie venture persistence despite (potentially chronic) resource constraints (Powell and Baker 2011: 376), the capacity for positive adaption under adverse conditions (Sutcliffe and Vogus 2003), and the ability to bounce back from failure or setbacks (Block and Kremen 1996; Lazarus 1998). While more is known about how entrepreneurs creatively bundle and deploy a limited set of resources as a *reflection* of resilience (Baker and Nelson 2005; Powell and Baker 2011), less is known about how entrepreneurial action has an *impact* on resilience.

In the context of postcrisis responses, exploring this gap is potentially very important: could organizing to alleviate others' suffering have positive (or negative) impacts on the actor's ability to cope with and function despite the disaster? To explore this gap, we draw on the clinical psychology literature on resilience. In this literature, *resilience* is described as more than the simple absence of psychopathology (i.e., posttraumatic stress disorder): it is defined as a *stable trajectory* of *healthy functioning* across time, as well as the capacity for both positive emotions and generative experiences (Bonanno 2004, 2005; Williams et al. 2017). It occurs in the context of *a discrete and identifiable crisis or shock*—a potentially traumatic event (Bonanno 2012), such as a disaster (Bonanno et al. 2007, 2010). Critical to the definition of resilience is the recognition that the discrete event for the individual is only potentially traumatic, for different people have different responses even when exposed to the same event (Bonanno and Mancini 2012). As explored in earlier chapters, a disaster exposes individuals to a variety of challenges that are different from those faced in traditional resource-scarce environments. Specifically, the challenge is a surprise, potentially violent, and inherently involves loss, such as the loss of friends, family members, pets, livestock, or property (Bonanno 2004).

Resilience is considered to be important as it can facilitate adaptation in postdisaster contexts. After a disaster, resilient individuals are able to regulate emotions (Bonanno, Westphal, and Mancini 2011; Westphal and Bonanno 2004; Westphal, Seivert, and Bonanno 2010), maintain a stable or slightly modified view of the world (Bonanno et al. 2007; Galatzer-Levy, Burton, and Bonanno 2012; Janoff-Bulman 1992), cope with stress (Bonanno et al. 2002, 2010 Bonanno et al. 2002), and maintain stable or healthy levels of psychological and physical functioning (Bonanno 2004). In connecting entrepreneurial action with resilience after a disaster, a number of researchers have explored the emergent actions of disaster victims to help those in need (e.g., Drabek and McEntire 2003; Majchrzak, Jarvenpaa, and Hollingshead 2007), specifically the creation of new ventures to alleviate suffering (Shepherd and Williams 2014; see also the previous chapters). These entrepreneurial actions play an important role for the people who are helped (consistent with the social entrepreneurship literature), including filling gaps left by the system and generally alleviating suffering (Drabek 1987; Drabek and McEntire 2003; Shepherd and Williams 2014). The questions we then ask are as follows: what influence does spontaneous venturing to help those suffering in the aftermath of a disaster have on the resilience of the entrepreneurial actor, and how could that shape our understanding of the value individuals derive from helping the victims of a disaster, over and above the economic, social, and environmental consequences of their actions for others?

To address these questions, we draw on theories of psychological resilience and entrepreneurial action to construct and test a model (based largely on Williams and Shepherd 2016a) that makes several contributions.

First, the growing literature on social entrepreneurship has established that key benefits from entrepreneurial action include those to the environment (Dean and McMullen 2007), communities (Peredo and Chrisman 2006; Peredo and McLean 2006), and targeted social groups (Mair and Marti 2006). In addition, some research has emphasized benefits to the individual actor, including satisfaction from doing good (Sonnentag and Grant 2012) and building a desired career (Haynie and Shepherd 2011; Shepherd and Williams 2018; Teal and Carroll 1999). However, this research has not explored the benefits of other-serving entrepreneurial action *for the entrepreneur* in terms of helping him or her overcome obstacles associated with a disaster. Although entrepreneurial action helps others after a disaster (Drabek and McEntire 2002, 2003), we found (Williams and Shepherd 2016b) that entrepreneurial action also helps the entrepreneur him- or herself psychologically, physically, and emotionally.

Second, entrepreneurship research has explored how entrepreneuring individuals and organizations rebound from failure or severe crises (i.e., Hayward et al. 2010). Similarly, resilience in the entrepreneurship space is often explained as an ability to overcome (Fergus and Zimmerman 2005), a unique strength to rebound (Sutcliffe and Vogus 2003), or an active resistance to environmental buffetings (Harris, Sapienza, and Bowie 2009: 410). However, little is known about the antecedents of entrepreneurial resilience in the aftermath of a disaster. In this chapter, we explore these relationships and extend our understanding of resilience as explored in the entrepreneurship and management literature to include the disaster context. We found that when certain individuals immediately responded to a disaster through spontaneous venturing they not only maintained functioning by continuing ongoing activities (doing their jobs, fulfilling predisaster responsibilities) but even demonstrated enhanced functioning in that they took on new roles, activities, and challenges that they previously had not dealt with (Williams and Shepherd 2016b).

Third, scholars have previously found that prior experience is important in identifying and exploiting opportunities (Autio, Dahlander, and Frederiksen 2013; Grégoire and Shepherd 2012; Shane 2000) and influences an entrepreneur's self-confidence and sense of control (Ucbasaran, Westhead, and Wright 2009). Entrepreneurial experience enables individuals to identify opportunities based on their existing path of activity generated by their unique stock of experience (Nelson and Winter 1982; Shane 2000) as well as the creation of an entrepreneurial path that combines knowledge in novel ways that may have been impossible for those without experience (Dosi 1984). However, owing to the general inexperience most have with a large-scale natural disaster, entrepreneurial experience could serve a detrimental role in an individual's adjustment if that person fails to take action. In this chapter, we explore the possible double-edged sword of entrepreneurial experience, specifically in terms of the influence it has on resilient outcomes for founders of spontaneous ventures. We find that on the one hand, entrepreneurial experience can promote action and thus resilient outcomes. On the other hand, if entrepreneurially experienced individuals do not act, their confidence will be shattered by a realization of their lack of control and lack of solutions in the disaster, leading to nonresilient outcomes. Our findings (Williams and Shepherd 2016b) add to research on the role experience and action play in influencing entrepreneur-level outcomes.

Finally, we contribute to the cognitive psychology literature, in which resilience has been construed as the ability of an individual who is exposed to a disaster to maintain stable, healthy levels of functioning (Bonanno 2004). While this approach has been useful in understanding variation in reaction to trauma, scholars acknowledge that resilience can be achieved by a variety of paths and that it is important to understand the many forms of resilience (Bonanno 2004: 26; see also Bonanno and Mancini 2012; Joseph and Linley 2005). Specifically, the conceptualization of resilience has typically been captured as a binary outcome (resilient or not), which leaves much to be learned in terms of varying reactions to disasters and broader aspects of adjustment (Bonanno and Mancini 2012). We hope to enlarge the picture of adjustment following a disaster and, in doing so, add to the conversation about the heterogeneity of disaster responding (Bonanno 2004; Curran and Hussong 2003) by identifying three types of resilient functioning—behavioral, emotional, and assumptive (Williams and Shepherd 2016b).

The Impact of Spontaneous Venturing on the Entrepreneur

To explore the key research questions outlined above, we investigate resilience after entrepreneurial action in the wake of a natural disaster. As illustrated throughout this book, especially in chapter 1, natural disasters are events, observable in time and space, in which a community incurs physical damages and losses (of persons or property) that severely deplete the resources available within that community (Drabek 2004; Kreps 1984). *Entrepreneurial action* involves the mobilization of resources in a coordinated way that will generate goods or services to produce a desired economic or social gain (Gartner 1985; Katz and Gartner 1988; Shane and Venkataraman 2000). Entrepreneurial action can result in the creation of a venture, although this is not a necessary condition (Shane and Venkataraman 2000) as entrepreneurial action can occur within existing firms or organizational entities (Amit, Glosten, and Mueller 1993; Casson 1982). Moreover, entrepreneurial action in the form of spontaneous venturing to help those suffering after a disaster appears to be quite common (Shepherd and Williams 2014; Williams and Shepherd 2016b; see also chapters 3 and 4). In the data set drawn on for this chapter, many of the individuals who took entrepreneurial action—that is, entrepreneurs—could be described as new venture creators, whereas others created new initiatives within existing organizational frameworks (similar to corporate entrepreneurship). This is similar to the picture presented in chapters 3 and 4.

With this background understanding of postdisaster activity, we draw on the theories of entrepreneurial action (Haynie et al. 2009; McMullen and Shepherd 2006; Shane 2001; Shane and Venkataraman 2000; Shepherd, McMullen, and Jennings 2007) and the clinical psychology conceptualizaton of resilience (Bonanno 2004, 2012; Bonanno and Mancini 2012; Williams et al. 2017) as the theoretical foundation for our spontaneous venturing model of resilience after a disaster. We illustrate this model in figure 5.1 (consistent with Williams and Shepherd 2016b). In building on these theories, we explore the influence that spontaneous venturing to help those suffering in the aftermath of a disaster has on the resilient outcomes of entrepreneurial actors. In our model, spontaneous venturing to help those suffering in the aftermath

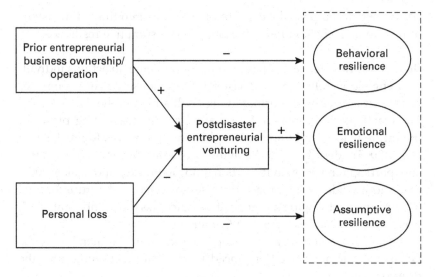

Figure 5.1
Factors Influencing the Effectiveness of Spontaneous Ventures in Alleviating Suffering

of a disaster plays both a direct and an indirect role in explaining resilience: spontaneous venturing mediates the relationship between attributes of the individual victims (i.e., prior entrepreneurial business experience, degree of personal loss) and resilience. In the discussion that follows, we detail the mediating role of spontaneous venturing in the relationships between prior entrepreneurial business experience and the three resilience dimensions. We also discuss the mediating role of spontaneous venturing in the relationships between the degree of personal loss an individual experiences and the three resilience dimensions.

Spontaneous Venturing and Resilience Outcomes

The primary emphasis in the clinical psychology literature on resilience is on functioning. Here, functioning does not imply the complete absence of a stress response, which would be a relatively rare occurrence after a disaster (Hobfoll et al. 2011; Ong et al. 2006). Rather, resilient individuals still express at least some degree of distress during or in the immediate aftermath of a disaster (Bonanno 2012). For resilient individuals, distress reactions are usually mild and temporary and tend not to interfere with their ongoing ability to function over time (Bonanno 2004, 2005, 2012). In this chapter (following Williams and Shepherd

2016b), we decompose the concept of resilience into three dimensions of functioning—behavioral, emotional, and assumptive resilience.

Behavioral Resilience   Behavioral resilience refers to actions individuals engage in following a disaster that demonstrate functioning or actions associated with normal living (Williams and Shepherd 2016b). These actions could include formulating and implementing plans for the future (e.g., rebuilding efforts, planning) (Bonanno, Rennicke, and Dekel 2005), identifying and solving problems (Bonanno 2004, 2005), and participating in activities (Bonanno, Rennicke, and Dekel 2005) that show evidence of proactivity—self-directed and future-focused action aimed at bringing about positive outcomes (Bonanno, et al. 1995; Coifman et al. 2007; Scheier and Carver 1992).

As an illustration of this concept, one community member, Anne Leadbeater, demonstrated enhanced behavioral functioning after the disaster:

After Black Saturday, I had a key role in coordinating the recovery efforts. ... I ran daily community meetings in Kinglake and its surrounds. I arranged for a number of relief and emergency services agencies to attend each meeting. I also chaired agency briefings twice a day. I helped to coordinate the delivery and dissemination of material aid and resources to the communities, and arranged transport for those wishing to leave the area within the first few days after the fires.

Victims who engage in spontaneous venturing to help those suffering in the aftermath of a disaster likely experience a different behavioral resilience trajectory over time than those who do not engage in such actions. First, by immediately focusing on an organized effort to address needs, victims who spontaneously venture concentrate on future-oriented problems and solutions, which in turn call for continued attention and action (Coifman et al. 2007; Scheier and Carver 1992). From the entrepreneurial action literature, we know that an early stage of the action process involves allocating attention to identifying possible solutions to address specific problems (McMullen and Shepherd 2006). When a solution is deemed feasible, the actor defines and executes a course of action (or series of actions), which again requires the allocation of attention and other resources, such as time, equipment, and money (Autio et al. 2013; Bakker and Shepherd 2017; Shepherd, McMullen, and Ocasio 2017). By taking entrepreneurial action, these individuals fill their time planning and executing ongoing activities, essentially committing themselves to function on an ongoing basis.

Therefore, a consequence of their action is a commitment to future action, activity, and engagement (Bonanno et al. 2005). For example, Anne Leadbeater explained, "I was involved across the recovery process—from the initial 'response' stage (on 9 February 2009) to the longer-term 'recovery stage,' continuing [from role to role] until ... August 2009."

Second, by spontaneously venturing, the entrepreneur makes connections with other individuals—both within (victims) and outside (relief providers) the community—that are specifically related to the objectives of the newly created venture. This increased contact leads to support from people in the social environment who are critical to successfully addressing various needs (Keltner and Bonanno 1997) and also increases the interactions and activities the entrepreneur engages in with others. As others recognize the entrepreneur as a source of resources as well as a critical component of rebuilding or disaster response (Tierney, Lindell, and Perry 2001; Tierney and Trainor 2004), additional activities and interactions are generated for the entrepreneur, again leading to a resilient behavioral functioning trajectory. As an illustration, one individual, Helen Kenney, explained how initial actions resulted in a "snowballing effect" of resources:

I started working in recovery on almost a full-time basis within two weeks of the fire, trying to balance that with monitoring the fire threat and re-establishing a safe haven for my children. ... I run a community breakfast barbecue once a month which assists community members to gather together and I also do personal outreach where I visit people in their homes. I am working with a panel of psychologists and other specialists to assist those who are experiencing ongoing emotional and physical trauma as a result of the fire. I am not a psychologist but I trained as a youth counsellor many years ago and I have the ability to listen and pick up on what people are saying. That helps, as does the fact that a lot of people know me through my association with the [community fire brigade] and feel comfortable talking to me.

Through Helen's connections and relationships, she managed to generate many activities that resulted in additional interactions and improved functioning.

Third, spontaneous venturing to help those suffering in the aftermath of a disaster places the actor in a role where he or she must think creatively, solve problems, and take leadership roles to achieve the goals of the venture (Long and McMullan 1984). The actor fulfills this role with uncertain information regarding resource availability or venture duration (Casson 2007; Casson and Wadeson 2007), which therefore requires ongoing engagement, planning, and decision making. Similarly, the potential outcome of the action remains uncertain (Knight 1921; McMullen and Shepherd 2006), triggering ongoing activities by the entrepreneur to enhance positive outcomes and reduce negative outcomes. This motivation for achieving positive action outcomes is perhaps even higher because of the strained environmental conditions (i.e., the presence of ongoing threats) surrounding the disaster and the dire consequences of failing to achieve the venture's objectives, such as ongoing suffering and additional property loss. We indeed found that those who engaged in spontaneous venturing to help those suffering in the aftermath of a disaster had higher behavioral resilience than those who did not engage in spontaneous venturing (Williams and Shepherd 2016b). As an illustration, Peta Whitford felt "inspired" after organizing a response. In particular, she was impressed by those who rallied to support her cause, and she found new leadership skills. She explained, "We all came together as a community. ... [Later] we contacted [everyone who was involved] and hosted a street party. Most people attended despite the trauma they were going through. ... We discussed with them what had worked and what had not [which helped them]." This individual had previously had no experience or expertise in such matters.

Emotional Resilience   Emotional resilience refers to emotional functioning, or the ability of individuals to voluntarily regulate their emotional responses following a traumatic event (Gross and John 2003; New et al. 2009; Williams and Shepherd 2016b) and to express relatively less negative emotion and greater positive emotion than other bereaved individuals (e.g., Keltner and Bonanno 1997). During potentially traumatic events (e.g., disasters), positive emotions co-occur alongside negative emotions (Folkman and Moskowitz 2000), with some individuals demonstrating higher levels of negative than positive emotions and vice versa. Emotionally resilient individuals demonstrate an emotionally adaptive flexibility following traumatic events (Bonanno 2005), or the ability to enhance or suppress sentiments of grief, distress, and anxiety in an effective manner (Bonanno et al. 2004). In addition, such people show increased levels of positive emotion and optimism compared to nonresilient individuals (New et al. 2009: 662; see also Tugade and Fredrickson 2007).

As described earlier, spontaneous venturing to help those suffering in the aftermath of a disaster involves directing attention to an opportunity, evaluating the opportunity, and then taking steps toward acting on that opportunity (McMullen and Shepherd 2006). By engaging in the activities of spontaneous venturing to help those suffering in the aftermath of a disaster, these entrepreneurs are likely to exhibit emotional resilience for three primary reasons. First, such entrepreneurial action requires both creativity (Baker and Nelson 2005) and an emphasis on constructing or creating (Shane and Venkataraman 2000) when identifying, developing, evaluating, and enacting entrepreneurial ideas (Ardichvili, Cardozo, and Ray 2003; see also Mair and Marti 2009), such as those intended to alleviate others' suffering. Entrepreneurial activity under extreme resource constraints (e.g., spontaneous venturing to help those suffering after a disaster) is especially reliant on creative and flexible thinking to find workable approaches (within extreme constraints) to problems (Baker 2007; Baker and Nelson 2005), in the context of damaged systems, an imperfect or absent resource pool, and a generally disabled external environment (Kreps 1984; Majchrzak, Jarvenpaa, and Hollingshead 2007; Tierney, Lindell, and Perry 2001). Acts of creative, flexible, and broad-based thinking are typically associated with positive emotions (Fredrickson 2001), and we expect that as individuals engage in these activities, they shift their attention from the obvious problems—damage to people, buildings, and the landscape—to possible solutions (consistent with Dunn, Aknin, and Norton 2008; Williamson and Clark 1989), thereby enhancing their resilience (Tugade and Fredrickson 2007) to the disaster. For example, Ann Leadbeater stated that she was "very busy" with the venture, initiating new efforts, and that made her feel "quite amazed," "fortunate," and "lucky" despite all of the destruction that had occurred around her.

Second, spontaneous venturing to help those suffering in the aftermath of a disaster allows entrepreneurs to interact with both victims and nonvictims. These interactions include coordinating operations, communicating needs and solutions, and participating in more therapeutic activities, such as debriefing, listening to fellow victims, and telling stories of survival (see Dynes 1970; Marcum, Bevc, and Butts 2012; Quarantelli 1996). By participating in and leading these activities, entrepreneurs engage recursively in problem-based coping or pragmatic coping (i.e., actions and cognitions aimed at addressing the underlying problem) and emotion-based coping (i.e., actions and cognitions aimed at ameliorating the negative emotions associated with the underlying problem) (Bonanno et al. 2004; Folkman and

Moskowitz 2004; Gupta and Bonanno 2011). These combined forms of coping (Galatzer-Levy, Burton, and Bonanno 2012) are likely a consequence of initiating the venture, facilitating emotional resilience. In utilizing both forms of coping—through spontaneous venturing to help those suffering in the aftermath of a disaster—the entrepreneur benefits from the distraction provided by problem-focused coping (Folkman and Moskowitz 2004) and the reprieve from negative emotions (Fredrickson et al. 2000) from talking through the emotions of the disaster with other individuals (see Shepherd 2003 for the importance of oscillating between a loss orientation and a restoration orientation for reducing grief over loss). For example, nearly all the entrepreneurs spoke to the value of meeting and interacting with people after the disaster. Just having the opportunity to talk to people about the event helped them sort through challenges. For some, this involved meeting new people, such as "politicians ... volunteers, and the local council," among others.

Third, spontaneous venturing to help those suffering in the aftermath of a disaster can generate personal utility for the entrepreneur in the form of fulfillment, interest, and intrinsic enjoyment (Evans and Leighton 1989; Goss 2005; Smith and Miner 1983). Entrepreneurial action is inherently social in nature and generates emotional energy (Goss 2005) both for the entrepreneur and for those around him or her, which can lead to self-efficacy and pride in the work being accomplished (Hatfield, Cacioppo, and Rapson 1994). In leading an initiative after a disaster, actors draw followers (Kershaw 1998), or individuals who trust them (Bryson, Crosby, and Stone 2006; Child and Möllering 2003; Majchrzak, Jarvenpaa, and Hollingshead 2007), and view them as legitimate actors in the new environment (Laufer 2007; Voorhees 2008). Engaging with these followers (or participants in the entrepreneurial activity), delivering services, and fulfilling very public roles (e.g., as communicator or coordinator) increase actors' visibility and often deepen the complexity of their entrepreneurial activities (Shepherd and Williams 2014; see also Drabek 1989). After a disaster, this escalation of entrepreneurial action likely generates a virtuous emotional cycle, triggered and perpetuated by entrepreneurial actions, that continues to grow while influencing the actor's emotional resilience. Indeed, we found that those who engaged in spontaneous venturing to help those suffering in the aftermath of a disaster were more likely to have higher emotional resilience than those who did not engage in this spontaneous venturing (Williams and Shepherd 2016b).

Assumptive Resilience   Assumptive resilience refers to the view that the world, or the environment one lives in, is benevolent (i.e., people generally have good intentions and everything will work out positively) and meaningful (i.e., causal relationships still exist, the world makes sense, and the self is capable of virtuous and positive acts) (Beder 2005; Janoff-Bulman 1992; Williams and Shepherd 2016b). After a traumatic event, an individual's assumptive view of the world is often threatened (Janoff-Bulman 1992), and the assumptions that previously provided coherence and structure for the individual can suddenly be perceived as illusions, leading to a "terrifying disillusionment" (Beder 2005: 258). For many individuals suffering through disasters, their previous views of others, world meaning, and the self are shattered (Kauffman 2013). In contrast, individuals with assumptive resilience maintain a balanced view of the world and continue fulfilling personal and social responsibilities while even engaging in new experiences or challenges (Bonanno, Galea, et al. 2007). These individuals still recognize the implications of the tragedy but find a way to maintain self- and worldviews that promote functioning (Janoff-Bulman 1992).

When pursuing entrepreneurial ideas, individuals are inherently pushed to investigate and interpret their surroundings, detect potential problems or barriers, and ultimately make conjectures in an uncertain environment about their world or environment (McMullen and Shepherd 2006; Shepherd et al. 2012). Therefore, we suggest that when individuals engage in spontaneous venturing to help those suffering in a disaster-stricken area, they are more likely to retain their previous view of the world, or only a slightly modified version of it. We suggest this occurs through three primary mechanisms.

First, insofar as entrepreneurial activity is inherently social in nature, with the entrepreneur interacting with customers, collaborators, and suppliers (Aldrich 1999; Burt 1992, 2000), he or she will be exposed to benevolent individuals seeking to assist with disaster recovery (Bryson, Crosby, and Stone 2006; Marcum, Bevc, and Butts 2012) who can help achieve the goals of the venture. By constantly interfacing with others, the entrepreneur likely relies on common standards (e.g., contracts, informal agreements) to accomplish the tasks at hand. Similarly, the entrepreneur relies on many others to coordinate action and deliver goods or services to individuals in need. As a result of this frequent interaction with others in the world, actors will likely put their beliefs in the benevolence of others to the test (Beder 2005) and will find evidence that benevolence exists (despite the chaos of a disaster). By immediately acting entrepreneurially to create a venture that helps disaster victims, the individual can quickly challenge, test, and validate ongoing assumptions, enabling assumptive resilience. For example, after the bushfires, many individuals expressed that they were "amazed," "grateful," and "inspired" by how their community responded. As one individual said, "Everyone has been really good. … We are just so grateful."

Second, because spontaneous venturing enables the entrepreneur to explore the various needs in the new, postdisaster environment and make decisions regarding what opportunities to pursue and whom to service, they will rapidly transition from a "meaning-making" mentality to "meaning made" (Park et al. 2008). Meaning making involves the effort or process to understand the event that has violated an individual's belief that the world is fair or just and that one's life is meaningful or ordered (Janoff-Bulman 1989; Park and Folkman 1997). Meaning made, on the other hand, is an outcome of meaning making, where meaning (as described above) is restored (Park et al. 2008). While meaning-making activities can be positive for an individual's response to a disaster, they can also lead an individual to overly focus on the disaster itself, thereby reducing adjustment (Nolen-Hoeksema 1996). As entrepreneurs pursue opportunities to help victims of the disaster, the new relationships they form, the products or services they deliver to others, and other consequences of taking action will likely lead to meaning made, such as a reinterpretation of their experience as positive (see Bellizzi and Blank 2006), a deepened sense of community and survivorship (see Brady et al.1999), and reduced inconsistency of beliefs in a just world (i.e., the focus on "why me?") (see Park et al. 2008), all of which are critical to assumptive resilience. For example, Helen said she "started off quite simply" by calling a few farmers, but this effort grew: "Once the [venture] started, we began calling for farmers to provide fodder, the whole thing became absolutely enormous. … Transport companies got involved and we were getting phone offers of assistance from all over Victoria. … [We took on the role] of organising distribution." All these activities helped create new meaning and relationships in the community, which cultivated resilience.

Third, through spontaneous venturing to alleviate victim suffering, an entrepreneur is able to reaffirm self-value despite all that may have been lost. Research has found that most of the emergent activities individuals pursue after disasters are "higher-purpose" activities, designed to ameliorate the critical needs of others, address gaps in a system, and so forth (Drabek and McEntire 2003). For this reason, individuals who act and provide for others will likely view their task as fulfilling (Sonnentag and Grant 2012) and end up helping themselves in the process (Penner et al. 2005; Sonnentag and Grant 2012). Indeed, initial labels for entrepreneurial activity following a disaster included the "altruistic community" (Barton 1969) and "utopian community" (Taylor, Zurcher, and Key 1970), wherein the dominant activity is prosocial in nature (Quarantelli 1986) and the affected persons are first to help themselves and others (Stephens 1997; Wenger, Quarantelli, and Dynes 1987). In this sense, acting to help others after a disaster does not appear to lead to assumptive disruption; rather, such action appears to spark the altruistic nature within individuals (Quarantelli 1986), further solidifying assumptive functioning. Again, we found that those who engaged in spontaneous venturing to help victims after a disaster were more likely to have assumptive resilience than those who did not engage in spontaneous venturing (Williams and Shepherd 2016b). As an illustration, Juliet Moore explained the following:

One of the projects I [started working on right after the disaster] and one that I'm really excited about is another neighbours' house. Their house was completely flattened. They had also been in the process of building a gym at Pheasant Creek. The gym equipment which was stored at their home was destroyed but they just got on and rebuilt it. And it is amazing, it has added such a sense of community because suddenly we all have an outlet to go to ...[and we] have a lot of admiration for their attitude towards the rebuilding process, which is "If it's going to happen, we've got to do it, because we can't expect someone else to do it, and if we talk about it, it's not going to happen and if we open it up to community discussion we'll just get 5000 opinions and arguments, so we'll just do it." ... I am also very excited to be involved in another project. The project is for a restaurant and the intention is that it will be provide a focal point for the community and potentially also provide training and jobs for young people in the community. We are currently in [discussions] regarding the opportunities the area can generate.

Spontaneous Venturing as a Mediating Mechanism

Role of Startup Experience   In the entrepreneurial context, experience is a critical resource (Shane 2000) that can help reduce uncertainty and therefore encourage action (McMullen and Shepherd 2006; Shane and Venkataraman 2000; Stevenson and Jarillo 1990). Expert entrepreneurs are able to leverage their experience to recognize opportunities by "uncovering new means-ends relationships, which, if fruitfully combined with the individual's idiosyncratic skills, experience, and resources, trigger entrepreneurial action" (Autio, Dahlander, and Frederiksen 2013: 9; Eckhardt and Shane 2003; Shane 2000).

In the disaster context, entrepreneurial experience likely promotes action for two reasons. First, having conducted business in the disaster-stricken area prior to the disaster, local entrepreneurs know how to serve the local market (Shane 2000) despite their possible lack of knowledge regarding disaster management. This local knowledge is likely accumulated through years of social relationships (i.e., social capital; Burt 1992), interactions with others, and a general understanding of how commerce functions at the local level (see Shepherd and Williams 2014; see also chapter 3). Previous entrepreneurial efforts provide the actor with experience in processing and framing information, both of which help individuals identify and take advantage of disequilibrium in the market (Kaish and Gilad 1991). Prior experience in generating ideas by evaluating a local market, obtaining feedback on existing products, and making adjustments over time, coupled with the knowledge attained in managing an entrepreneurial firm, likely prepares one for the creation of a venture to alleviate the suffering caused by a disaster. For example, many of the victims who started ventures in the aftermath of disaster did so in areas in which they had practical experience (e.g., farming, psychology) or in which they had prior experience starting a business (e.g., architecture, construction, animal care).

Second, entrepreneurs who are themselves victims of a natural disaster can draw on the newly established, potentially tragic common experience of having endured the natural disaster as a way both to gain legitimacy and to more accurately and rapidly address customer needs. Experience-induced awareness of issues or needs in a system can lead to opportunity recognition (Autio, Dahlander, and Frederiksen 2013). Those with prior experience are more likely than less experienced individuals to be aware of solutions (e.g., managerial, product) to problems (Autio, Dahlander, and Frederiksen 2013) and to recognize the needs of potential customers (Companys and McMullen 2007). These individuals, having endured the disaster, are often more aware of victims' needs and are "more innovative in solving their problems ... than they are given credit for" (Drabek and McEntire 2003: 99). Knowledge of the victims (and thereby the potential customers of the spontaneous ventures) in these instances comes from the maintenance (and even strength) of the social structure (Dynes and Tierney 1994; see also Shepherd and Williams 2014), as well as from the shared experience of having endured the disaster together (Wenger, Quarantelli, and Dynes

1987). For example, Juliet Moore recognized a unique opportunity to build homes for those who had lost their residences and to do so in a fast, unique way. Most permanent disaster shelters were taking months to arrive; however, this entrepreneur was able to produce and deliver a customized solution in fewer than ninety days. She was motivated to address the suffering of her neighbors, recognizing that they wanted both to stay on their property and live in a suitable home. She made this happen.

Potential Downside of Experience Though experience has benefits, entrepreneurial experience could also inhibit resilient outcomes when entrepreneurial action does not occur. Experience then acts as a double-edged sword, positively influencing experienced individuals who take action and negatively affecting those experienced actors who do not.

First, those with entrepreneurial experience might be more subject to overconfidence, resulting in the illusion of control (Forbes 2005; Gaglio 1997; Hayward, Shepherd, and Griffin 2006; Simon and Shrader 2012). At the moment of the disaster, this perception of control and self-confidence could come crashing down as the individual faces a postdisaster reality that may result in near total loss of control (Wenger, Quarantelli, and Dynes 1987). If individuals with prior entrepreneurial experience fail to transfer their self-confidence and entrepreneurial skill set into entrepreneurial action to address emerging needs, they could experience a greater fall than those without such experience in terms of a resilient outcome. For example, Andrew Berry lost his café and felt aimless. Before the disaster he had felt "in control" and capable of directing his own path, but after seeing that path dismantled in just a few minutes, he was left searching for other options.

Second, an experienced entrepreneur might rely excessively on past decisions, processes, and solutions (Hayward, Shepherd, and Griffin 2006), even though the environment requires new thinking to address emergent needs (Drabek and McEntire 2003). While experience is useful in sensitizing an individual to solutions and opportunities that resonate with that individual's idiosyncratic knowledge (Autio, Dahlander, and Frederiksen 2013; Shane 2000), it could also limit the individual's openness to new processes or solutions required for functioning in the postdisaster environment. A disaster creates problems, social structures, and institutional challenges that are new to (previously unexperienced by) most of the people who are exposed to them (Drabek and McEntire 2003). The incongruence or misapplication of existing processes, decision-making criteria, and predetermined solutions to the postdisaster environment could therefore lead to frustration, stress, and despondency and could ultimately reduce an individual's resilience. For these reasons, if individuals with entrepreneurial experience do not initiate new ventures, we expect they will have lower resilience. Further, we suggest that experience can cut both ways, either benefiting or hurting individuals, depending on whether or not they take entrepreneurial action to create a spontaneous venture. We found that prior entrepreneurial business experience positively related to spontaneous venturing to alleviate others' suffering in the aftermath of a disaster, which in turn mediated the relationship between prior entrepreneurial business experience and behavioral, emotional, and assumptive resilience (Williams and Shepherd 2016b). In addition, we found that those who had previous entrepreneurship experience but did not take action were less likely to experience behavioral, emotional, and assumptive resilience.

Role of the Degree of Loss   For response groups (e.g., spontaneous ventures) to emerge after a disaster, material resources (Bonanno et al. 2007) such as equipment, means of transportation, and goods (Quarantelli 1996) must be available. Similarly, research has found that the "loss of psychosocial and material resources [is] associated with the level of distress experienced" (Hobfoll et al. 2011: 1405), which in turn can affect one's response trajectory (Bonanno 2004). While individuals have demonstrated the ability to make do with limited resources in helping themselves after disasters (Drabek and McEntire 2003) and in penurious environments, cobbling together unique and valuable bundles of resources seemingly "from nothing" (Baker and Nelson 2005; Shepherd, Parida and Wincent in press), the change in resource availability at extreme levels can increase stress levels (Hobfoll et al. 2003; Norris and Kaniasty 1996). In particular, research has found that the presence of personal resources, including material resources, such as income; work resources, such as employment; and interpersonal resources, such as social support or affinity groups (Hobfoll and Lilly 1993), is more likely to lead to positive personal outcomes (Hobfoll et al. 2003) as personal resources provide a sense of control or impact over important elements of the environment despite the difficult circumstances (Bandura 1997; Kobasa and Puccetti 1983). Therefore, the more the disaster results in the loss of these personal resources, the less likely an individual is to take entrepreneurial action and in turn exhibit a resilient response trajectory. This could occur for two primary reasons.

First, excessive uncertainty is believed to limit entrepreneurial action (McMullen and Shepherd 2006; Shane and Venkataraman 2000; Stevenson and Jarillo 1990). When an individual has experienced extensive loss—for example, the loss of home in its entirety, the loss of property, physical injury, the death of a family member or friend—the uncertain future could potentially block or delay action (Lipshitz and Strauss 1997: 150). While perceptions of uncertainty have been shown to vary among individuals experiencing the exact same circumstances (Lipshitz and Strauss 1997), as the severity of the loss increases, individuals likely experience greater interruption of routines and are forced into choosing among many unappealing options (Yates and Stone 1992). In turn, these events could drive an individual to focus inward, or on narrow, more self-oriented activities or actions (e.g., filing insurance claims, sorting through debris) (Fredrickson 2001). For example, Anja Toikka, who lost friends as well as her home in the bushfires, explained the following:

It is hard to understand and accept that life will never be the same again. At times the grief for the lost life and resentment and pain for the sudden change forced upon us has been unbearable. There have been many days when I have sat inside and thought "where do I start?" ... The whole vastness of the tasks overwhelmed me completely and at the end of each day nothing got done.

Second, while entrepreneurs have been shown to make do with resources on hand under situations of resource scarcity (Baker and Nelson 2005), it would appear that as the extent of lost resources increases, an individual's ability to act on opportunities eventually begins to decrease (Hobfoll 1989, 2001), and he or she could even fall into a "loss spiral" (Hobfoll 2001: 337). To function as an entrepreneur, the individual must be able to take responsibility for the judgmental decisions that influence the location, form, and use of goods or resources (Hébert and Link 1988). In making these judgment decisions in the disaster context, an entrepreneur needs to have attentional capacity to determine unique resource combinations (Shepherd, McMullen, and Jennings 2007) while also attempting to survive the ongoing threats in the unstable postdisaster environment (Drabek 1987). As a result of a diminished resource supply, the individual could lose a sense of control to offset stressors, a belief that action in the world has meaning, and trust that the world is benevolent, thereby disrupting his or her assumptive resilience (Beder 2005; Janoff-Bulman 1985, 1992). Indeed, we found that after the Black Saturday bushfires, the extent of personal loss negatively related to spontaneous venturing to help others, which in turn mediated the relationship between prior entrepreneurial business experience and behavioral, emotional, and assumptive resilience (Williams and Shepherd 2016b).

For example, Andrew Berry explained how initial losses led to disruptions in functioning, which in turn led to additional losses (underemployment):

Our closest neighbours were approximately 70–80 feet from [our door] ... they all died. They should have been in our bunker, we had capacity to take all those people but none of us expected the [degree of crisis]. ... Although we've now moved away from the area we still struggle. I don't have the capacity to work five days a week but I'm still trying to work. ... [Until now] I had never been on unemployment benefits in my life. I know many people [like me] who are not going back to their previous job as they are in no mental state to cope with work. ... Everybody has been affected in some way.

Although experience and resource loss explain whether an individual is more or less likely to engage in spontaneous venturing to alleviate others' suffering (Williams and Shepherd 2016b), it is also important to explore the underlying motivations of these entrepreneurial actions, to which we now turn.

Motivating Spontaneous Venturing

Recent research on motivation has distinguished between prosocial, intrinsic, and extrinsic motivation (De Dreu and Nauta 2009; Grant 2008; Grant and Berry 2011). *Prosocial motivation* refers to feeling compelled to put forth effort based on the desire to aid or contribute to others (Batson 1998; De Dreu 2006; Grant 2008; Grant and Berry 2011; Grant and Sumanth 2009) and can help fulfill many victim needs after disasters (Batson et al. 2008). According to Grant, prosocial motivation is

a more temporary psychological state, involves a momentary focus on the goal of protecting and promoting the welfare of other people. ... [It is a state of] introjected or identified regulation ... [driven] by introjected goals of avoiding guilt and protecting self-esteem or by identified goals of fulfilling core values and identities ... a telic state in which the work is instrumental to a purpose or goal ... [a state] concerned with achieving a meaningful outcome upon completing the work. (Grant 2008: 49)

In contrast, *intrinsic motivation* refers to feeling compelled to put forth effort based on an interest in and the pleasure of the work itself (Amabile 1993; Ryan and Deci 2000), and *extrinsic motivation* refers to being compelled to put forth effort based on the desire to receive some external reward, such as feedback, praise, or financial incentive (Amabile 1993; Grant 2008). Because the differentiation between extrinsic and intrinsic motivation has been investigated (Amabile et al. 1994; Deci, Koestner, and Ryan 1999) and because many scholars see a closer alignment between prosocial and intrinsic motivation than between intrinsic motivation and extrinsic motivation (De Dreu and Nauta 2009; Grant 2008), recent empirical research has emphasized how intrinsic and prosocial motivations differ (Grant 2008). This research has found that "intrinsic motivation takes a hedonic perspective by emphasizing pleasure and enjoyment as drivers of effort, whereas prosocial motivation takes a eudaimonic perspective by emphasizing meaning and purpose as drivers of effort" (Grant 2008: 49). Furthermore, Grant (2008) found that intrinsic and prosocial motivations differ along three dimensions: self-regulation, goal directedness, and temporal focus (Grant and Berry 2011). Indeed, empirical research has shown that prosocial motivation and intrinsic/extrinsic motivation (i.e., self-interested motivation) are empirically independent and that they can be positively related (De Dreu and Nauta 2009; Grant and Berry 2011). Moreover, prosocial motivation has been found to be impactful in motivating individuals' actions when those individuals "have vivid, proximal exposure to the human beings affected by their contributions" (Grant 2012: 458; see also Grant et al. 2007). By being close to the recipients of their job or organizational outputs, individuals "see the tangible, meaningful consequences of their actions for a living, breathing person," which establishes a powerful motivational force and is associated with higher effort, persistence, and job performance (Grant 2012: 459–460).

First, after the bushfires, the entrepreneurs of the spontaneous ventures we studied were not drawn to creating a new venture because they believed that the work of creating and/or running a venture would be inherently interesting to them—as would be the case if they were intrinsically motivated (Kehr 2004)—or because their particular venture promised to be profitable (consistent with extrinsic motivation). Rather, they were motivated by the "introjected goal" to achieve an outcome of alleviating the suffering of people they identified with—consistent with the identified regulation of prosocial motivation (Grant

2008: 49). For example, one entrepreneur (Lachlan Frazer) expressed his motivation in creating a marathon festival was "his passion for his home town Marysville and surrounding communities. His vision to create the [festival] was all about bringing people back to Marysville. He wanted to be sure the town and surrounding communities got the support they needed to get back on their feet" (Judy Frazer-Jans).

Similarly, another venture founder (Bruce Morrow) was motivated by a desire to relieve victims of the incredible stresses of living in a disaster zone by offering them a holiday to relax, receive counseling from psychologists, and listen to inspiring stories from motivational speakers. A news article described the motivation in the following way, acknowledging the founder's ability to generate interest from a variety of sources:

The Qantas Group, through Jetstar, recently pitched in to help a true Aussie hero arrange a Dreamer Trip to the Gold Coast for 43 children and 15 adults affected by the Victorian bushfires. Father of two and Salvation Army member Bruce Morrow from Marysville, Victoria, lost his home and his livelihood on Black Saturday, 7 February, as well as friends and a community he loved. Mr. Morrow saw the need to help affected families and went about organising a holiday for the children and their families. (Jetstarmag 2009)

Despite his personal setbacks, Bruce Morrow's prosocial motivation translated into rapid action, enabling victims and their families to obtain critical psychological relief within six weeks of the fire.

As further evidence of the role prosocial motivation played over other types of motivation in compassion organizing, many entrepreneurs of spontaneous ventures created to alleviate others' suffering after the Black Saturday bushfire disaster even expressed an outright lack of intrinsic motivation in their work because of the emotional, physical, and time constraints it imposed. This is consistent with the compassion organizing literature, which explains that compassion organizing is "both effortful and potentially draining" (Lilius, Worline, et al. 2011: 875; see also Figley 2002; Frost 2003; Jacobson 2006). One entrepreneur, Judy Frazer-Jans, explained her experience this way:

Those of us involved in [the venture] from the beginning have worked extremely hard. It is draining, and at times we have had to support each other. I have found the recovery process exhausting, particularly as my husband has had to travel a lot, in order to keep our consultancy business operating. I have devoted so much time and energy to the rebuilding and recovery efforts that I have only left Marysville five times since the day of the fires.

Ann Leadbeater explained, "Like many people in the recovery period, I was profoundly tired and often overwhelmed by the enormity of the job ahead of us. We cried a lot during those meetings. I got pretty good at crying in public. ... It was a very raw and emotional environment." Finally, another entrepreneur, Vicki Ruhr, explained her experience this way:

I experience a wide range of human emotion on a daily basis. I am exhausted, I feel despair and dismay every day and I have immense trouble thinking about the future. ... I'm sick and tired of dealing with bureaucracy, paper work, and processes. I hear my friend, Suzanne Hyde, who perished in the fires. I hear her voice and I hear her screams; often. I worry about my husband and my children. I miss my community, my home, my garden and my farm animals.

Amazingly, despite these challenges, these individuals were motivated to organize compassion for others.

Second, there was little evidence to suggest that those who engaged in spontaneous venturing to help alleviate victim suffering were process focused—that is, seeing the work as an end in and of itself—when creating their ventures, which typically characterizes intrinsic motivation (Amabile 1993; Grant 2008; Wrzesniewski et al. 1997). Indeed, we found evidence of disregard for process (e.g., cutting corners, disobeying authorities) in venture creation to achieve the desired outcome of alleviating victim suffering, which is consistent with seeing work as a way to reach certain goals that benefit others (Grant 2008). For example, when explaining how his venture delivered supplies to members of his community, Doug Walter described the various means he and other locals used to circumvent roadblocks imposed by the authorities. He explained that "residents forded the river in their vehicles, travelled bush tracks and avoided that road block" to procure supplies and communicate with the outside world. Similarly, James Kennedy explained that he was able to procure resources for his impromptu relief this way: "Initially we had a fair stock of food and we ran that for the first three or four days. Then we were able to smuggle in some food and some supplies from different places past some of the roadblocks that we had." The actions of spontaneous-venturing entrepreneurs were guided by the desire to alleviate suffering using any means and resources possible. As Graeme Brown explained, there was a need to use "unconventional means to address an unconventional circumstance," something understood by local victims motivated to alleviate suffering. As a result of the intense motivation to alleviate suffering, "unconventional methods" were used to deliver food to victims weeks before others arrived with food via traditional methods, animal fodder and other goods were delivered in customized bundles in mere hours and days after the fires versus weeks and months, and temporary housing solutions were provided a full six months before formal temporary housing units could be erected.

Third, the entrepreneurs of the spontaneous ventures founded to alleviate suffering after the Black Saturday disaster were all local victims of the bushfires and thus the most proximate to the recipients of their products or services, which suggests a strong likelihood of prosocial motivation (Grant 2012; Grant et al. 2007). As these entrepreneurs rallied support both within and outside the community, they were able to appeal to the core values of followers, were recognized as legitimate actors, and drew the snowballing support of many individuals toward achieving their prosocial goals. Thus, spontaneous venturing not only demonstrated prosocial motivation but also served as a recognizable conduit for other prosocially motivated individuals (e.g., donors, volunteers) through which they could assist in alleviating suffering in the most rapid and customized way possible.

Finally, although Grant (2008) proposed that prosocially motivated individuals are future focused—that is, they wish to achieve a consequential outcome *at the conclusion* of the action (Batson 1998)—and intrinsically motivated individuals are present focused—that is, they wish to experience performing the work *during* the action (Quinn 2005), we found that prosocial entrepreneurs are not future focused, or at least not in the way described in the literature (Batson 1998; Grant 2008), because they do not have a planned goal for some later period when the task can be considered complete. Rather, the temporal dimension of the prosocial behavior underlying spontaneous venturing is best described as repeatedly immediate—these entrepreneurs are concerned with achieving the outcome of alleviating a victim's suffering and doing so immediately, and then immediately alleviating another victim's suffering, and so on. That is, in the environment faced by the entrepreneurs of spontaneous ventures after the bushfires, the drive to "benefit others" through the alleviation of suffering was urgent, emerging, and constantly evolving, requiring an intense present focus, or an emphasis on the immediate needs at hand. In this sense, respondents were not focused on a specified end goal but rather on quickly identifying needs, issues, and threats and then coordinating responses. This present focus on alleviating suffering allowed the rapid and customized delivery of goods and services that evolved to match the constantly changing needs of victims. For example, James Kennedy explained his experience moments after the fire had passed this way:

I decided that we [James and his wife] would go for a drive to inspect any damage to the local area. When we arrived at the Narbethong township, we saw that it had been almost completely destroyed and that the fire had ruined buildings in a way that I had never seen before. In the past, I had seen buildings destroyed by bushfires which still had parts of walls and floors intact— this bushfire left almost nothing behind except concrete stumps. One of the buildings in Narbethong which survived the bushfire was a ski hire shop and when we arrived there, we found several cars parked out the front. We went in and found a large group of people huddled together in a shelter underneath the building. We told them that our hotel had not been affected and that they were welcome to go there for a meal when they felt ready. Most of the people seemed too frightened to leave immediately but we saw some of them at the hotel later in the evening. ... When we woke up on 8 February 2009, we went outside to find a number of CFA tankers in our car park. We gave the fire fighters breakfast. Local people whose houses had been destroyed by the fire also started to arrive and we also gave them breakfast. We did not charge anyone for these meals. These were the first of thousands of meals which were prepared for local people, fire fighters and police at our hotel over the coming weeks.

After initially serving meals for locals, the Black Spur Relief Centre rapidly evolved, offering critical services to rescue personnel and victims. Remarkably, these changes all occurred over the course of four weeks, roughly the time the relief center was in full-time operation. The Victorian Parliament captured the transformation to match delivery of goods and services to meet urgent community needs this way:

The [Black Spur Inn] is now a temporary home to firefighters, emergency personnel and relief workers. [They] are providing breakfast, lunch and dinner to everyone, from the visiting forensic teams to locals who have lost their homes and have nowhere else to go. They got on the phone straightaway and rang one of the Bass Strait oil crews, which donated all its chefs. The chefs have been doing all the cooking for free. The army has set up a camp out the back. One of those buildings is now a relief store. There is a structure known as Jim's shed, which is now holding bay for generators and fodder. ... The day I was there volunteers were all unloading a huge semitrailer of tools that had been donated by Dahlsen hardware. Community meetings are now held there. Half the community is helping in some way, and the pub's housekeeping supervisor is now in charge of the whole operation. That really exemplifies and highlights what has been happening in so many parts of the state. (Brumby 2009: 296–297)

Similarly, the Bayles Relief Centre, initially established solely for the purpose of addressing the suffering caused by lack of animal fodder, evolved rapidly in response to victim needs. Again, this transformation occurred in a very compressed time period, over the course of three weeks, changing daily to rapidly resolve emerging community needs. Throughout the process, Karleen Elledge maintained a focus on conditions in the present, designing customized solutions to address a wide array of needs. She described some of the activities this way:

After a short time, the relief centre started offering all sorts of things—not just feed and fencing. ... During the three-week period following Black Saturday, we re-fenced about 70 properties. We had 642 volunteers work for us during those three weeks. ... As well as providing agistment, we distributed plenty of medical equipment for injured animals. We had a big list of people who volunteered [to] agist animals including cows, dogs and other farm animals. ... Volunteers also helped us provide a range of services, particularly as part of clean-up crews. ... Next door to the [fire] station is two acres of public land and we decided to use that as part of the relief centre. We sectioned off a yard into different areas so that when visitors came into the driveway each section had a particular product type. For example, to the left of the driveway we stored our fencing materials. We then had an area at the back which contained our grain stores. We also set up a cool room where we stored boxes of donated fruit and baked biscuits and slices, which were being made by the local Girl Guides and Lions Club. We also had a drinks store, which contained about 20 pallets of drinks, which were primarily for the volunteers' lunch packs, but we also gave out bottles of water to residents who had contaminated water tanks. We also had the use of a donated 40-foot shipping container, which we used to store all the loose horse equipment. ... The relief centre became huge—it was a bit like Bunnings. We installed tower lights in the yard because we were working day and night. We also needed to put in big traffic signs and flashing lights. Because of the increased number of people using the centre, we had to install extra toilets and convert one of the existing toilets into a shower. All of these things were donated. We also provided six donated 40-foot shipping containers to residents who needed somewhere to store their belongings.

Therefore, the initial evidence indicates that spontaneous venturing is largely prosocially motivated. The individuals were motivated by the introjected goal of alleviating suffering in the aftermath of Black Saturday, experienced the suffering personally and through those close to them, had little regard for the process of how suffering was alleviated (they often cut corners), and were focused exclusively on repeatedly achieving immediate outcomes.

Discussion

Prior research at the individual level of analysis has focused on the noneconomic or psychic benefits of entrepreneurial action (Gimeno et al. 1997), such as enhanced identity, satisfaction, and autonomy (Evans and Leighton 1989; Oyserman, Terry, and Bybee 2002; Haynie and Shepherd 2011; Smith and Miner 1983), as well as the enjoyment and self-efficacy entrepreneurs experience in creating innovative solutions in resource-scarce environments (Baker and Nelson 2005; Hayward et al. 2010). Although this research has investigated topics beyond the creation of economic value, valuable opportunities remain to learn more about how entrepreneurs generate noneconomic value for themselves through entrepreneurial action, especially in the aftermath of a disaster. Throughout this chapter, we have filled this gap by investigating how and when spontaneous venturing to alleviate victim suffering after a disaster affects the actor's behavioral, emotional, and psychological resilience.

Drawing on the theory of entrepreneurial action and the clinical psychology literature on resilient adjustment following a disaster, we made two sets of theoretical arguments. First, spontaneous venturing to alleviate victim suffering after a disaster promotes resilience by (1) committing individuals to future actions and engaging them socially (supporting behavioral resilience), (2) enabling the cultivation and sharing of positive and negative emotions (supporting emotional resilience), and (3) connecting individuals with others who are providing support while also enabling the fulfillment of other-serving tasks that enhance their view of self, the world, and the benevolence of others (supporting assumptive resilience). Second, spontaneous venturing mediates the relationship between attributes of the individual victims (prior entrepreneurial business experience and degree of personal loss) and resilience and, in the case of prior entrepreneurial experience, provides a positive alternative to a double-edged sword, namely, the negative impact on resilience when no entrepreneurial action is taken versus the positive impact on resilience when entrepreneurial action is taken.

Entrepreneurial action has been explored in a variety of contexts, including extremely turbulent environments that have sustained exogenous shocks. While prior research on entrepreneurial action after one type of environmental shock, natural disasters, typically couched the phenomenon of entrepreneurial action within broad conceptualizations of disaster planning, detailing benefits for society or the environment, in this chapter we explored the impact that such spontaneous venturing to help victims of a natural disaster has on the actor doing the venturing. We drew on the action theory of entrepreneurship and the clinical psychology research on resilience to explore the "self-help" received through entrepreneurial action, which comes in the form of behavioral, emotional, and assumptive resilience.

Practical Implications

In this chapter we pivoted from focusing on how venturing benefits others in the aftermath of a disaster to how it also provides relief—in the form of resilience—to the entrepreneur. Furthermore, we found that those who are equipped to take action should indeed do so as failure to act leads to a greater likelihood of poor functioning. This suggests that when faced with a disaster, victims would do well to seek opportunities to engage in efforts to help others. Organizing to help others will provide purpose, social interaction, structure, and cohesion for people in a postdisaster context, all of which will work together to benefit the actor.

For those seeking to help victims of a disaster, we hope that our results will lead to greater reflection on what it means to help. While we explore this topic more in the next chapter, it is worth mentioning here that helping efforts should be done while considering the potential benefits for victims of taking effortful action to alleviate others' suffering despite the actors being victims themselves. That is, those helping should not assume that victims are helpless and need to have all their needs fulfilled with little to no effort on their part. While there certainly are people who are completely reliant on others after a crisis, research tells us that the vast majority of people have a strong capacity for resilience—we simply need to find better ways to develop and cultivate resilience.

The following points summarize the primary practical implications of this chapter:

1. If you have prior experience that may be relevant following a disaster, use it! It is likely to benefit both you and others. Failure to use it could result in regret and other disruptions to functioning.
2. Do not assume victims are helpless—they often are not. Furthermore, they may just hold the key to their own recovery.
3. For those skeptical of entrepreneurial efforts after a disaster, keep in mind that cases of exploitation and abuse after a disaster are extremely rare. While sometimes hyped in the media, in reality, disasters tend to draw out the compassionate side of people, not the exploitive side.

4. When confronted with a difficult scenario, think of how to organize to help others, as this can end up providing self-help. Of course, certain conditions require clinical support; we are not offering that type of advice. Rather, we suggest that actions of venturing to help others appear to provide a vehicle for greater functioning and resilience.

5. Outsiders coming to help should cultivate and engage action from victims. This aligns with previous findings that victims are often the best positioned to solve problems. Even more, when victims engage in helping, they too will be helped.

6. Outsiders should be on the lookout for overgeneralized postcrisis interventions. Research has shown that these interventions can actually lead to greater psychological dysfunction than had nothing been done at all. Consistent with our other chapters, we suggest that responses be customized to local needs and driven by local decision makers and experts.

7. As individuals, communities, and organizations plan for disaster events, they should consider how to cultivate various forms of motivation. For example, are there ways to encourage prosocial behaviors?

6   Building Better Resilience in a Least Developed Country

You want me to tell you what the Haitians did to help Haitians after the earthquake? Not the NGOs? Well, nobody has ever asked me that! There is a lot we did, so much that has gone untold.

—Jean François, victim entrepreneur in Haiti

To this point in the book, we have focused primarily on developing the concept of spontaneous compassionate venturing, the way it fits into the broader conversations of disaster response, and the impact it has both on the entrepreneurs and on those being helped. To isolate our focus on those aspects, we developed three different studies focused exclusively on a single disaster context in Australia as this helped us develop a robust foundation for our main ideas concerning spontaneous venturing. Furthermore, our approach extends research that explores how actors in developed countries interpret and respond to crises through compassionate venturing.[1]

As we progressed in our thinking on the topic of spontaneous venturing, we began to wonder whether the phenomenon was limited to economically well-to-do contexts. Are compassionate ventures merely the product of a wealthy economic context? That is, were victims of the Australian bushfires who started ventures able to act because they were in a national context that was rich in resources? How would victims in less developed economies respond to a crisis? Would they be similarly well equipped to provide rapid, customized, and high-magnitude responses to disasters, or would they require more outside support? While considering these questions, we also noted some disheartening data on disasters, namely, that disasters tend to disproportionally affect the most economically vulnerable (UN 2015). A recent book (Guha-Sapir, Santos, and Borde 2013) summarizes the situation this way:

Since the turn of the millennium, more than 2.3 billion people have been
directly affected by natural disasters—several of these have killed nearly
100,000 people within a matter of 24 hours. Moreover, the global alarm generated during the last decade by events such as the 2004 tsunami in Asia, Hurricane Katrina in the United States in 2005, the Sichuan earthquake in China in
2008, and more recently the 2011 tsunami in Japan ... has renewed the policy
and academic interest on understanding the ... consequences of natural disasters. ... Poverty remains the main risk factor determining the long-term impact
of natural hazards. Furthermore, natural disasters have themselves a tremendous impact on the poorest of the poor, who are often ill-prepared to deal with
the natural hazards and for whom a hurricane, or earthquake, or a drought can
mean a permanent submersion into poverty. (p. 1).

Catastrophic disasters ... can set the development process back for decades. In
addition to the immediate effects, low-intensity asset loss and livelihood disruption over extensive areas where people and economic activities are exposed
to localized hazard events, steadily erode the coping capacity of families and
communities, pushing them into increasing marginalization.
    Poor communities living in high-risk areas ... [experience] permanent or
temporary loss of the communities' productive base, aggravating their level of
poverty, and, in some cases, triggering migration. ... While death is often the
immediate and tragic consequence of a disaster, economic losses and the inability of the underprivileged to recuperate over the medium and long term add
additional burdens (p. vii).

One of the main arguments made for countries that are the "poorest
of the poor" is that they generally lack the resources to adequately
prepare for and respond to a disaster (Guha-Sapir, Santos, and Borde
2013). While we certainly agree there is merit to this argument in terms
of poor infrastructure, inadequate disaster preparedness, and so forth,
we were curious to see whether such countries might have other
resources (similar to those described in chapter 4) that could be
deployed to build or develop resilience (see chapter 5) in an underdeveloped context. This chapter explores the topic of compassionate venturing in an extremely poor context, Haiti. Specifically, we examine the
local compassionate venturing that occurred after a devastating earthquake struck Haiti in 2010.

As we explore spontaneous venturing in this context, we hope to
apply the insights and observations discussed in earlier chapters and
also introduce new insights from the Haitian context that expand
our knowledge. In particular, we introduce the concept of building
resilience in a community, which extends concepts introduced earlier,
including the nature of being local and launching a venture, the role
of networks in the types and applications of resources, and the

performance of spontaneous ventures. We also discuss the potential drawbacks to creative resourcefulness. In earlier chapters, we talked about the benefits of bundling resources to achieve a new venture's goals. By exploring resourcefulness in the extreme setting of post-earthquake Haiti, we are able to pinpoint difficulties that may arise when ventures take resourcefulness too far.

Haiti is a country with a rich history and legacy. It had the first successful self-liberation of an enslaved population (from 1791 to 1804), which had a substantial impact on the history of the slave trade throughout the world. Despite this significant past, Haiti has gone from crisis to crisis throughout its entire history. These crises have inevitably drawn in external actors; a tradition that continues today. In a recent article exploring the role of external organizations in Haiti following the earthquake, Edmonds (2013: 440–441) explained the following:

Before the earthquake, Haiti was routinely referred to as the poorest nation in the Western hemisphere, the prototypical failed state—a little piece of sub-Saharan Africa only 750km off of the Florida coast. In the midst of all of these derogatory references, there has been little to no discussion in the media about how the "basket case of the hemisphere" has been predominately engineered through slavery, colonialism, genocide, economic terrorism, political manipulation and foreign military occupation.

After the success of the Haitian Revolution in 1804, the colonial powers of the time decided that an independent Haiti would pose a threat to the entire system of slavery and colonialism in the Americas. After numerous attempts to recolonize the newly established republic through military force alone were defeated, the international powers of France, the USA, England and Holland put aside their colonial rivalries in a determined effort to destroy the revolution in its infancy by bleeding it to death financially.

Facing extreme isolation, and with a French war fleet sitting offshore, in 1825 Haiti agreed to take out a loan from a designated French bank and pay compensation to the French plantation owners for their "loss of property," including freed slaves and stolen land. In effect Haiti was paying twice for its freedom; first with blood, and second with money. The amount of the debt totalled 150,000,000 francs. Today that amount would equal US$21b dollars (Schuller 2006).

Haiti may have been the first nation to escape colonialism through revolution, but Haiti also became the first 'third world' nation in the traditional sense, as it was poor and overburdened with debt. The Haitian Government could not build schools, hospitals or roads because nearly all of the available money went to pay France. In 1915, for example, 80 percent of government revenues went to debt service (Farmer 2003). Haiti did not finish paying the loans that financed this odious debt until 1947 (Regan 2005). Over a century after the global slave trade was recognized and eliminated as the evil it was, the Haitians were still paying their ancestors' masters for their freedom ([Concannon and] Phillips 2006).

As illustrated by this brief historical account, Haiti has been exposed to obstacles from a number of fronts throughout its entire history. Beyond these historical accounts, Haiti endured a number of challenges during the twentieth century including years of instability in government from multiple coups, a nineteen-year occupation by the United States (ending in 1933), hurricanes and other disasters, the reign of multiple dictators, military rule, and so forth. The early part of the twenty-first century (2004) saw the arrival of UN peacekeeping troops, who remain in Haiti to this day.

In recent years, Haiti has seen a proliferation of outsiders—in particular, nongovernmental organizations (NGOs) and foreign governments—seeking to "help" Haiti with its many challenges. However, as Haitian experts (Edmonds 2013; Schuller 2007) have noted, this outside help often does the opposite. As Edmonds (2013: 445) has suggested, "The reality of NGOs in Haiti and in the developing world in general is along the lines of a twisted, but suitable idiom which states, 'Give a man a fish, you feed him for a day. Allow a man to fish and you ruin a perfectly good business opportunity.'"

Despite the many efforts over the years to alleviate Haiti's impoverished situation, the situation remains difficult. As summarized in a 2013 U.S. government report:

Plagued by chronic political instability and frequent natural disasters, Haiti remains the poorest country in the Western Hemisphere. Haiti's poverty is massive and deep. Over half the population (54%) of 9.8 million people live in extreme poverty, living on less than $1 a day; 78% live on $2 or less a day, according to the World Bank. Poverty among the rural population is even more widespread: 69% of rural dwellers live on less than $1 a day, and 86% live on less than $2 a day. Hunger is also widespread: 81% of the national population and 87% of the rural population do not get the minimum daily ration of food defined by the World Health Organization. In remote parts of Haiti, children have died from malnutrition. (Margesson and Taft-Morales 2010: 23–24)

Interestingly, and as it relates to our discussion in chapter 2, much of the logic undergirding NGO and international governmental interventions in Haiti is consistent with the command-and-control theory of crisis management: central management by those in the know (outsiders) should take command and control of Haiti to provide the solution. However, this approach is not working. Klarreich and Polman (2012) explained the situation this way:

Welcome to the NGO Republic of Haiti, the fragile island-state born, in part, out of the country's painfully lopsided earthquake recovery. ... Thousands of aid organizations came to Haiti with the entire international aid budget in their bank accounts (several billion dollars among them) and built a powerful parallel state. ... [But] the Haitian people themselves [are] impoverished, unemployed, homeless and trapped in a recovery effort that has all too often failed to meet their needs. ... Hundreds of thousands of people are [in Haiti] delivering aid, but they are doing functions that should be done by the Haitians. ... The international relief effort after the 2010 earthquake [in many ways] excluded Haitians from their own recovery.

Because of this history and what we had learned from our other studies, our interest in studying the postearthquake venturing led us to focus not on what outsiders did but on whether and how Haitians organized to help their fellow victims. Is it possible that Haitians are and were part of the solution following the devastating earthquake of 2010, just as the Australians were after the Black Saturday bushfires?

In telling this story, we first discuss the impact of disasters on the "poorest of the poor." This is an important shift in the book because disaster often has its greatest impacts in underdeveloped economic environments. Therefore a thorough conceptualization of spontaneous venturing requires that the concept be tested in a variety of contexts. We then discuss the Haiti earthquake and the degree of destruction it caused. This helps highlight just how debilitated the infrastructure was, underscoring even more the incredible value of spontaneous venturing in coming to the rescue. Finally, we compare and contrast two different types of spontaneous ventures that emerged. Specifically, we explore how and why they differed in their approach to alleviating suffering and the consequences of these differences. This discussion builds on material presented in earlier chapters and offers yet another important perspective on differences in the performance of spontaneous ventures.

Disasters and Least Developed Countries

A select group of nations form what the UN categorizes as least developed countries (LDCs). These nations have the lowest levels of income and human capital and are considered the most economically vulnerable (Cuervo-Cazurra and Genc 2008; UN 2015). Helping LDCs overcome the tragic effects of poverty has been a priority for the UN as LDCs are home to nearly 900 million people, or 12 percent of the world's population. Efforts to help have involved both formal government programs and extensive efforts from NGOs and, more recently, multinational corporations (MNCs). Despite these efforts, addressing risks and crises in LDCs remains a global challenge.

Similarly, natural disasters pose a challenge as they threaten human life, critical infrastructure, and economic stability (Shah 2012; USAID 2015). Global governments and organizations recognize natural disasters as a challenge, giving special attention to anticipating, avoiding, and responding to natural disasters. Though disasters occur all over the world, they most frequently (77 percent of the time) wreak their effects on LDCs (Strobl 2012), which are most vulnerable to the economic and social consequences of disasters, such as high mortality rates, loss of infrastructure, and economic and governmental failure (Guillaumont 2010; Peduzzi et al. 2009; UN 2015). Disasters in LDCs and their devastating consequences pose a grand challenge to society and have resulted in billions of dollars of aid dispensed (Norris et al. 2002), government programs (Drabek 2007), and NGO activities (Eikenberry, Arroyave, and Cooper 2007) designed to alleviate victim suffering. We wanted to understand how the broader global community can participate in identifying solutions to prevent losses when LDCs experience disasters, and to identify the best approaches for responding to crises in the moment.

As suggested by our brief historical review at the beginning of this chapter, the Republic of Haiti offers an extreme example of these grand challenges. Currently ranked as the twentieth LDC in the world (for gross national income per capita) (UN 2015), Haiti has gone from crisis to crisis for decades, with each crisis deepening divisions that result in economic, political, and social dysfunction (International Crisis Group 2013). Already suffering from widespread chronic poverty, in January 2010 Haiti was hit by a catastrophic earthquake that destroyed nearly 80 percent of its capital city, Port-au-Prince, killed hundreds of thousands of people, displaced hundreds of thousands of other people, and substantially increased Haitians' already high susceptibility to disease, poverty, and death (International Crisis Group 2013; Zanotti 2010). Because of Haiti's status as an LDC, outside governments and NGOs responded in full force to help victims recover after the earthquake. These groups donated billions of dollars, and volunteers from thousands of NGOs traveled to Haiti, providing an array of "solutions" to Haiti's problems. Many of these foreign governments and NGOs already had a substantial presence in the country and therefore simply took charge of various relief efforts.

The initial response thus differed substantially from the initial response to the Black Saturday disaster. While there was an outpouring of external resources from NGOs, foreign governments, and organizations after the bushfires, those resources were not already embedded in the context, and those aid organizations did not act in lieu of the Australian government in coordinating and distributing resources. In Haiti, however, the fragmented network of more than 10,000 NGOs and countless UN peace-keepers and foreign government actors simply took over, overseeing everything from security to transportation to temporary housing and other relief measures.

Because of the sheer size of outsiders' commitment of resources in responding to the 2010 earthquake, many investigators have used the Haitian example to examine the effectiveness of foreign government and NGO activities in LDCs following natural disasters. (Some instances of ineffective response are highlighted by Eikenberry, Arroyave, and Cooper [2007] and Jobe [2011].) By contrast, there has been little research on the actions of local people and organizations in these LDCs working to help fellow citizens. Specifically, evaluations of the earthquake response have largely assumed that LDC local residents are victims, are helpless, or lack the political and organizational infrastructure needed to respond appropriately (for reviews, see Tierney 2012; Zanotti 2010). This belief is consistent with the command-and-control logic we explored in more developed contexts (see chapters 2–5). Though this is the prevailing view regarding LDCs, in light of the prevalence of local venturing in other contexts (Drabek and McEntire 2003; Shepherd and Williams 2014), there is reason to believe that despite obstacles, LDC-led organizing efforts likely contribute to endeavors to overcome the major issues associated with widespread, disaster-related suffering. Indeed, a recent report on the crises in Haiti suggested that "the key to fixing Haiti is that Haitians have to do it" (International Crisis Group 2013: 14).

The above observations lead us to our research questions for this chapter: Did Haitians overcome incredible environmental challenges to engage in spontaneous venturing after the earthquake? If so, how did Haitian-initiated ventures identify and pursue potential opportunities to alleviate suffering, and to what effect? Owing to the lack of research and theorizing in this area, we used an inductive method to explore the activities and outcomes of six Haitian-led ventures that emerged to alleviate suffering after the January 2010 earthquake (Williams and Shepherd 2016a). While inductively exploring these ventures, we found each fell into one of two groups (three in each group) with respect to how they alleviated suffering. Specifically, we explain how ventures identified potential opportunities to alleviate suffering, how these choices influenced the development and evolution of the ventures over time, and how these combined actions differentially influenced recovery. In developing an inductive model of local venturing after a disaster in an LDC, we hope to open pathways for the organization and management research communities to apply their collective knowledge of organizing and entrepreneurial action toward addressing the intersecting grand challenges of disaster response in LDCs. Further, building on material presented in previous chapters, we demonstrate the widespread applicability of spontaneous venturing following a disaster.

In this chapter we first discuss the literature on poverty alleviation and disaster response, to set the theoretical background. We then discuss the findings of our research and share many quotations from informants to illustrate our main findings. Finally, we discuss the theoretical and practical implications of this study.

Poverty Alleviation in Least Developed Countries

To further illustrate the context in which we sought to observe spontaneous venturing, we first highlight the various actors that are most active in alleviating poverty in underdeveloped countries and LDCs. Poverty alleviation as a subject has garnered increasing attention among a diverse set of global actors as wealthier nations have sought to eradicate suffering. These efforts often focus on providing basic services and amenities, such as medicine, shelter, food, and water. Again, these efforts are ongoing independent of natural disasters. However, when disasters strike, needs become even more pressing and draw a heightened response from external actors.

Research on poverty alleviation in LDCs focuses on three primary kinds of actors, governments, NGOs, and MNCs, which we now briefly discuss.

Government Actors and Poverty Alleviation   Research on the role of government actors in alleviating poverty is extensive and has focused primarily on the topic of foreign aid (Dickovick 2014; Mansur and Rao 2004, 2012). Foreign aid can include a wide range of resources, such as military (Peksen 2012; Pickering and Peceny 2006) and financial (Easterly and Pfutze 2008; Fuchs, Dreher, and Nunnenkamp 2014) support, the provision of goods and medical supplies (Annen and Moers 2012;

Knack and Smets 2013), and infrastructure development (Parmigiani and Rivera-Santos 2015; Winters and Martinez 2015). It is estimated that in the last fifty years, more than $2.5 trillion has been given to developing countries (excluding private aid); however, the effectiveness of these donations remains very much in question (Easterly 2006; Easterly and Pfutze 2008), snd criticisms reflect many of the issues we discussed in chapter 2 relating to the command-and-control model of disaster response. Acknowledging these criticisms, recent research (e.g., Mansuri and Rao 2004, 2012) has highlighted the importance of community-based projects—programs that engage local participation in project design and implementation—as a way to sharpen "poverty targeting, [improve] service delivery, [expand] livelihood opportunities and [strengthen] demand for good governance" (Mansuri and Rao 2012: 1). This is again consistent with our discussions in previous chapters that emphasized the importance of local and customized responses to crises. Furthermore, it goes a step further by suggesting that engaging the receiver of a charitable donation as a participant in the process can provide significant benefits over simply providing resources. Most such programs focus on helping governments and organizations develop LDCs' formal institutions. Thus, while these programs acknowledge organic local organizing efforts, such efforts are typically not the focus of aid efforts (Gulrajani and Moloney 2012; Mansuri and Rao 2012).

Though disappointing, in light of what we discussed earlier in the book, this observation is not all that surprising: those "coming to the rescue" of victims often view the victims in a certain light—as helpless, incapable of taking action, and in need of outsiders who can efficiently provide food, shelter, employment, and so forth. This logic aligns closely with the faulty assumptions of the command-and-control model (for a review, see Jensen and Waugh 2014; see also chapter 2).

Nongovernmental Organizations   Often working in close collaboration with foreign governments (Batley 2006), NGOs play a prominent role in efforts to alleviate poverty in LDCs (Lecy, Schmitz, and Swedlund 2012; Smith 2012). As an example, prior to the January 12 earthquake, between 8,000 and 9,000 NGOs operated in Haiti. Research on NGOs in LDCs has focused on their role in such activities as state-building (Batley and Mcloughlin 2010; Zanotti 2010), developing a civil society to protect human rights (Bold, Collier, and Zeitlin 2009; White 1999), enhancing education (Newcomer, Baradel, and Garcia 2013; Rose

2009), providing health services (Brinkerhoff 2008; Palmer 2006), and improving economic development (Elbers, Knippenberg, and Schulpen 2014; Gazley 2008). In LDCs, NGOs often have the highest priority (over local government and citizen groups) for receiving foreign funding because of the trust and relationships they have built with donors and aid recipients. However, little is known about the effects of delivering services, developing societies, and state-building through NGOs in postconflict or postdisaster contexts (Zanotti 2010: 756) when needs are greatest and LDCs are flooded with foreign actors seeking to pursue various missions.

Multinational Corporations   The third major type of actor in LDCs is MNCs, which seek to provide goods and services to millions of individuals with unmet needs who are located at the "base of the pyramid" (Prahalad 2004; Prahalad and Hart 2002). Base-of-the-pyramid markets include LDCs as well as populations from developing countries. These markets represent nearly four billion people, or about 70 percent of the world's population, who live on roughly $2 a day (Hart 2005; Prahalad 2004; Webb et al. 2010). The primary approach of MNCs to base-of-the-pyramid markets has been to develop products and services that both generate profits (for the MNC) and alleviate poverty by providing individuals access to affordable products essential to health and well-being (London 2008; Seelos and Mair 2007). While the opportunities in these markets appear abundant, prior research has found mixed results in terms of the financial value created for MNCs and the social value created for recipients in base-of-the-pyramid markets (Kandachar and Halme 2008). MNCs face a number of challenges in these markets, including the necessity of navigating cultural and institutional environments (Kistruck and Beamish 2010), matching business models and products to local needs (Hart and Christensen 2002; London and Hart 2004), and realizing desired objectives (Easterly 2006). Though efforts to merge market-based thinking with the alleviation of poverty provide considerable opportunities (Brugmann and Prahalad 2007), there is an ongoing search for solutions that engage "participants [those in base-of-the-pyramid markets] in the design of a more inclusive process" (London 2007: 6) to understand the complex multidimensional nature of poverty (Sen 1999). Similarly, there is an increased focus on identifying longer-term market-based solutions that would allow the poorest of the poor to rise to the first rung of the economic development ladder (Sachs 2005).

Most of the literature on poverty alleviation in LDCs has focused on the role of external actors—governments, NGOs, and MNCs—in developing programs, investment portfolios, and business opportunities. While all three bodies of literature call for greater engagement with local actors, there is a noticeable gap in research on locally led efforts to alleviate poverty, especially in the aftermath of a disruptive event that, while devastating, provides numerous opportunities to transform communities and individual lives—or to "build back better."

Disaster Response
Despite what we have learned from the literature, as well as what we discussed in chapters 2–5, "much remains to be learned about the internal dynamics of these emergent response groups" (Majchrzak, Jarvenpaa, and Hollingshead 2007: 147), especially with regard to responding to crises in LDCs. There is still much to learn about how venturing emerges to alleviate the large-scale suffering caused by a disaster in the most vulnerable economies. We discuss our exploration of these concepts in relation to spontaneous venturing in response to the 2010 Haitian earthquake.

**Research Setting: The January 12, 2010, Haitian
Earthquake Disaster**
On January 12, 2010, a magnitude 7.0 earthquake struck Port-au-Prince. This was the worst earthquake on record in Haiti. It led to widespread death (estimated at 316,000), injury (300,000), and displacement (1.5 million) and affected one-third of Haiti's entire population (Margesson and Taft-Morales 2010). The financial impact on Haiti was also catastrophic, with damage estimated at 117 percent of Haiti's annual economic output (Margesson and Taft-Morales 2010), which led the Inter-American Development Bank to call the tragedy "the most destructive event a country has ever experienced" (Cavallo, Powell, and Becerra 2010: 3). After the earthquake, basic services, such as transportation, telephony, and electricity, were almost completely destroyed, and many homes, hospitals, schools, and government buildings collapsed (Margesson and Taft-Morales 2010). Out of Haiti's seventeen government ministries, fifteen were severely damaged, including the presidential palace, further weakening Haiti's already "thin layer" of administrative infrastructure (Zanotti 2010: 756). Because of the scale of the destruction and the Haitian government's call for assistance, nearly $14 billion in donations and other aid were sent to the shaken

nation in an attempt to alleviate suffering. However, most of this aid only indirectly reached the Haitians as it was directed through non-Haitian governments, NGOs, and international government bodies such as the UN.

Beyond the actual destruction of the earthquake, additional suffering also occurred do to "numerous man-made aftershocks which ... seriously undermined the ability of the Haitian people to establish a state run in accordance with the demands of the poor majority." (Edmonds 2013: 445). In particular, the international policies of organizations involved in Haiti, such as the UN and USAID,

> privileged NGOs as the favored recipients of international support ... [which] contributed to the cacophony of aid and the lack of accountability of politicians to local constituencies in Haiti and that, by siphoning human and monetary resources from the [Haitian people], these NGOs have *de facto* jeopardized the building of sustainable institutions in [Haiti]. Furthermore, because of the rigidity of their mandate or administrative functioning some major international NGOs have ended up producing negative impacts on the local economy and on the durable and consistent availability of services to the population. (Zanotti 2010: 768)

For these reasons, while much of the literature has focused on the large international relief response to the earthquake, we focus on venturing to alleviate suffering that was initiated by local Haitians in the Port-au-Prince region in the immediate aftermath of the earthquake. We sought to find examples of community building and development initiated by local residents because of LDCs' prominent need for such venturing.

Case Selection

To achieve our goals, we identified extreme cases that would help shed light on our research questions. Through a number of steps, including systematic internet searches, making connections through Haitian diaspora communities, and visiting Port-au-Prince, we identified six local compassionate ventures that emerged after the earthquake to alleviate fellow Haitians' suffering. In assessing these six different ventures, we found fundamental differences between two kinds (three ventures each) of venture. To facilitate writing about our findings, we created a fictional name for each venture: Sogeun, Seleco, Sagesse, Toujours, Tangage, and Travailleurs. Similarly, we provide a fictional name for each individual who served as an informant. In table 6.1, we provide details about the six ventures' core activities, total members, the informants for each venture, and additional data sources.

Table 6.1
Background Characteristics and Data Sources for Cases

Characteristic	Sogeun	Seleco	Sagesse	Toujours	Tangage	Travailleurs
Core activities	Food, shelter, tent city management, government activism	Food, shelter, part-time work, tent city management, government activism	Food, shelter, tent city management, government activism	Food, housing, career, job training	Food, housing, career, psychological services, job training, medical	Food, housing, career, psychological services, job training, medical
Members (at peak)	38	34	38	49	42	51
Venture life span	3 years/ongoing	3 years/ongoing	3 years/ongoing	2 years	2.5 years	3 years/ongoing
Informants (role) 41 in total (510 pages)	Founder 1 (Stephan) Founder 2 (Sebastian) Employee 1 (Spencer) Employee 2 (Sanders) Employee 3 (Sachin) Employee 4 (Suzanne) Customer 1 (Clint) Customer 2 (Seth) Customer 3 (Luanne)	Founder 1 (Lane) Founder 2 (Laren) Employee 1 (Lacey) Employee 2 (Leone) Employee 3 (Leslie) Customer 1 (Leigh)	Founder 1 (Adan) Founder 2 (Addison) Employee 1 (Akiva) Customer 1 (Aisley) Customer 2 (Alain) Customer 3 (Alba) Customer 4 (Alba)	Founder 1 (Tristan) Founder 2 (Tariq) Employee 1 (Tate) Employee 2 (Torrey) Customer 1 (Tianna) Customer 2 (Terrin)	Founder 1 (Gabi) Founder 2 (Gail) Employee 1 (Garuda) Employee 2 (Gili) Employee 3 (Glyn) Customer 1 (Gwyn) Customer 2 (Greta) Customer 3 (Gaymnor)	Founder 1 (Raine) Founder 2 (Remi) Employee 1 (Rio) Customer 1 (Rory) Customer 2 (TR-C2)

Note: Names have been changed to protect anonymity.
Source: Modified from Williams and Shepherd (2016a).

Introduction to Our Findings

Before discussing the details of our findings, we first summarize some major points. In answer to our first research question, we did identify instances of spontaneous venturing immediately after the Haiti earthquake. Second, all of the venture founders were local Haitians who were themselves victims of the disaster; that is, they had experienced loss of property or loss of a loved one. Third, the majority of these ventures sought to organize relief efforts around providing food, shelter, medical care, and access to water. Finally, these ventures differed in how they evolved over time and the approach they took toward those they served. We discuss the factors that shaped these differences and highlight how these influenced long-term outcomes.

Alleviation of Suffering: Primary Differences between the Two Kinds of Ventures

We found that Haitian victim-led ventures designed to alleviate suffering after the 2010 earthquake displayed distinct patterns in their identification of opportunities to alleviate suffering, their pursuit of these opportunities, and the degree to which they alleviated suffering. The most striking difference between the two kinds of ventures was seen in the alleviation of suffering. Ventures in one group promoted behaviors associated with *sustaining people* by providing systemic relief that helped victims survive postdisaster conditions. In the other group, the ventures promoted behaviors associated with *transforming people* by facilitating the transition from a state of crisis to one of autonomy, self-reliance, and advancement out of extreme hardship.

Sustaining Ventures

Three ventures alleviated suffering by sustaining people: Sogeun, Seleco, and Sagesse (hereafter referred to as sustaining ventures). *Sustaining ventures* were those that alleviated suffering by providing for victims' most basic needs and continually working toward achieving the venture's short-term objectives and delivering relief to victims. That is, sustaining ventures alleviated suffering in three primary ways. (1) First, sustaining ventures alleviated suffering by *providing for basic needs*. For example, one founder (Stephan) explained that in response to the crisis, "We organized ourselves to obtain necessary resources, such as food, water, and housing. ... We continue to live in tent camps in unsatisfactory conditions. ... People can live in temporary shelters for three months, but they should not have to live in such conditions for three years (as we have) ... but at least we have our lives." (2) Sustaining ventures also alleviated suffering by achieving *short-term objectives* related to improving victim survival. That is, these ventures were interested in addressing immediate and pressing needs, but not in evolving to meet other needs. Furthermore, these ventures had minimal concern for long-term planning, which led them to approach each day as a relatively isolated, discrete set of problems. For example, one founder (Adan) explained, "Each day we get up, look for resources, and seek to survive. ... Then we get up and do it again the next day. We are stuck like this." (3) Finally, sustaining ventures alleviated suffering by *exclusively providing relief,* that is by coordinating activities to deal with the symptoms of problems instead of the sources of those problems. For example, Stephan, who founded an organization to provide long-term relief, said: "Instead of progressing and becoming richer, my people and I have become poorer ... but our goal remains to provide at least one meal a day for those in the camp. ... I will keep doing this even if it takes years to help people." As illustrated by these examples, sustaining ventures focused primarily on survival. While critical, this method of aid provision did not necessarily lead to a long-term ability for those receiving products and services to sustain themselves. This finding adds nuance to what we learned in earlier chapters in discussing the Black Saturday bushfire responses regarding the quality of a compassionate response. While some responses do offer help, we can question whether this help is in the best interest of victims in the long-term.

Transforming Ventures
In contrast, three ventures, Toujours, Tangage, and Travailleurs, alleviated suffering by transforming people. *Transforming ventures* addressed a broad and evolving set of causes of suffering by providing both longer-term solutions and aid in multiple stages of recovery that led to the transformation of victims' lives. That is, these ventures focused on addressing needs in stages, helping people overcome challenges until they became autonomous and self-reliant in meeting their physical, social, and psychological needs.

Transforming ventures alleviated suffering in three ways. (1) They provided for a *wide range of urgent and emerging needs* because although they understood the early need for basic survival resources, they eventually began helping victims move toward autonomy and self-reliance.

For instance, Raine, who founded a venture providing psychological services as well as food and housing, explained: "We analyzed people's needs so we could help them moving forward, including housing, jobs, and so forth." (2) Transforming ventures alleviated suffering by offering *long-term solutions* that included providing education and career opportunities to victims. This kind of aid not only brought postdisaster relief but often led to significant improvements from predisaster conditions. For example, one founder (Tristan) explained, "We had short-term and long-term projects. ... Short-term included providing tents, hygiene kits, food, and medical care [first three months]. ... Long-term involved plywood homes that they would help build—to maintain their dignity—job training, and psychological support." (3) Finally, transforming ventures alleviated victim suffering through their pursuit of *multiple stages of recovery,* including creating customized solutions that both met people's specific needs and enabled the progressive development of autonomy among those being helped. For example, after they reached their goal of helping individuals find housing, these ventures provided entrepreneurship training to individuals with limited education so they could sell goods on the street, and provided computer and language training as well as other opportunities to individuals with higher educational backgrounds. This approach demonstrated a staged model to addressing the problem by providing a use case for the venture both in immediate disaster response and in moving into the future once basic needs for food, water, and shelter were met.

As we considered these two starkly different groups of cases, we wanted to better understand why they had such different models for alleviating suffering. In evaluating the statements of founders, employees, and customers of these ventures, we found seven primary themes that appeared to explain the differences in outcomes: (1) social resources, (2) founding mindset, (3) potential opportunities (4) resourcefulness, (5) entrepreneurial action, (6) role emergence, and (7) deviance. Figure 6.1 shows a general model of how these themes worked together to shape outcomes. That is, differences in each dimension appeared to shape the trajectory of the spontaneous venture as it emerged in response to suffering. The goal of our modeling and analysis is to better understand how certain combinations of actions resulted in a more resilient, self-reliant community whereas other helping actions appeared to result in long-term dependence and stagnation.

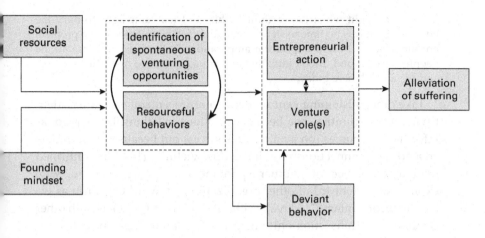

Figure 6.1
Factors Influencing the Effectiveness of Spontaneous Ventures in Alleviating Suffering

In this section, we discuss two different pathways based on the seven themes identified above. In doing so, we try to identify how various thematic groupings resulted in divergent outcomes.

Pathways of Sustaining Ventures in the Aftermath of a Disaster
Social Resources Social resources denote social relationships that provide access to important resources for opportunities aimed at easing suffering. As highlighted in chapters 3 and 4, network relationships are important in facilitating quick action. This appears to be the case as well in an LDC. However, there were differences in the nature of the social resources between the two groups of ventures (sustaining or transforming), which shaped subsequent choices and actions. Sustaining ventures had a small (if any) endowment of social resources from which to draw. These ventures were largely isolated from both local and international communities and therefore identified transaction-based strategies as the most effective means of acquiring resources to help victims. It was evident that for all sustaining ventures, the earliest identification of opportunities for spontaneous venturing to alleviate suffering primarily reflected where founders were located at the time of the disaster. For example, one founder (Stephan) explained the following:

On January 12, 2010, I was right over there across the way [motions across the field]. The majority of these people lived across the street as well. ... I was here in this area right when the earthquake hit. ... I led campaigns to bury the bodies—there was no time to sit around and reflect because we had a problem on our hands. ... I had to perform amputations in the field. ... Since all the people were around, I took initiative to form a committee to continue acting, and we are still here today.

Like other sustaining ventures, this venture's members started identifying opportunities not because previous relationships served as information sources (on available resources) but because the founders created new connections with individual victims. This was confirmed by one employee of another spontaneous venture, Sagesse, who explained, "We heard of other organizations by word of mouth as we had no prior contacts" (Akiva). Without established contacts with other groups, the transaction-only nature of relationships in the post-earthquake environment eventually took its toll: "Many organizations [NGOs] have come to visit us, but then we never see them again. We never see them, you understand? We need people to collaborate with us, but we don't have access to those people" (Adan). It appears that the lack of networks led to certain assessments about the strategic options of the new venture—they could only make do with what they had. While these ventures recognized the need to develop new local social ties, their efforts to connect with both local and international groups were only moderately successful. As a result of this lack of connections, sustaining ventures blamed outsiders for their inability to progress and grow the venture, viewing them negatively and with distrust, which in turn affected the ventures' subsequent resource acquisition approaches and the scope of the services they offered.

Founding Mindset   A founding mindset was also influential in creating sustaining spontaneous ventures. As a founding mindset, sustaining ventures possessed a strong sense of *patriotism,* feeding an "us versus them" inclination. For example, one founder explained, "My motivation was that I am a Haitian and I am a patriotic person. I couldn't stand there and watch my country in crisis" (Adan). Another founder introduced himself by detailing his ancestry, something he does whenever he describes his work to others. He explained, "I always introduce myself in the context of my ancestry because I am very proud of my country's history. ... I will never become discouraged because my history does not allow me this. ... This is why I was motivated to act" (Stephan). Because of this national pride, sustaining ventures often proclaimed that they would independently "do whatever it takes to survive" (Adan, Lane, Spencer), just as their ancestors had. A national patriotism orientation, coupled with the social resource constraints, shaped how sustaining ventures operated: they sought to function independently, and viewed outsiders with distrust. This combination of features often led to deviant and aggressive behaviors, including seizing resources from "threatening" outsiders.

Although it motivated action, these individuals' patriotism was confounded by a suspicion of non-Haitians to the point that some victims began blaming non-Haitians for the earthquake itself, setting up an entitlement mindset. For example, one founder (Sebastian) asserted the following:

We are not here to start fights ... but we demand that victims receive reparations for the injustices they have suffered [He saw the earthquake itself as a criminal act]. ... The Haitian government along with foreign governments need to provide land on which those rendered homeless by the earthquake can resettle. ... I have found that there is a lot of land and we demand that these people receive it for reparation.

Likewise, another founder noted, "There is no organization that takes care of us in reality. ... If foreigners would just get us the supplies most necessary, the population's needs would be met" (Addison). This patriotic, entitled mindset led sustaining ventures to focus on demanding resources to alleviate the most pressing and visual forms of suffering with a short-term horizon for recovery (i.e., immediate relief issues). Thus, these ventures faced a paradox: on the one hand, they relied out outsiders for ongoing resources (food, water, etc.), which they accepted when donated; on the other hand, these ventures were unwilling to partner with outsiders for long-term investment and growth because oftheir resource structures and founders' mindset.

Identification of Potential Opportunities to Alleviate Suffering Ventures' social resources and the founders' mindset influenced their identification of opportunities to alleviate suffering through spontaneous venturing. First, sustaining ventures identified opportunities that offered perpetual relief to their community. That is, they saw an opportunity to be a long-term provider of services typically associated with emergency relief, such as burying the dead, acquiring water, and helping individuals obtain shelter. After these activities were completed, sustaining ventures moved on to gaining access to basic resources from donors indefinitely. For instance, one founder (Adan) trained individuals in how to talk with aid workers to facilitate ongoing resource deliveries, and another founder (Spencer) instructed colleagues "not to rush the aid workers. ... Rushing them will make them not want to come back." These most basic victim needs were the simplest to recognize, and they were always the most pressing. As one founder reported, "The first immediate need was water and food, but ... people also needed shelter (tents), because they can't sleep with their young babies in the streets. ... We recognized this need and continue to provide it today; this is why we organized ourselves" (Sebastian).

Second, sustaining ventures identified opportunities that provided additional power and improved social status for themselves (and their founders). After the earthquake, the Haitian government essentially failed to provide basic services, including policing, governance, and health care, which created numerous opportunities for enterprising individuals and ventures to fill the leadership void. For example, Stephan, the founder of Sogeun, said:

I had previous experience with campaigning and mobilization work before starting this organization, so it was not overly difficult for me to get the hang of organizing people in the camp. ... I organized various groups of people here, seeing the government had a weakened capacity. ... Now, whenever something needs to be done, they call me because I'm the boss.

Similarly, one employee (Akiva) described how he and other founders organized themselves by putting up shelters and then leading efforts to "obtain necessary resources. This helped us search for water, food, and supply kits. ... Eventually, we were able to establish ourselves in the manner that you see today." In addition to helping others, sustaining ventures recognized opportunities to position themselves as informal ruling bodies of large tent cities. These ventures often made important decisions regarding food and water procurement, judged crimes in the community, hosted visitors, and so forth. It became clear during our interviews with these individuals and our observations of their situation that they had become conflicted. On the one hand, they sincerely sought to fulfill the needs of those they were helping. However, the nature of their help required that individuals *need* basic services of food, water, medical care, and security. They provided these things but did not offer a pathway for individuals to support themselves. As the founders and their teams took over these communities, they created new community-level titles that transformed them from creators of ventures to impromptu governors of tent cities.

Resourceful Behavior   Consistent with the other themes identified for sustaining ventures, founders of these ventures engaged in high-level resourceful behavior to pursue and test the validity of their spontaneous venture ideas. This resourceful behavior eventually became perpetual and permanent, meaning it was their sole means of operating. This became problematic and further fueled the short-term orientation of the firm. Rather than identify new resources or invest in relationships, these ventures simply identified and consumed what they could every day. They did this in a number of ways. First, sustaining ventures cunningly seized non-owned resources for long-term use, which affected both their subsequent detection of opportunities and their entrepreneurial actions. For example, one founder (Adan) reported, "We faced a problem, which was that [our operations] were set up on private lands, and the landowners wanted to reclaim their lands. The proprietors started pressuring us to make all the people leave. … This was a big problem we faced and overcame by staying on the land." These ventures believed the appropriation of other peoples' land was "a right" that was "owed to us by the government and wealthy landowners" (this statement was endorsed by Stephan, Spencer, Lane, and Aisley).

Second, sustaining ventures maintained an enduring resourcefulness mindset—a perspective on resource gathering that relied on daily search for resources, the constant repurposing of readily available resources to new ends, and living exclusively in the immediate present. This way of thinking reinforced the identification of opportunities for sustaining themselves and those they helped and led to additional action. For example, one founder (Lane) told us the following:

[After getting settled on the land] we bought a truckload of water, put it in the container, and then sold it to the population at a low price. … This is a way to ensure that we will always have money for water to continue filling up the storage tank with water. … We sell it for 4 gourdes [$.08] a bucket, but on the street, it is sold for 5 gourdes [$.10] a bucket.

Similarly, an employee (Spencer) described the actions he took:

We constantly searched for food. The children do not get the kind of nutritious foods that they really should be eating, but we managed to eat regardless. … Every time you find someone who gives you a little something to tide you over, you are in a better situation … and you keep searching every day.

As people continued to search for food and other basic resources, as time passed, the subsequent identification of opportunities became further entrenched in providing relief, forming the basis for a continuous cycle. Similarly, as long-term relief and the opportunity for power in a community deepened, ventures pursued even greater resourceful activities to meet basic needs and thereby provide victim relief. Taken together, these factors influenced entrepreneurial action.

Entrepreneurial Action Sustaining ventures engaged in two primary forms of entrepreneurial action that influenced both venture roles as well as the nature of the suffering alleviated by those actions. First, although sustaining ventures focused on providing shelter, they also provided a location for entrepreneurial action in the form of a "space" for the creation and operation of new microbusinesses. Specifically, as sustaining ventures developed, they provided meeting "houses" for group gatherings (Stephan and Lane), "liquor shops" (in tents), where individuals could purchase bootleg alcohol sold out of old anti-freeze bottles (Sanders), and other microbusinesses. One founder described his intention to continue using non-owned land to provide basic resources: "We would like to build out a reservoir for water. ... We also want to have a fish hatchery; we believe strongly in animal husbandry. People could use this fish hatchery as a business and also a source of food" (Lane). Although these ventures' efforts provided victims access to services that met some basic life needs, they also prevented people from moving out of the largely temporary setup, thus hindering their forward movement. For example, while eating a meal in a makeshift tent restaurant, a customer who was both a resident of the camp and a recipient of the venture's services said the following: "Where will we be in five years? ... We will still be here in two, three, four, ten, even thirty years from now [living the same way on this land]" (Luanne).

Second, sustaining ventures were involved in considerable government, NGO, and foreign national lobbying as a key entrepreneurial action. This is understandable in light of the large presence of NGOs and MNCs in the region. Indeed, an important part of the entrepreneurial process is acquiring resources to exploit potential opportunities and to organize and grow the business (Webb et al. 2009; Winborg and Landström 2001). For example, one employee said, "A big part of what we do is bringing people [NGOs, government agencies, others] to the camp to provide resources" (Sanders). Similarly, a founder (Adan) explained the combination of lobbying and organizing needed for resource delivery:

We tried to help people find activities and programs to participate in. ... We helped people learn about where to get aid, including food, money for leaving tents, and so forth. ... We helped people get food in an orderly way. ... We even did this with vaccinations. We had an organized system for distributing all types of materials and supplies.

Over time, sustaining ventures became more complex, structured, and committed to providing housing and meeting basic needs while increasing the number of microbusinesses in the tent cities and lobbying everyone within earshot (including one of the authors and a research assistant) to exploit their potential opportunities to alleviate suffering.

Venture Roles   Sustaining ventures established their role as a relief provider as a result of early success in finding and delivering resources to meet victims' most basic needs. As time progressed, this role of providing basic resources became further entrenched and resulted in additional entrepreneurial action focused on sustaining people's lives with basic resources.

First, the sustaining ventures developed symbols and representations that reinforced their *authority and power* in the new communities. For example, one employee (Akiva) explained the following:

We have a logo and coat of arms. ... A gold crown over a shield representing Haitian pride behind two crossed swords symbolizing the struggle for a better tomorrow. ... Two lions represent the potential of young people. ... Finally a mosaic of red, blue, and black colors combining past and present Haitian flags. ... These symbols are recognized in our community and give us authority to direct others.

Similarly, another employee (Spencer) described his organization's symbols this way: "Our flag symbolizes that we will always be the rulers and lords over our territory. ... The guinea fowl symbolizes guile and prudence because it is always difficult to find a guinea fowl's nest, and it is even more difficult to kill a guinea fowl if you spot one." He went on to explain that all individuals in his organization had an identification badge with this guinea fowl on the back to reinforce their venture's position in the community as they walked about. The authority role represented a new sense of community importance and power, connecting a strong sense of patriotism with current actions. One founder (Sebastian) explained, "In my new role here, I am channeling my Haitian spirit going back to our ancestors who survived crossing the Atlantic without food [on the slave ships]. ... We are still standing today, and now I am a leader of thousands in this big community!"

Second, in expressing their role of authority, sustaining ventures typically exaggerated their importance and accomplishments.[2] For example, one founder (Stephan) estimated that his venture had helped 32,000 people, even though only 15,000 or so had lived in the community since its inception. Similarly, another founder (Adam) stated, "We indirectly helped 11 million people," an incredibly high estimate insofar as the total population in Haiti was less than ten million at the time of the earthquake. Actions and perhaps the (over) statement of impact reinforced the ventures' authority role. As one founder (Sebastian) explained, "Since we did our part to take action and search for resources, people gradually gained hope until everyone who had initially been discouraged was eventually filled with hope [in our ability to help]." This authority created and sustained victims' dependence on these ventures and victims' expectation that the venture would continue to provide basic resources. As such, the role resulted in an increased focus on seeking basic resources, which further solidified the ventures' static role of basic resource provider.

Third, sustaining ventures created new rules and pressured others for basic resources, which reinforced and even enhanced their role as "the" relief provider. For example, two founders (Adan and Addison) produced a complex organizational structure that depicted organizational members responsible for community management, governance, document preservation, security, and so forth, all of which fell outside the established structures of the Haitian state. These roles were designed to be rigid and limited in scope (i.e., fulfilling basic needs), and they contributed to ongoing dependency among victims. In doing so, sustaining ventures reinforced their position of authority and systematized entrepreneurial activities, including resource gathering and lobbying. As one employee (Akiva) explained:

We formed a core team to respond. ... I assigned people responsibilities. This helped me to manage the venture more easily because when I need to speak, I don't call everyone; I just call the leaders of each group. ... I have experience managing people; I have a system that I use for organizing people so that things stay under my control.

Finally, as sustaining ventures were in a position of power, they could pressure both their members and (current and future) resource providers into giving them what they asked for. As one employee (Leslie) explained, "We do not vote [for our leaders] because ever since the venture was founded, there has been a leader, and everybody knows that individual is the leader. ... If this person gives instructions to do something, it will really happen." Ventures formed committees and assigned tasks, many of which involved procuring resources "at all costs." Other times, founders did the lobbying themselves. For instance, one founder (Lane) explained, "We currently are pressuring and lobbying the government to implement a water project in our area."

Deviant Behaviors Sustaining ventures' venturing activities often involved deviant behaviors: nonsanctioned or illegal activities to accomplish their ends. We observed two primary modes of deviant behavior, namely, deception in resource acquisition and property seizure. As an example of deception, one founder (Adan) explained the following:

I dressed in a manner similar to a military personnel and went to the military to get gasoline. ... They assumed I was part of the military. ... I told them I needed gasoline, and they told me no problem, they had a lot of gasoline. There were obstacles, but I overcame them. ... Many people were afraid of the military ... but not me. I told others I'm not afraid of the military because I am in the military too! I did this often to get resources.

Deception is also noticeable one employee's (Spencer's) description of his actions to procure water:

I found gallons of water in destroyed stores and broke down the walls with a tractor I took. I then took the gallons and brought them back. ... We had to act quickly and resourcefully because we felt a sense of responsibility to find solutions to all of these problems.

Other stories included details of confiscating water tanks (Lane), tricking foreign NGOs into leaving food trucks (Addison and Stephan), and stealing vehicles and other resources to survive (Sanders and Adan). Some founders (Adan, Stephan, Laren) explained how they threatened to harm NGOs, border agents, and other individuals unless they handed over food containers. These types of actions allowed them to gain access to the basic resources they needed.

Sustaining ventures also acquired and retained land that they did not own and continued to fend off attempts by landowners to reclaim their land, as one founder (Sebastian) explained:

We want to take advantage of the resources the government already has [i.e., land]. ... Only 5% of privately owned lands in the country have titles to the land ... so many of these lands are under the government's jurisdiction. ... It is OK for us to occupy these lands because they are under the control of the rich elite. ... All of us here are children of the land, and we all should have the right to a place to live.

Similarly, after sidestepping an owner who brought police to evict their group from the land, one founder (Lane) explained, "We are on the land [going on three years], but it is an injustice for the landowner to take us off the land!"

As we have illustrated above, sustaining ventures combined their existing resources, motivations, and skills to launch spontaneous ventures. While these efforts resulted in the alleviation of suffering, it did so in a way that led to dependence. This is an important addition to our conversation so far, demonstrating how not all actions provide concrete benefits and may, in fact, be detrimental if maintained over the long term. In the next section, we compare transforming ventures across the same seven dimensions above. In doing so, we highlight how differences across these seven dimensions appeared to significantly alter the nature of the spontaneous ventures that emerged as well as the outcomes they realized.

Pathways of Transforming Ventures in the Aftermath of a Disaster

Social Resources Those involved with transforming ventures explained the importance of social relationships, describing their use of and heavy reliance on *local ties* and their access to and use of extensive international ties in facilitating the identification opportunities for spontaneous venturing. This contrasted significantly with sustaining ventures. These connections resulted in multinational teams in which locals and outsiders were viewed as important collaborators, which enabled individuals from these ventures to harness their existing personal relationships for new purposes. For example, one founder (Tariq) described how access to local ties positively affected his ability to identify and fund potential opportunities to alleviate suffering:

We used a lot of local contacts. For example, there was a man who had helped with previous construction projects, including working on all of our church buildings, and he has an engineering company. This man opened up his house for our use in relief efforts, and we housed groups of foreign volunteers there when they came to Haiti to help out. ... He also had a large depot full of construction materials that he lent to us for our use. We used the depot as a receiving point for all of the food trucks that came from the DR [Dominican Republic], and we stored the food supplies in the depot after unloading the trucks.

A different founder (Gail) explained that his personal international network opened up access to needed resources: "I was already friends with these people [from the United States] since before the earthquake. ... After the earthquake, they just asked me what they could do to help. I told them what to do, and they went right into action." Similarly, a customer detailed one transforming venture's collaborative approach and the ways it helped ease suffering: the venture collaborated with "the Americans, French, and Canadians, who genuinely showed interest in learning who we were as a Haitian people and what we needed before they got to work," resulting in the generation of opportunities to help victims recover" (Gwyn). As these examples show, social resources played a critical role in helping founders launch new ventures. Furthermore, they provided access to a variety of important inputs, including ideas and resources, that could help shape the scale, scope, and direction of the new organization.

Founding Mindset   Transforming ventures described their founding mindset primarily in terms of doing the right thing for the community and assisting others in achieving self-reliance. This prosocial mindset influenced the identification and resourcing of spontaneous ventures. For example, one employee (Rio) explained, "I have a passion for helping people; it is what I love to do. I am not someone who will only help others out for money because I feel that if I am getting paid for what I do, I am not really helping the person. If I'm going to help someone, I need to do it with all my heart." Similarly, one founder (Tristan) described his mindset as an example of the overall venture mindset in this way:

I should have died [when the roof collapsed inches from my head]. ... This has been pretty hard to deal with. However, no matter what obstacle is presented. ... This [helping others] always gives me strength and drives me. ... This mentality is shared by those in our organization.

Importantly, these ventures helped others in ways beyond simply giving victims materials or resources; these ventures had goals to ensure those receiving aid retained their "dignity through work" (Raine, Tristan, Gili); that is, they maintained self-reliance through work. For example, one founder (Raine) described how his desire to help his fellow community members become autonomous influenced his venture's actions and how he is now seeing some of the positive outcomes of those actions:

Although we are coming up on three years since the earthquake and there haven't been any huge changes or improvements, we are still better off than we were in January 2010, and I know that things will continue to get better. Today, more people have jobs and businesses than back then, and this was the motivation I had all along! ... This is something that Haiti and Haitians want—a chance to find a job and to be independent instead of constantly having to ask for food and other forms of international aid.

Transforming ventures' founding mindset led these ventures to draw on a wide set of social resources (local and international) to identify any opportunities linked to their resources. This mindset differed substantially from that exhibited by founders of sustaining ventures, who were motivated primarily by national pride. It appears that this deep motivation to help others and to do so while allowing victims to retain dignity and autonomy through participation was critical for generating a transformative outcome

Identifying Potential Opportunities for Spontaneous Venturing to Alleviate Suffering Transforming ventures opportunities by transitioning the community through a staged recovery approach (rather than the single-step approach used by sustaining ventures). These spontaneous ventures were influenced by network connections as well as a mindset emphasizing victim autonomy and self-sufficiency as a long-term objective. Right after the earthquake, transforming ventures recognized the pressing need for immediate relief—that is, for food, water, shelter, and care for the injured—but they also understood that they could not and should not continue providing for people's basic needs in the long term. Rather, they knew they needed to encourage and help victims to "stand on their own feet" (Raine). For example, one founder (Tristan) stated, "Initially we gave people hygiene kits, food, and medical care. ... This was intended to be done in the short term. ... Our focus on everything [food, shelter, etc.] was transitional," that is, moving people from one stage of recovery to the next until victim autonomy was realized.

After addressing basic survival needs, as the second and third stages of recovery, the transforming ventures concentrated on providing job and career training, recognizing this would help victims not only recover but would perhaps put them in a better life situation than before the disaster. These ventures realized locals had numerous opportunities to gain employment through the many international organizations seeking to help Haitians. Thus, instead of continuing to lobby donor organizations for additional resources, these ventures focused on positioning community members as workers (translators, laborers, drivers, caregivers) to provide not only a service to these international organizations but also jobs and potentially careers to local victims.

Finally, transforming ventures were drawn to opportunities that enabled them to fulfill a felt obligation to act and to improve the community. One founder (Gail) stated, "I knew it was my responsibility to help [those in my community]." Similarly, an employee (Gili), a nurse by profession, explained, "I took an oath to act, and I take that seriously." The ventures emphasized the obligation they had to look out for their communities after the disaster, which influenced subsequent actions. Indeed, informants from all three transforming ventures described their early decision to pursue venturing as an obligation to help those in need. As these ventures took action to help others, they undertook numerous activities that would later position them well for more comprehensive entrepreneurial action. These activities included searching for survivors in rubble (Garuda), burying victims who had died (Gabi, Gail), organizing work parties for NGOs in exchange for resources or salaries (Raine), and pursuing resources in the Dominican Republic (Tate, Tristan).

Resourceful Behaviors   Transforming ventures engaged in transitional resourcefulness behaviors, temporarily appropriating non-owned resources toward new ends. As these ventures harnessed existing organizational structures and resources in their initial resourceful activities, they recognized that this use was only meant to be temporary. As summarized by one founder (Tariq), "The church ground was supposed to be primarily a place of worship and not a long-term camp." Rather than appropriating resources as sustaining ventures did, these individuals accessed, used, and then returned non-owned resources in the early stages of opportunity formation, which in turn influenced their subsequent action. These resources included land, medical equipment and facilities, buildings, and even loaned helicopters and an airplane. In most cases, buildings were appropriated for new purposes, including food services, shelter, and medical services (e.g., surgical procedures were performed in the main chapel), and so forth, but this repurposing of venues was always intended to be temporary, and the resources and assets were all eventually returned to their owners.

Furthermore, transforming ventures emphasized a transition from resource seeking to an investment mindset, which influenced entrepreneurial action and the alleviation of suffering. For instance, one employee (Tate) described how he and his team worked nonstop to help people gradually move toward autonomy, focusing on investing in the future through education and other efforts addressing the sources of victim suffering (including poverty). He stated,

Each time the problems or issues changed, we had to meet together to plan how we were going to resolve the root causes of the new problems that had come up. ... We continued holding meetings with the needs evolving until our primary goal was met, which was people were again living in their own homes and on their own lands [living autonomously].

Similarly, one founder (Raine) said,

[Many other groups believed that] NGOs would continue giving them things for free [indefinitely]. ... Because of this, there are groups of people who are still living in tents even to this day [on land they do not own]. ... We did not function this way toward those we helped; we wanted them to be self-reliant by getting training, education, or what they needed to function on their own.

Sustaining ventures recognized that a state of perpetual, resourceful resource seeking would not lead to the long-term resolution of suffering. Therefore, an investment mindset bounded beliefs about opportunities by a respect for private property and motivated and provided for more extensive entrepreneurial actions. As such, ventures' initial beliefs about opportunities had a significant effect on the implementation of difficult transitions, such as urging individuals to leave temporary camps and start the challenging process of learning to live autonomously in order to eventually "build back better."

Entrepreneurial Action Transforming ventures engaged in two primary forms of entrepreneurial action: developing need-based solutions to housing and other basic needs and developing self-reliance-based solutions to enable victim autonomy. These forms of action influenced changes in the ventures' roles and subsequently the alleviation of suffering. First, transforming ventures took a customized approach to meeting critical basic needs, such as obtaining housing, food, and water, while focusing on helping people restore their lives in such a way that their life circumstances would be better than they were before the earthquake. That is, rather than providing one solution for all (i.e., tents to anyone without housing), they explored different types of solutions based on victims' pre-earthquake life situations, such as whether these individuals were renters or home owners. This customization relates to our findings described in previous chapters but highlights an important extension: customization appears to facilitate transformative change as well as evolutionary change (staged and progressive) over time.

To accomplish the customized solutions, these ventures provided structural assessments of individuals' houses, which enabled victims to repair their homes when the damage was not too extensive (Tristan, Gabi). To address basic needs, transforming ventures took the long view; that is, they focused on helping people provide for themselves as soon as possible rather than relying on outside donors over the long run. This perspective resulted in sometimes difficult transitions from one living situation to another. While the victims making these transitions expressed difficulty with the "forced" change, they later recognized how important it was to move beyond surviving and immediate relief toward a higher level of well-being. For example, one customer (Terrin) explained, "It was hard leaving the tents; things were desperate ... but I fixed up my house and later helped with other projects like delivering food and water. ... This led to a job with an NGO, which would not have happened if I [had] stayed in a tent!"

Second, to help victims transition to long-term solutions, transforming ventures customized solutions based on individuals' baseline skill sets. All of these customized solutions were designed to enable self-reliance. For example, one founder (Tristan) described how his organization identified and provided for a variety of needs, such as loans for "those who couldn't read or write ... [to] open a small business." One employee (Rio) explained that after initially providing basic resources, "We developed a partnership with a technical school and a language institute because computer skills and English language skills could lead to quality long-term careers." By enabling victims to ultimately achieve autonomy, transforming ventures helped build communities in a way that improved pre-earthquake life situations, or building back better (Tariq, Raine, Remi, Gaymnor).

Ventures' Roles   As transforming ventures acted to address evolving physical needs and enable autonomy, they developed fluid roles that reinforced entrepreneurial actions. This stands in stark contrast to sustaining ventures, whose static roles as resource providers were reinforced through their successful actions of seeking and procuring resources to satisfy basic needs. Transforming ventures' fluid roles centered on enabling autonomy, adapting previous rules to new settings, and need finding.

First, one founder (Raine) explained how his primary role went from working as a local laborer before the disaster to working with his venture to enable others to be self-sufficient, which evolved over time: "All of the programs we [now] run are geared toward helping others be autonomous. There are people currently attending English classes, and other people attending computer literacy courses. There are people who have successfully launched small businesses, and they are now business owners." As illustrated by this founder's statements, transforming ventures' roles were fluid, from meeting basic needs and security to setting up career development programs, because of their focus on others' self-sufficiency. As one employee (Gili) explained, in working with others after the disaster, the venture had to fulfill a role that would "encourage victims and make them feel like they are capable." This focus on enabling others naturally led the ventures to alter and adjust their roles to best fit the evolving needs of those they helped. To realize fluid roles that best addressed victim needs, ventures negotiated roles for themselves, those on their leadership team, and the recipients of their services in collaboration with others, which enabled both role flexibility and victim autonomy. For example, one founder (Tariq) told us the following:

I didn't make decisions by myself ... but everyone came to my home to coordinate. There were leaders from the different communities, as well as men and women over men's, women's and children's groups that came to plan. ... I just started planning and doing things—I didn't really have a defined role as our roles were more need based. We simply met together as a committee and discussed problems and issues so that we could come up with solutions and action plans. ... Then, we all got to work to accomplish them. ... Our roles would change over time in line with the needs we uncovered.

As indicated by this comment, enabling autonomy was fundamental to the role of a venture's leadership team (enabling each member to be a contributing member) and to empowering those they helped. This stands in stark contrast to sustaining ventures, whose leaders held absolute power in decision making and actions within their communities and whose roles remained static.

Second, and in contrast to sustaining ventures that created new roles that fell outside Haitian community and legal systems, transforming ventures successfully built on and repurposed legitimate roles for new ends. Specifically, in the immediate aftermath of the disaster, transforming ventures drew heavily on and adapted existing rules and routines associated with church and community leader roles to achieve their goals. However, these routines evolved as individuals (i.e., those being helped) progressed. For example, one founder (Gabi) explained that he used the existing role structure of his church organization to gather information on a range of needs as well as to prioritize his role in an appropriate response. As such, he "activated" his role as a church leader and the connections that it provided by adapting the "rules" governing those relationships to the postdisaster setting. By adapting roles from previous relationships, the venture was able to draw on existing leadership structures (and associated roles) to quickly develop new roles (and associated rules and routines), which continued over time.

Finally, and related to the previous point, transforming ventures prioritized identifying and addressing the root causes of problems as opposed to taking a lobbying role to provide relief to the symptoms of these underlying causes of suffering. One founder (Tristan) explained the following:

Our overall process was simple. The various members of the leadership committee [i.e., overseeing women, children, and all parties] assessed the needs and evaluated the necessary resources. They would sort out what families have what problems. Then, they presented those needs to us [the committee leadership], and we drew upon all our resources, including our international church infrastructure, to fulfill those needs.

Similarly, other venture founders (Remi, Tariq) described situations in which people wanted to wait for government assistance when moving from tents to homes but realized it could take a long time and would trap victims in a negative and unproductive mindset. To avoid such a dependency trap, transforming ventures forced hard transitions, which required ventures to align their next role with the subsequent phase of recovery (e.g., transition from providing basic resources to providing education). Achieving this objective required an openness to role fluidity. Another founder (Raine) explained that providing food or short-term solutions on a long-term basis (i.e., not altering activities and roles to alleviate suffering) actually masked the real issues:

We desired to help people more in the long term so that they do not continue relying on assistance in the future. ... If you come to us and say that you do not have food, it is more likely that we will help you find a job [instead of giving you food only]. Thus, the next time you are hungry, you can just take the money you make from your job and buy food to eat. ... [Otherwise] the root problem [lack of jobs] is eventually going to resurface.

Transforming ventures recognized that role fluidity was essential to achieving their objectives through entrepreneurial action. If the ventures failed to evolve their roles, they recognized that victims would be forever trapped in seeking and receiving relief for their most basic needs. The emergence of these fluid roles influenced and reinforced subsequent entrepreneurial action, which in turn influenced the ongoing fluidity of the ventures' roles.

Deviant Behaviors   Transforming ventures differed from sustaining ventures in that they employed both creative and legal techniques to access and distribute resources. First, transforming ventures engaged in legitimate resource acquisition—that is, acquiring resources through legal means. For example, one founder (Raine) explained that instead of stealing others' resources, such as food and water, his venture encouraged and enabled individuals to pool what few resources they had on hand to ride out the most trying times:

Imagine that you have flour, I have salt, and someone else has oil, and a fourth person has rice—it doesn't make sense for us to each try to make food with our limited resources. Instead, we pooled all of our food supplies together and cooked food for everyone; we distributed it equally among everyone even if each person got only one or two spoonfuls. ... You have to know each person's talents and capabilities. ... You need doctors to form a medical committee, and you need lawyers to form a legal committee. ... We knew people's capabilities, so we could deploy them.

Transforming ventures were also creative in accessing and distributing resources through legitimate methods from outside the disaster area. One founder (Tariq) explained that his team would bring resources into Haiti from the Dominican Republic at night to avoid having the supplies taken or redirected (e.g., by sustaining ventures). He described a typical evening this way:

We traveled to another commune called La Vallée de Jacmel. We finally arrived at 4:00 a.m., dropped off the supplies, and then turned right around to go back without a break. We were so tired on the way back that we switched places every 10 minutes. ... There was nobody around on the roads to see that we were carrying valuable food supplies—we were able to travel with no hindrances.

With these creative resource-acquisition and distribution tactics, transforming ventures were able to access and engage their connections to obtain vital resources in pursuit of their potential opportunities to alleviate suffering.

Second, transforming ventures demonstrated a respect for private property in acquisitions. For example, one founder (Gabi) recalled how he helped establish a surgical center in a neighboring building to quickly treat individuals with severe and life-threatening injuries as hospitals were "overflowing and mostly full of dead bodies." The use of the building was temporary, however, as the venture worked toward long-term solutions (and corresponding roles) once the need for immediate medical relief lessened. Similarly, all three ventures explained that the use of non-owned buildings, property, and facilities was always meant to be temporary. As such, these ventures helped individuals transition out of camps in as few as three months, with no one remaining in tents after one year. They also helped people with property titles rebuild their homes and helped renters find available housing for rent.

In summary, transforming ventures differed greatly from sustaining ventures in their social resources, founding mindset, identifying opportunities for spontaneous venturing, resourceful behavior, entrepreneurial actions, roles, and deviant behaviors, which resulted in different outcomes in the alleviation of suffering. These differences highlight how there are likely considerable differences in the performance of spontaneous ventures. We anticipate that there is much to be learned about how to be efficient and yet customized in identifying needs for long-term and sustainable alleviation of suffering.

Discussion

In this chapter, we provided a unique examination of six ventures that emerged to alleviate suffering after a disaster in an LDC. This work adds to our broader discussion of compassion venturing and demonstrates that these types of ventures did (and do) emerge even in the most hostile of contexts. We showed that individuals who are already living in poverty before a disaster event and who endure even further resource loss through a disaster have much to offer in alleviating others' suffering. For example, one founder (Aidan) explained (and nearly all our informants reaffirmed), "Much of the story of the earthquake has been about foreign aid ... but what is missing is the Haitian story, the story of locals who rose up to help fellow Haitians in need. Please share that story with the world!"

Contributions to Research on Poverty Alleviation in Least Developed Countries

This chapter provides new insight into how individuals, organizations, and communities seek to alleviate poverty in LDCs, which is an ever-growing challenge. Scholars have presented a variety of (sometimes competing) perspectives on how governments and other organizations should involve themselves in addressing poverty, including work on foreign aid (Dickovick 2014), NGO–foreign government collaborations (Lecy, Schmitz, and Swedlund 2012), and base-of-the-pyramid investment (Prahalad 2004). As the observations in this chapter show, focusing on local venturing in the aftermath of a disaster extends our understanding of alleviation of suffering (including poverty) by directly considering the role of local venturing. Specifically, we found distinct differences between two groups of ventures that highlight the important actions of local ventures, the ways these ventures interact with outsiders, and the influence both have on the alleviation of suffering. Explaining how these ventures alleviated suffering has three primary implications for the literature on poverty alleviation.

First, recent studies have focused on governments' and NGOs' efforts to implement "community-based programs" (Mansuri and Rao 2012; Zanotti 2010) that engage local people in developing responses to poverty. Despite these efforts, many of these programs fail to achieve the desired outcomes (Mansuri and Rao 2012) and may even result in a victim dependence that proves destructive for local communities (Easterly 2006; Easterly and Pfutze 2008). While scholars have focused on community-based programs, they have largely ignored programs that originate in affected communities. Our findings show an important form of local response, venturing to alleviate suffering, that opens pathways for future research on ventures that originate in impoverished areas specifically designed to alleviate others' suffering. Consistent with the literature on poverty alleviation, we found evidence of both the benefits of international actors in collaborating with local ventures (i.e., transforming ventures' outcomes) and the potential risks (i.e., sustaining ventures' outcomes). Specifically, and counterintuitively, those ventures that engaged with international donors such as NGOs and government organizations as collaborators were able to break the cycle of dependence from those donors as they built back local residents' autonomy. In contrast, those who did not actively engage with international donors as collaborators but instead treated them as transactional resource providers became increasingly dependent on them and eventually grew to actively despise them, seeing them as a necessary evil. This finding has implications for those hoping to invest in community-based programs as some investments aid in transforming victims by providing broad solutions to alleviate suffering and foster a more complete recovery and perhaps even growth (i.e., collaboration with transforming ventures), while others bring relief through satisfying basic needs, which can create dependence, stagnation, and resentment (i.e., providing resources to sustaining ventures). This finding contrasts with previous research focusing more on the actions of the donating party—an NGO, government agency, or MNC— as opposed to matching and partnering with local actors.

Second, in exploring how spontaneous venture opportunities were identified and exploited, we explained two different perspectives on alleviating suffering. One important mechanism driving differences in ventures' alleviation of suffering was that transforming ventures focused on a multistage response to recovery, whereas sustaining ventures focused on a perpetual relief state response toward providing relief. Specifically, transforming ventures anticipated and encouraged difficult transitions between different stages of recovery. These steps, though uncomfortable for victims, were critical in moving toward long-term recovery and the lasting alleviation of suffering by helping clients exit extreme poverty. In contrast, sustaining ventures drew on international resources to perpetuate a subsistence-oriented way of living for disaster victims. Rather than moving on to advanced stages of recovery, they held out for government payouts, free land and food, and other services, even three years after the earthquake. This created a dependency that, while enabling people to survive, limited their ability to make progress in their lives. This finding about sustaining ventures highlights why international organizations have a difficult time knowing how and when to transition individuals to subsequent stages, resulting in perpetual aid with disappointing results (Easterly 2006; Zanotti 2010). Subsequent research can focus on the transitional stages beyond relief and the ways donors can best recognize and connect with transitioning ventures. Focusing on moving people through the stages of recovery, as opposed to implementing one-size-fits-all solutions for providing relief, is likely to improve the effectiveness of both local and foreign efforts to alleviate poverty in LDCs.

Finally, recent research has emphasized the importance of engaging participants to find more inclusive and appropriate solutions that address the multidimensional nature of poverty (London 2007; Sen 1999). While this research emphasizes the need to engage local residents, it does so primarily from the perspective of an external MNC attempting in a for-profit manner to deploy a product that is believed to have positive implications for poverty reduction. Our findings suggest that engaging local residents in recovery efforts is complicated, as those in LDCs have access to varying levels of resources and differing mindsets, which can influence success in poverty alleviation. Specifically, we found that local people who created ventures and possessed considerable social resources, including strong ties to other community members, were more likely to identify, pursue, and deliver transformative solutions for alleviating suffering. In contrast, ventures founded with limited social resources and that had primarily transaction-based ties were more likely to identify, pursue, and deliver a narrow range of solutions focused on meeting basic needs to provide immediate relief from adverse conditions. That is, transforming ventures were likely better able to engage foreign organizations (and governments) in developing long-term solutions.

Contributions to Research on Disaster Response

Researchers acknowledge the inevitable convergence of individuals on disaster areas in an effort to alleviate suffering (Quarantelli 1996; Waugh and Streib 2006), including local victim-actors (Drabek and McEntire 2003; Shepherd and Williams 2014). In exploring this phenomenon in an environment that was impoverished even before the disaster, we uncovered findings that make two primary contributions to the literature on disaster response (Drabek and McEntire 2003; Quarantelli 1996).

First, our findings extend research focused on relief from suffering by uncovering ventures that focused on transformation, or building individuals and communities back better than they were prior to the disaster. Traditional disaster research has focused on how disaster responders facilitate the restoration of order and normality following a crisis (for a review, see Drabek and McEntire 2003). As such, researchers have considered how to most rapidly respond to ongoing suffering, how to minimize subsequent suffering, and how to transition to clean-up activities as soon as the crisis has passed (Stallings and Quarantelli 1985; Waugh and Streib 2006). This study highlights the importance of seizing opportunities for positive change when disasters disrupt people's lives and the ways in which local venturing can facilitate this process (i.e., transforming ventures). Similarly, we showed how not all local venturing efforts will result in these positive changes. For example, in Haiti, some individuals lived in worse conditions—in tent cities rather than in cinderblock houses—for several years after the disaster and have yet to transition from a surviving state to one of autonomy and self-reliance. This study opens up the possibility for deepening disaster research to focus on fostering and supporting transforming ventures rather than on simply sustaining ventures.

Second, our findings contribute to the emerging management literature on disaster response, including compassion organizing (Maitlis 2012; Majchrzak, Jarvenpaa, and Hollingshead 2007; Shepherd and Williams 2014), by identifying variability in ventures' roles, the habits of mind that influenced these roles, and the ways these roles affected the alleviation of suffering. Prior studies have demonstrated that an "ethic of care" is likely to influence the emergence of compassionate responses to negative events (Maitlis 2012) and that community membership can embody this ethic of care when actors perceive others' suffering (Shepherd and Williams 2014). Our work extends this compassion organizing literature by highlighting differences in ventures' founding mindsets. Specifically, while some ventures were founded on principles of helping others (transforming ventures), others took action to help out of a sense of patriotism and to obtain power (sustaining ventures). This finding underscores the variation in the ethic of care among local LDC ventures founded to ease victim suffering after the 2010 Haiti earthquake, which led to differences in their organizing the alleviation of suffering and the outcomes of such organizing. Similarly, prior research has emphasized the importance of narratives in fostering an ethic of care (Maitlis 2012). We found that sustaining ventures used symbols such as images, badges, and slogans to demonstrate national pride and its authority within local communities within the LDC, which reinforced a continuous focus on basic and short-term forms of relief from suffering. Disaster response scholars will likely benefit by further exploring roles, the uses of symbols and narratives, and how these influence the identification, pursuit, and outcomes of spontaneous venturing opportunity pursuit.

Practical Implications

The outcomes from this chapter generate a number of practical implications. First, we show that under certain conditions, actors in disaster-stricken LDCs can be best positioned to identify and address their own needs despite incredible resource loss and suffering. For this reason, we argue that disaster responders in LDCs need to assess how they can support and facilitate these actions. In particular, how can local transformative efforts be supported, rather than just sustaining efforts? In the context we studied, not all actors were positioned to work toward long-term recovery, which resulted in ongoing poverty and suffering for some community members. Second, transforming ventures focused their disaster relief efforts on building back better, allowing them to simultaneously address disaster-induced suffering and causes of long-term poverty (e.g., lack of career training, lack of education, lack of permanent housing). This is an important finding and suggests that as aid organizations converge on LDC disaster zones, there are likely to be local people ready, willing, and able to make substantial long-term change after the disaster that could result in building a better future. In this way, disruptive events provide a unique opportunity for transformative change, which may be difficult to achieve without a disaster as a catalyst.

Third, NGOs and foreign investors need to be mindful that they may potentially harm by their mode of helping: in some of the cases we studied, the parties' actions encouraged an environment of entitlement, resentment, and perpetual poverty. Thus, any relief effort by outsiders should first focus on developing NGO and foreign investment competencies in identifying and facilitating stages of recovery that help transition victims toward autonomy.

Fourth, we found that actors who possessed strong local and international connections before the disaster were more likely to take action resulting in transformative outcomes. This is consistent with our findings in chapters 3 and 4 and further suggests that outsiders need to find more effective ways to identify and support well-connected local residents.

Finally, we found that a prosocial mindset proved beneficial to actors in identifying transformation-focused opportunities to alleviate suffering. This again is consistent with our observations previous chapters and further exposes the need for organizations to learn how to develop a prosocial way of thinking to facilitate the development of ventures that provide social benefits (e.g., alleviating suffering) in both disaster and nondisaster LDC environments.

The primary practical implications of this chapter are listed below:

1. When helping those in LDCs, do not assume they have nothing. The Haitians proved to have the most critical knowledge needed for real transformative recovery.
2. Actors getting involved in LDCs must constantly ask themselves, "Am I really helping, or am I creating long-term dependence?"
3. The standards of developed economies should not be applied to LDCs. For example, housing, food, and education solutions in LDCs will be very different from those in established economies. The key is to listen to the local residents and have them identify opportunities to help people advance in stages.
4. The human capacity for resilience is amazing. The Haiti earthquake disaster was one of the worst in modern history, yet we heard countless tales of resilience and innovation. This further demonstrates the validity of the ideas shared here and the need to better understand how to support and develop resilience.
5. The "best" technology or solution may not be the one needed. The best solution is the one that is managed by the locals and has local buy-in. These solutions will have greater capacity for sustainability.
6. Do not assume people who were exposed to extreme trauma are helpless.
7. Do not underestimate local people's creativity and resourcefulness. At the same time, be mindful that an expectation of extreme resourcefulness may lead to downstream challenges, such as distrust.
8. Determine how to identify subcommunities (see chapter 4). Do not blindly treat individuals in a similar neighborhood or physical location as a "community."
9. Encourage individuals to self-identify their communities. This will help reveal the tacit networks people actually use to get things done.
10. Outside resources do have a place in addressing locals' needs. Despite all the negative things that have been said about NGOs and foreign governments in Haiti, there is a way these groups can help. However, the key to success lies with the Haitians.

7   Where to Next?

If you don't know what to do, that's okay. But do something. Start somewhere.
... There is no model for this [responding to unique disasters] ... but we're
smart enough around here and we're well connected enough that we're going
to create [something].

—Pete Williams, Black Saturday entrepreneur

Disasters and crises abound. Recent data even show that disasters are
increasing in frequency and severity. Now more than ever, we need to
be better prepared as individuals, communities, and organizations to
respond to the crises of others in meaningful ways. Organizing compassionate responses to crises is both timely and timeless. It is timely
in that human suffering is widespread throughout society (Rynes et al.
2012) and has various causes, including conditions at work (Dutton,
Workman, and Gardin 2014), personal tragedy (Hazen 2008), and
adverse environmental conditions, such as natural or human-caused
disasters (Frost 2003). It is timeless because crisis, loss, and disaster are
fundamental aspects of the human experience, and all individuals will
be exposed to some sort of tragedy at some point in time (Bonanno
2004).

We hope that some of the ideas shared in *Spontaneous Venturing* will
generate new ways of thinking in terms of both academic research and
practical disaster response. In particular, we believe the stories from
which we developed this book provide clear paths for how current
programs can be enhanced and new ideas can be developed:

• In chapter 1, we told of the personal costs of disaster. Disasters
touch many people, and often continue to impact communities for
years following the initial destruction. However, while disasters are
horrific and destructive, they also reveal a compassionate, resilient,

and enduring side of humanity, whereby victims help fellow victims overcome crisis.

• In chapter 2, we explained the traditional perspective of responding to disasters: the command-and-control model. This model clearly has a place in responding to crises in that it allows for the engagement and coordination of institutional actors (e.g., emergency responders) and generates or passes through many resources. However, the assumption that the command-and-control model is best suited for all scenarios is fundamentally inaccurate. Disasters are idiosyncratic and surprising, and they have an unequal impact on victims. As a result, it is nearly impossible to fully prepare for a disaster. Therefore, disaster planning should include ideas that incorporate spontaneous compassionate venturing as such efforts occur in the aftermath of nearly every disaster, are driven by local residents, and provide the most effective response—one that is customized, speedy, and of appropriate magnitude.

• In chapter 3, we shared the stories of local people who organized in the aftermath of the Black Saturday bushfires. Individuals immediately took action despite being victims themselves, demonstrating the value of local knowledge and relationships in mobilizing resources to help others. Amazingly, we found these individuals generally had to work around rather than with those acting within a command-and-control framework. Furthermore, we also learned the incredible destruction and loss experienced by the Black Saturday actors and how, despite all this, they were far from helpless.

• In chapter 4, we extended the concepts developed in chapter 3 to better understand just how those affected by the disaster managed to mobilize resources despite experiencing considerable losses. We highlighted the value of social networks, in particular brokerage relationships, whereby compassionate entrepreneurs bridged the relationship between resource providers and victims. Furthermore, we found that entrepreneurs accessed resources in different ways: some bundled and repurposed what was available locally, whereas others sought (and received) resources from outside investors and donors. In short, entrepreneurs did everything possible to resource their efforts to alleviate suffering. Finally, this chapter provided a way of measuring just how helpful response actions might be. For example, if a response is rapid and large in magnitude but is insufficiently customized, it may not help at all. This type of response may end up hurting victims more than helping them. As individuals, communities, and others respond to suffering, rather than responders simply assuming they are helping, they should be mindful of how much they are actually helping.

• In chapter 5, we further expanded on how venturing to help others helps victims. In particular, we highlighted how when victims take action to help others, it helps them by strengthening their behavioral, emotional, and assumptive resilience. This is important in that victim organizing to help others appears to create a virtuous cycle for the victim-actor: venturing leads to social interaction, community connections, and other positive outcomes that further reinforce resilience. From the stories we shared, we found that when victims were capable of providing a response but did not, they were more likely to experience increased dysfunction. Therefore, it is critical that victims not be treated as helpless, as victims themselves appear to hold a key to their own recovery.

• Finally, in chapter 6, we explored spontaneous compassionate venturing in the least developed country of Haiti. We wanted to see whether compassionate venturing was a phenomenon limited only to resource-rich countries or whether it could also occur in the most unlikely of locations. We found that after one of the most devastating disasters ever to hit a nation, victims still organized and provided effective responses to suffering. However, these responses differed in *how* they alleviated suffering. Some ventures helped victims transform their situation, whereas others maintained an ongoing subsistence model. We advocate for efforts to transform victims by helping them move through stages to "build back better." While these processes are difficult, they ultimately provide greater freedom, growth, and functioning for victims.

So What? Who Cares? A Call to Action

What can be done to better prepare for the future? In the remaining pages of this book, we develop some ideas for how various stakeholders can personally embrace the principles of compassionate venturing.

There Is a Role for Centralization—But It Is Not the *Only* Role or Even the *Most Important* Role for All Disaster Situations

Though we have perhaps been hard on the command-and-control approach, we do not mean to imply it has no place. Quite the

contrary—there is clearly a very important role for emergency responders and institutional resource providers, which deliver incredible services after a crisis. For example, the Red Cross and other international
aid organizations are often among the earliest responders to a disaster
area and most often draw on local personnel for this response. Furthermore, the sheer scale of destruction caused by disasters inevitably requires an infusion of resources well beyond the capabilities of
victim-organizers.

However, alleviating others' suffering is not just about restoring lost
resources. Victim needs are multiplex in nature, involving psychological, physical, and emotional needs. Many of these needs cannot be met
by outsiders, who simply cannot fully understand or relate to victims'
experiences and needs. Furthermore, victims gain benefits from engaging in the intensive and often exhausting process of venturing. While
counterintuitive, it is critical that outside responders avoid setting
aside or undermining victim efforts to alleviate suffering, for allowing
and enabling this type of action may be the most effective outside
approach to alleviating suffering.

In sum, the most important role of outsiders is likely not just to offer
basic resources but to truly enable the autonomy and action of victim-
actors. Though disaster responders may feel an urge to be efficient in
addressing needs as soon as possible by taking command and exercis-
ing control, they should be mindful that these actions could generate
untoward long-term consequences. For example, a command-and-control response could result in the appropriation of outside resources
away from victim-actors; it could lead to unhelpful, overgeneralized
responses that cause more damage than good (e.g., off-the-shelf psychological interventions); it could promote long-term dependencies for
basic needs (e.g., shelter, food, health care services) that are not sustainable and do not promote transformation; and it could discourage actors
from trying to be part of their own solutions.

Thus, to those in emergency response institutions, while we honor
your contribution, we implore you to be mindful of the various costs
of the command-and-control model for the long-term recovery of disaster victims. We invite you to seek innovative ways to support and even
encourage local action after a disaster. We encourage you to have faith
in local people and businesses in all different kinds of economies, to
trust that they will know best, that they will be equipped, psychologically and physically, to provide effective solutions, and that they will
take steps to participate in their own recovery.

Every Situation Is Unique. Identify What Will Work Best for You and Your Community

As suggested throughout this book, but especially in chapter 5, research suggests that everyone will at some point be exposed to a potentially traumatic stressor or crisis. Though these crises may not come in the form of a disaster, they will likely provide opportunities for compassionate action. When encountering these experiences, trust your knowledge of yourself and your community. If outsiders try to tell you "That's not how things are generally done," but you know it is how your community functions, what you are doing is probably correct! Disasters hit communities in different ways. For example, the Black Saturday bushfires completely destroyed certain communities while leaving others virtually untouched. This is common and leads to unique circumstances for each individual community in terms of recovery. In light of the disproportionate way the Black Saturday fires affected communities, it would be inaccurate to say "All Black Saturday victims need X or "What happened to affected Black Saturday victims was Y." Statements such as these are too general and do not reflect the real experiences and needs of disaster victims.

As a community actor, trust your specific knowledge of your community. Who are the people who can be relied on to take action? What resources do you have immediately at hand that you could deploy? Get creative! By simply believing in your community's capacity to self-heal, you are already halfway to taking generative action. Furthermore, be aware that after a crisis, outsiders are searching for ways to truly help. If you have outside connections, consider ways to deploy their capabilities. There are so many needs after a crisis that nearly any skill or capability is useful. For example, in our Black Saturday examples, these outside sources put to use cooking skills, legal knowledge, IT knowledge, medical expertise, communication skills, an understanding of temporary housing, psychological resources, insurance help, and so forth. Most important, know that as a local person, you have the best knowledge about what resources are needed to help you and your community heal. You are the expert!

But Do Not Go It Alone. Learn from Those Who Came Before

Despite what we just said about you being the expert of your own community, you are not alone when it comes to developing long-term solutions. While no two disasters are alike, there are similarities that can be useful, especially when the goal is long-term recovery. In all our studies, we found that many local actors made impromptu connections with disaster actors from other contexts (e.g., California forest fires in the United States, the earthquake in Mexico). That is, as the recovery evolved from the earliest stages toward an effort to rebuild communities, entrepreneurs often reached out to others to learn how they could best "build back better."

At least two features make this approach effective. First, the pull rather than push approach to gathering outside input allows local customization of outside ideas. That is, local residents *sought* (pulled from other sources) the most relevant information for their situation rather than having general disaster information pushed from the top down. This led locals to actively explore various options in other contexts, allowing them to hand-pick aspects that transferred over. In particular, the act of seeking information from outsiders made local people more open to outside ideas that could be relevant.

Second, local residents seeking outside support could receive information that was *timely*. For example, when the town of Flower Dale, Australia, burned to the ground, it took a little time before residents were ready to consider rebuilding. However, they were ready to begin considering building back better sooner than outsiders might have assumed. Within a couple of weeks, they were already plotting to create a model of helping for future disaster victims to follow. They surprised outsiders with their ambition, in light of the destruction their town had experienced, with the loss of homes, lives, and property, and the general isolation they experienced after the disaster. As with other aspects of disaster response, timeliness appears to be one of the most critical aspects in customizing a response. When is the time right to get outsider advice on the recovery? Ask the local people!

Embrace Action and a Revitalized View of Potential Opportunities
Action is a fundamental principle of traditional entrepreneurship and the pursuit of opportunities. When it comes to potential opportunities to alleviate suffering, action is critical as well. We encourage a bias toward action. If you see a problem that needs solving, solve it! In our data, we found all different types of action: some volunteered for a number of hours or days, others initiated ventures that lasted months, while still others developed ventures that continue to this day. The long-term outcome should not be the determining factor in whether or not to do something; rather, locals should simply take action when they

notice suffering and feel they might be able to help, experimenting with what they have on hand.

When it comes to traditional opportunities, entrepreneurial actors may need to carefully weigh whether or not the business will succeed long term and the costs of taking action. In contrast, successful action to alleviate suffering may mean that a venture ceases operation once it has successfully addressed the need in the community. Furthermore, the cost of *not* taking action may be much higher than the cost of acting, both for the community and for the entrepreneurial actor.

Start Where You Are and Then Be Prepared to Think Big
Every venture or project has to start somewhere, so when alleviating others' suffering, start where you are! Taking on too much will feel daunting and may inhibit action. So start small and start with what you have. As victims of a disaster, you might consider what your own needs are. Many in our data set did just this. For example, farmers who had lost all of their fencing realized others may have experienced the same loss, so they created a fencing venture. In doing so, however, they first started by just seeing if they could organize to fence their own properties. Similarly, another victim recognized that the local community needed a sense of community. She spoke with a local church pastor and within hours set up an impromptu community center in the parking lot of the church. This community center became the temporary "hub" of the community where fellow victims could share stories over a hot meal, obtain information on the status of the fires and the recovery, and so forth.

While both these examples could be considered success stories at that point, the founders of these ventures transitioned from the initial idea to something much, much bigger. This surprised them but highlights the importance of thinking big when it comes to spontaneous venturing. In the first example, the local fencing venture became an international sensation, with volunteers coming from all over the world to participate. The organizers converted their small farm quarters from a private home for two into headquarters for the operation. They housed and fed volunteers while coordinating refencing programs across the affected area. As time went on, the founders realized they had created a network and organization capable of doing even more. They have responded to an array of disasters from 2011 to today, hewing to the mantra, "We are not just rebuilding fences, but helping rebuild lives." The lesson? Do not underestimate the potential impact you have; it may be much larger than you anticipate!

This principle is further exemplified in the second case noted above. The woman who founded the community center realized that the community in need was much larger than her immediate neighborhood. She partnered with two other women to create a network that reached a widespread community of people who suffered from the Black Saturday bushfires. This network led to the organization of retreats, with the founders organizing a host of resources to address the needs of the broad fire community, seeking to help people "create a new normal and realise their dreams." Today this entrepreneur is still serving her community as the venture has continued to evolve, with new needs emerging over time.

In short, do not hesitate to think big! If it looks like there is a substantial unmet need, be the one to fill the gap. If people are flocking to your effort as volunteers, funders, or customers, you may be on your way to solving a problem even bigger than the immediate disaster response. Run with it, and be prepared for what those in our studies called an "ongoing evolution" of the venture. As the venture changes, it may end up changing you in ways you never imagined. However, it all starts with taking action, beginning where you are, and trying to address real needs in a customized way.

Don't Have the Resources? Think Again!

So you have an idea, and you know what you want to do. Now, you just need some resources! Not so fast! You have much more on hand than you might think. Do not fall victim to the "I would have … if only I had had …" attitude; it is debilitating and inhibits action. Remember, if you have identified a real need after a crisis, you are already far ahead of many responders—you actually know what is needed! With this in mind, now think of creative ways to address that need!

In every situation there are ideal tools or resources that fit a need, but postdisaster responding is not the context to wait for the ideal to happen. If you wait for an ideal situation to exist before stepping up to respond, you will likely be waiting forever. In Haiti, for example, an ideal world would be one in which all of Haiti's roads and infrastructure were replaced, but this may never happen. Rather than wait, venture responders can take action with what they have. This requires several things. First, be more open in considering what resources you do have. What skills do you have? Break this list down into small chunks. Are you talented at mobilizing people? Organizing? Transporting? Getting resources from the outside? Leadership? Communication? Conducting a more detailed inventory of what you can do can lead to solutions. This will also help you push through any debilitating stance of waiting for a prepackaged set of solutions. Second, consider your network. You are more than your own skills—you are your network as well! Whom do you know who could contribute to the effort? Does that person have additional contacts? Can you create new contacts by generating publicity for your efforts? Think about how you can magnify your current network and capabilities to fill the need. Finally, think about your full set of resources (yours and your networks) and consider how you could alter or repurpose those resources for alternative purposes. Could equipment, buildings, or infrastructure be used in different ways? Now is not the time to worry (at least initially) about the long-term redeployment of resources. Instead, think: "What could be repurposed today for the short term?" As suggested throughout this book, needs will evolve. The resources needed today may not be needed tomorrow. Worrying about how long you can redeploy a resource will only inhibit action.

As in Pursuing Traditional Opportunities, There Will Be Variance in Spontaneous Ventures' Performance

The performance of spontaneous ventures will vary, primarily with respect to response speed, customization, and magnitude. This means that there will be a number of responses, all providing different degrees and levels of value. Some responses may be small but highly customized; others may be large and more generic, such as the solicitation of financial donations. Because of this variance, responders should not try to be all things to all victims but rather should focus on alleviating suffering in whatever way is most possible. That is, all actors should be aware of others and their possible roles in providing an effective response. Command-and-control responses have a place and may be most capable of a large-scale response but will likely lack in customization and speed. Similarly, local actors may feel their response is "too small"; however, the reality is that local responses, no matter how big or small, can often be the fastest and most customized in meeting critical victim needs. For this reason, spontaneous responders should not let the fear of poor performance inhibit action. No matter how large or small their contributions, the importance of spontaneous actors cannot be overstated.

Be More Aware as a "Helper": Are You Really Helping?

While we have emphasized in no uncertain terms a bias toward action, it is also necessary to add one small but important qualification: responders who are "helping" need to constantly question whether or not they are indeed helping. Even the best of intentions can lead to negative or less desirable outcomes. We illustrated this in great detail in chapter 6, where we highlighted sustaining ventures. While these ventures continue to provide some value—food, shelter (tents), and access to water—they also stand in between those they help and real transformative solutions.

As with any form of venturing, compassionate venturing can evolve: prosocial motivations can shift into motivations for power or financial resources. Helping others can be rewarding—it feels good to see that you have provided for others. However, as we saw in our data, converting others into dependents is not helpful for the victims. While compassionate responders may feel good continuing to provide for others' livelihoods, this approach is problematic in the long term. It is not sustainable, and at some point it stops being a form of help.

We suggest that any effort to help others needs to establish mechanisms to assess whether and how a venture is helping. It is critical that the venture be honest in this process by asking, "Are we doing more good than ill?" These issues are further complicated by the donation and aid provision complex that typically surrounds disasters. Millions of dollars may be poured into a disaster area that has very limited capabilities to manage and deploy those resources. We found shipping containers of materials being stored in warehouses on receipt, rather than being distributed (Black Saturday), billions of dollars donated to NGOs and foreign governments went unspent (Haiti), and thousands of volunteers flocked to disaster areas to offer aid, complicating ground logistics (both Black Saturday and Haiti). With all these resources coming into an area, waste is inevitable: resources are misappropriated, exploited, or simply forgotten until they spoil. It is our hope that by raising the profile of local spontaneous ventures as a more promising path to disaster response, future efforts can avoid waste and instead pour resources into the local ventures doing the greatest amount of good.

Conclusion

Disasters and crises are regular occurrences that have impacts on individual well-being, communities, and even global economies. However, disasters also highlight some of the best in the human experience. It is our hope that readers of this book might be as inspired as we were in reading the accounts of the courageous actions of compassionate entrepreneurs. Furthermore, our hope is that by sharing these accounts, we may help future postdisaster actors of all varieties learn from the actions of spontaneous entrepreneurs to consider taking action (for local persons), incorporating the actions of local residents and businesses in broader planning efforts (for institutional actors), and providing resources that sustain the ongoing efforts of spontaneous ventures (for outside donors).

Notes

Chapter 3: Spontaneous Venturing to Organize Compassion in the Aftermath of
a Disaster

1. This chapter is based on our inductive study (Shepherd and Williams 2014).

2. After three weeks, however, Elledge reopened her business and transitioned her
impromptu relief center to state-run institutions.

Chapter 4: Spontaneous Ventures Brokering to Alleviate Suffering

1. Chapter 4 is based on our quantitative study (Williams and Shepherd in press).

2. Gould and Fernandez (1989) discussed brokerage roles in terms of subgroup membership, which refers to any exogenous social category membership position that can be
seen as "fixed" in terms of the brokerage role itself (Spiro, Acton, and Butts 2013). As we
discuss in the methods section, everyone is our data set is associated with self-identified
subgroups within the disaster area.

3. See Williams and Shepherd (in press) for a detailed explanation of the methodology,
analysis, and results of this and other findings mentioned in chapter 4.

Chapter 5: Self-Help by Spontaneously Venturing to Help Others

1. This chapter is based on our quantitative study (Williams and Shepherd 2016b).

Chapter 6: A Focus on Building Resilience Rather Than Providing Sustenance

1. This chapter is based on Williams and Shepherd (2016a).

2. This assessment was corroborated by meeting with more than twenty individuals
influenced by these ventures, including customers, other ventures, and those living
within immediate proximity of the ventures.

References

Aldrich, D. P. 2012. *Building Resilience: Social Capital in Post-Disaster Recovery.* Chicago: University of Chicago Press.

Aldrich, H. 1979. *Organizations and Environments.* Englewood Cliffs, NJ: Prentice-Hall.

Aldrich, H. 1999. *Organizations Evolving.* Thousand Oaks, CA: Sage.

Aldrich, H. E. 2000. *Organizations Evolving.* Englewood Cliffs, NJ: Prentice-Hall.

Aldrich, H. E., and M. Ruef. 2006. *Organizations Evolving.* 2nd ed. Thousand Oaks, CA: Sage.

Amabile, T. M. 1993. "Motivational synergy: Toward new conceptualizations of intrinsic and extrinsic motivation in the workplace." *Human Resource Management Review* 3 (3): 185–201.

Amabile, T. M., K. G. Hill, B. A. Hennessey, and E. M. Tighe. 1994. "The Work Preference Inventory: Assessing intrinsic and extrinsic motivational orientations." *Journal of Personality and Social Psychology* 66 (5): 950.

Amit, R., L. Glosten, and E. Muller. 1993. "Challenges to theory development in entrepreneurship research." *Journal of Management Studies* 30 (5): 815–834.

Anderson, A. I., D. Compton, and T. Mason. 2004. "Managing in a dangerous world: The National Incident Management System." *Engineering Management Journal* 16 (4): 3–9.

Anderson, A. I., D. Compton, and T. Mason. 2005. "Managing in a dangerous world: The National Incident Management System." *IEEE Engineering Management Review* 33 (3).

Anderson, C. R., D. Hellriegel, and J. W. Slocum. 1977. "Managerial response to environmentally induced stress." *Academy of Management Journal* 20:260–272.

Annen, K., and L. Moers. 2012. *Donor Competition for Aid Impact, and Aid Fragmentation.* Washington, DC: International Monetary Fund.

Ardichvili, A., R. Cardozo, and S. Ray. 2003. "A theory of entrepreneurial opportunity identification and development." *Journal of Business Venturing* 18 (1): 105–123.

Armstrong, S., M. Curtis, R. Kent, D. Maxwell, F. Mousseau, F. Pearce, K. Sadler, P. Tamminga, and G. Tansey. 2011. *World Disasters Report 2011: Focus on Hunger and Malnutrition.* Lyon, France: Imprimerie Chirat.

Audia, P. G., E. A. Locke, and K. G. Smith. 2000. "The paradox of success: An archival and laboratory study of strategic persistence following radical environmental change." *Academy of Management Journal* 43 (5): 837–853.

Auf der Heide, E. 1989. *Disaster Response: Principles and Preparation and Coordination.* St. Louis, MO: C. V. Mosby.

Austin, J., H. Stevenson, and J. Wei-Skillern. 2006. "Social and commercial entrepreneurship: Same, different, or both?" *Entrepreneurship Theory and Practice* 30 (1): 1–22.

Austin, P. 2009. "How the government failed all Victorians." http://www.theage.com.au/national/how-the-government-failed-all-victorians-20090817-enp5.html.

Autio, E., L. Dahlander, and L. Frederiksen. 2013. "Information exposure, opportunity evaluation and entrepreneurial action: An empirical investigation of an online user community." *Academy of Management Journal* 56 (5): 1348–1371.

Baer, M., K. T. Dirks, and J. A. Nickerson. 2013. "Microfoundations of strategic problem formulation." *Strategic Management Journal* 34 (2): 197–214.

Baker, T. 2007. "Resources in play: Bricolage in the Toy Store(y)." *Journal of Business Venturing* 22 (5): 694–711.

Baker, T., and H. E. Aldrich. 2000. *Bricolage and Resource-Seeking: Improvisational Responses to Dependence in Entrepreneurial Firms.* Chapel Hill, NC: University of North Carolina Press.

Baker, T., A. S. Miner, and D. T. Eesley. 2003. "Improvising firms: Bricolage, account giving and improvisational competencies in the founding process." *Research Policy* 32 (2): 255–276.

Baker, T., and R. E. Nelson. 2005. "Creating something from nothing: Resource construction through entrepreneurial bricolage." *Administrative Science Quarterly* 50 (3): 329–366.

Bakker, R. M. 2010. "Taking stock of temporary organizational forms: A systematic review and research agenda." *International Journal of Management Reviews* 12 (4): 466–486.

Bakker, R. M., and D. A. Shepherd. 2017. "Pull the plug or take the plunge: Multiple opportunities and the speed of venturing decisions in the Australian mining industry." *Academy of Management Journal* 60 (1): 130–155.

Bandura, A. 1997. *Self-efficacy: The Exercise of Control.* New York: Macmillan.

Bansal, P. 2003. "From issues to actions: The importance of individual concerns and organizational values in responding to natural environmental issues." *Organization Science* 14 (5): 510–527.

Bansal, P. 2005. "Evolving sustainably: A longitudinal study of corporate sustainable development." *Strategic Management Journal* 26:197–218.

Barney, J. B. 1991. "Firm resources and sustained competitive advantage." *Journal of Management* 17:99–120.

Barney, J. B., and A. M. Arikan. 2001. "The resource-based view: Origins and implications." In *Handbook of Strategic Management*, ed. M. A. Hitt, R. E. Freeman, and J. S. Harrison, 124–188. Oxford: Blackwell.

Barton, A. H. 1969. *Communities in Disaster: A Sociological Analysis of Collective Stress Situations.* Garden City, NY: Doubleday.

Batley, R. 2006. "Engaged or divorced? Cross-service findings on government relations with non-state service-providers." *Public Administration and Development* 26 (3): 241–251.

Batley, R., and C. Mcloughlin. 2010. "Engagement with non-state service providers in fragile states: Reconciling state-building and service delivery." *Development Policy Review* 28 (2): 131–154.

Batson, C. D. 1998. "The psychology of helping and altruism: Problems and puzzles." *Contemporary Psychology* 43 (2): 108–109.

Batson, C. D., N. Ahmad, A. A. Powell, E. L. Stocks, J. Shah, and W. L. Gardner. 2008. In *Handbook of Motivation Science,* ed. J. Y. Shah and W. L. Gardner, 135–149. New York: Guilford.

Baum, J. R., and E. A. Locke. 2004. "The relationship of entrepreneurial traits, skill, and motivation to subsequent venture growth." *Journal of Applied Psychology* 89 (4): 587–598.

Baum, J. R., E. A. Locke, and K. G. Smith. 2001. "A multidimensional model of venture growth." *Academy of Management Journal* 44 (2): 292–303.

Becerra, O., E. Cavallo, and I. Noy. 2014. "Foreign aid in the aftermath of large natural disasters." *Review of Development Economics* 18 (3): 445–460.

Bechky, B. A. 2006. "Gaffers, gofers, and grips: Role-based coordination in temporary organizations." *Organization Science* 17:3–21.

Bechky, B. A., and G. A. Okhuysen. 2011. "Expecting the unexpected? How SWAT officers and film crews handle surprises." *Academy of Management Journal* 54 (2): 239–261.

Beder, J. 2005. "Loss of the assumptive world: How we deal with death and loss." *Journal of Death and Dying* 50 (4): 255–265.

Beggs, J. J., V. A. Haines, and J. S. Hurlbert. 1996. "Situational contingencies surrounding the receipt of informal support." *Social Forces* 75 (1): 201–222.

Bellizzi, K. M., and T. O. Blank. 2006. "Predicting posttraumatic growth in breast cancer survivors." *Health Psychology: Official Journal of the Division of Health Psychology, American Psychological Association* 25 (1): 47.

Bento, R. F. 1994. "When the show must go on: Disenfranchised grief in organizations." *Journal of Managerial Psychology* 9 (6): 35–44.

Bhagavatula, S., T. Elfring, A. van Tilburg, and G. G. van de Bunt. 2010. "How social and human capital influence opportunity recognition and resource mobilization in India's handloom industry." *Journal of Business Venturing* 25 (3): 245–260.

Bigley, G. A., and K. H. Roberts. 2001. "The incident command system: High-reliability organizing for complex and volatile task environments." *Academy of Management Journal* 44:1281–1299.

Bingham, C. B., and K. M. Eisenhardt. 2011. "Rational heuristics: The 'simple rules' that strategists learn from process experience." *Strategic Management Journal* 32 (13): 1437–1464.

Block, J., and A. M. Kremen. 1996. "IQ and ego-resiliency: Conceptual and empirical connections and separateness." *Journal of Personality and Social Psychology* 70 (2): 349–361.

Bold, T., P. Collier, and A. Zeitlin. 2009. *The Provision of Social Services in Fragile States: Independent Service Authorities as a New Modality.* Oxford: Oxford University, Centre for the Study of African Economies.

Bonanno, G. A. 2004. "Loss, trauma, and human resilience: Have we underestimated the human capacity to thrive after extremely aversive events?" *American Psychologist* 59 (1): 20–28.

Bonanno, G. A. 2005. "Resilience in the face of potential trauma." *Current Directions in Psychological Science* 14 (3): 135–138.

Bonanno, G. A. 2012. "Uses and abuses of the resilience construct: Loss, trauma, and health-related adversities." *Social Science & Medicine* 74 (5): 753.

Bonanno, G. A., C. R. Brewin, K. Kaniasty, and A. M. L. Greca. 2010. "Weighing the costs of disaster consequences, risks, and resilience in individuals, families, and communities." *Psychological Science in the Public Interest* 11 (1): 1–49.

Bonanno, G. A., N. P. Field, A. Kovacevic, and S. Kaltman. 2002. "Self-enhancement as a buffer against extreme adversity: Civil war in Bosnia and traumatic loss in the United States." *Personality and Social Psychology Bulletin* 28 (2): 184–196.

Bonanno, G. A., S. Galea, A. Bucciarelli, and D. Vlahov. 2006. "Psychological resilience after disaster New York City in the aftermath of the September 11th terrorist attack." *Psychological Science* 17 (3): 181–186.

Bonanno, G. A., S. Galea, A. Bucciarelli, and D. Vlahov. 2007. "What predicts psychological resilience after disaster? The role of demographics, resources, and life stress." *Journal of Consulting and Clinical Psychology* 75 (5): 671.

Bonanno, G. A., D. Keltner, A. Holen, and M. J. Horowitz. 1995. "When avoiding unpleasant emotions might not be such a bad thing: Verbal-autonomic response dissociation and midlife conjugal bereavement." *Journal of Personality and Social Psychology* 69 (5): 975–989.

Bonanno, G. A., and A. D. Mancini. 2012. "Beyond resilience and PTSD: Mapping the heterogeneity of responses to potential trauma." *Psychological Trauma: Theory, Research, Practice, and Policy* 4 (1): 74–83.

Bonanno, G. A., A. Papa, K. Lalande, M. Westphal, and K. Coifman. 2004. "The importance of being flexible: The ability to both enhance and suppress emotional expression predicts long-term adjustment." *Psychological Science* 15 (7): 482–487.

Bonanno, G. A., C. Rennicke, and S. Dekel. 2005. Self-enhancement among high-exposure survivors of the September 11th terrorist attack: Resilience or social maladjustment? *Journal of Personality and Social Psychology* 88 (6): 984–998.

Bonanno, G. A., M. Westphal, and A. D. Mancini. 2011. "Resilience to loss and potential trauma." *Annual Review of Clinical Psychology* 7:511–535.

Borrell, J., L. Vella, and S. Lane. 2011. *Bushfire Response and Recovery Evaluation: Community Experiences and Service Responses after the 2009 Victorian Bushfires.* Vol. 1, 1–123. Victoria, Australia: Kildonan Uniting Care. .

Boston Consulting Group. 2009. *Royal Commission Submission: Leadership Lessons from the Victorian Bushfires*, 1–8. Melbourne: Boston Consulting Group.

Bourguignon, F., and M. Sundberg. 2007. "Aid effectiveness—opening the black box." *American Economic Review* 97 (2): 316–321.

Bradley, S. W., H. E. Aldrich, D. A. Shepherd, and J. Wiklund. 2011. "Resources, environmental change, and survival: Asymmetric paths of young independent and subsidiary organizations." *Strategic Management Journal* 32 (5): 486–509.

Bradley, S. W., D. A. Shepherd, and J. Wiklund. 2011. "The importance of slack for new organizations facing 'tough' environments." *Journal of Management Studies* 48 (5): 1071–1097.

Brady, M. J., A. H. Peterman, G. Fitchett, M. Mo, and D. Cella. 1999. "A case for including spirituality in quality of life measurement in oncology." *Psycho-Oncology* 8 (5): 417–428.

Brinkerhoff, D. 2008. "From humanitarian and post-conflict assistance to health system strengthening in fragile states: Clarifying the transition and the role of NGOs." USAID, HealthSystems2020.org, https://www.hfgproject.org/wp-content/uploads/2015/02/From-Humanitarian-and-Post-Conflict-Assistance-to-Health-System-Strengthening-in-Fragile-States.pdf.

Britton, N. 1989. "Anticipating the unexpected: Is bureaucracy able to come to the dance?" Working Paper 1. Sydney: Cumberland College of Health Sciences, Disaster Management Studies Centre.

Brown, S. L., and K. M. Eisenhardt. 1997. "The art of continuous change: Linking complexity theory and time-paced evolution in relentlessly shifting organizations." *Administrative Science Quarterly* 42:1–34.

Brugmann, J., and C. K. Prahalad. 2007. "Cocreating business's new social compact." *Harvard Business Review* 85 (2): 80–90.

Brumby, J. M. 2009. *Parliamentary Debates: Condolences*. Melbourne, Australia: Victorian Government Printer.

Brush, C. G., P. G. Greene, and M. M. Hart. 2001. "From initial idea to unique advantage: The entrepreneurial challenge of constructing a resource base." *Academy of Management Executive* 15 (1): 64–78.

Brush, C. G., T. S. Manolova, and L. F. Edelman. 2008. "Properties of emerging organizations: An empirical test." *Journal of Business Venturing* 23 (5): 547–566.

Bryson, J. M., B. C. Crosby, and M. M. Stone. 2006. "The design and implementation of cross-sector collaborations: Propositions from the literature." *Public Administration Review* 66 (S1): 44–55.

Buehler, R., D. Griffin, and M. Ross. 1994. "Exploring the 'planning fallacy': Why people underestimate their task completion times." *Journal of Personality and Social Psychology* 67 (3): 366–381.

Burt, R. S. 1992. *Structural Holes: The Social Structure of Competition*. Cambridge, MA: Harvard University Press.

Burt, R. S. 1997. "A note on social capital and network content." *Social Networks* 19: 355–373.

Burt, R. S. 2000. "The network structure of social capital." In *Research in Organizational Behavior*, ed. B. M. Staw and R. I. Sutton. New York: Elsevier.

Burt, R. S. 2005. *Brokerage and Closure: An Introduction to Social Capital*. New York: Oxford University Press.

Cable, D. M., and S. Shane. 1997. "A prisoner's dilemma approach to entrepreneur-venture capitalist relationships." *Academy of Management Review* 22 (1): 142–176.

Caldwell, A. 2009. Radio systems failed on Black Saturday. ABC (Australia) News, May 18. http://www.abc.net.au/news/2009-05-19/radio-systems-failed-on-black-saturday/1687098.

Cameron, K. S., and A. Caza. 2004. "Introduction contributions to the discipline of positive organizational scholarship." *American Behavioral Scientist* 47:731–739.

Cannon, T., and L. Schipper. 2014. *World Disasters Report*. Lyon, France: Imprimerie Chirat.

Cardon, M. S., C. E. Stevens, and D. R. Potter. 2011. "Misfortunes or mistakes? Cultural sensemaking of entrepreneurial failure." *Journal of Business Venturing* 26 (1): 79–92.

Carlyon, P. 2009. "Marysville's last moments before disaster hit." http://www.heraldsun.com.au/news/marysvilles-last-moments-before-disaster-hit/story-e6frf7jo-1111111884 6958. Accessed 28 June 2013.

Carter, N. M., W. B. Gartner, and P. D. Reynolds. 1996. "Exploring start-up event sequences." *Journal of Business Venturing* 11 (3): 151–166.

Casson, M. 1982. *The Entrepreneur: An Economic Theory*. Lanham, MD: Rowman & Littlefield.

Casson, M., and N. Wadeson. 2007. "The discovery of opportunities: Extending the economic theory of the entrepreneur." *Small Business Economics* 28 (4): 285–300.

Cavallo, E., A. Powell, and O. Becerra. 2010. "Estimating the direct economic damages of the earthquake in Haiti." *Economic Journal (Oxford)* 120 (546): F298–F312.

Charles-Edwards, D. 2000. *Bereavement at Work: A Practical Guide*. London: Duckworth.

Cheng, J. L., and I. F. Kesner. 1997. "Organizational slack and response to environmental shifts: The impact of resource allocation patterns." *Journal of Management* 23 (1): 1–18.

Child, J., and G. Möllering. 2003. "Contextual confidence and active trust development in the Chinese business environment." *Organization Science* 14 (1): 69–80.

Clark, C. 1997. *Misery and Company: Sympathy in Everyday Life*. Chicago: University of Chicago Press.

Clegg, S. R., C. Hardy, T. B. Lawrence, and W. R. Nord, eds. 2006. *The Sage Handbook of Organization Studies*. London: Sage.

Cohen, B., and M. I. Winn. 2007. "Market imperfections, opportunity and sustainable entrepreneurship." *Journal of Business Venturing* 22 (1): 29–49.

Coifman, K. G., G. A. Bonanno, R. D. Ray, and J. J. Gross. 2007. "Does repressive coping promote resilience? Affective-autonomic response discrepancy during bereavement." *Journal of Personality and Social Psychology* 92 (4): 745.

Comfort, L. K. 1985. "Integrating organizational action in emergency management: Strategies for change." *Public Administration Review* 45:155–164.

Comfort, L. K. 2007. "Crisis management in hindsight: Cognition, communication, coordination, and control." *Public Administration Review* 67 (s1): 189–197.

Comfort, L. K., M. Dunn, D. Johnson, and R. Skertich. 2004. "Coordination in complex systems: Increasing efficiency in disaster mitigation and response." *International Journal of Emergency Management* 2 (1): 62–80.

Comfort, L. K., K. Ko, and A. Zagorecki. 2004. "Coordination in rapidly evolving disaster response systems the role of information." *American Behavioral Scientist* 48 (3): 295–313.

Companys, Y. E., and J. S. McMullen. 2007. "Strategic entrepreneurs at work: The nature, discovery, and exploitation of entrepreneurial opportunities." *Small Business Economics* 28 (4): 301–322.

Concannon, B. Jr., and A. Phillips. 2006. "Haiti needs justice, not charity." *The South Florida Sun-Sentinel*, July 24.

Cooper, C. 2009. "Witness describes Black Saturday fireballs." *ABC News*, May 13.

Cope, J. 2011. "Entrepreneurial learning from failure: An interpretative phenomenological analysis." *Journal of Business Venturing* 26 (6): 604–623.

Covin, J. G., and M. P. Miles. 2007. "Strategic use of corporate venturing." *Entrepreneurship Theory and Practice* 31:183–207.

Cuervo-Cazurra, A., and M. Genc. 2008. "Transforming disadvantages into advantages: Developing-country MNEs in the least developed countries." *Journal of International Business Studies* 39 (6): 957–979.

Curran, P. J., and A. M. Hussong. 2003. "The use of latent trajectory models in psychopathology research." *Journal of Abnormal Psychology* 112 (4): 526–544.

Currier, J. M., R. A. Neimeyer, and J. S. Berman. 2008. "The effectiveness of psychotherapeutic interventions for bereaved persons: A comprehensive quantitative review." *Psychological Bulletin* 134 (5): 648–661.

Davis, M., M. Reeve, and B. M. Altevogt. 2013. Forum on Medical and Public Health Preparedness for Catastrophic Events. In *Nationwide Response Issues after an Improvised Nuclear Device Attack: Medical and Public Health Considerations for Neighboring Jurisdictions. Workshop Summary*, ed. M. Davis, M. Reeve and B. M. Altevogt. Washington, DC: National Academies Press.

Dean, T. J., and J. S. McMullen. 2007. "Toward a theory of sustainable entrepreneurship: Reducing environmental degradation through entrepreneurial action." *Journal of Business Venturing* 22 (1): 50–76.

Deci, E. L., R. Koestner, and R. M. Ryan. 1999. "A meta-analytic review of experiments examining the effects of extrinsic rewards on intrinsic motivation." *Psychological Bulletin* 125 (6): 627–668.

De Dreu, C. K. W. 2006. "Rational self-interest and other orientation in organizational behavior: A critical appraisal and extension of Meglino and Korsgaard (2004)." *Journal of Applied Psychology* 91:1245–1252.

De Dreu, C. K., and A. Nauta. 2009. "Self-interest and other-orientation in organizational behavior: Implications for job performance, prosocial behavior, and personal initiative." *Journal of Applied Psychology* 94 (4): 913.

Delacroix, J., and M. Solt. 1988. "Niche formation and foundings in the California wine industry, 1941–1984." In *Ecological Models of Organizations*, ed. G. R. Carroll, 53–68. Cambridge, MA: Ballinger.

Delbecq, A. L. 2010. "Organizational compassion: A litmus test for a spiritually centered university culture." *Journal of Management, Spirituality & Religion* 7:241–249.

Denzin, N. K. 1970. *The Research Act: A Theoretical Introduction to Strategies of Qualitative Inquiry.* Chicago: Aldine.

Department of Homeland Security. 2004. "The national incident management system: Enhancing response to terrorist attacks." Washington, DC: Government Printing Office. http://www.gpo.gov/fdsys/pkg/CHRG-108hhrg25602/html/CHRG-108hhrg25602. htm.

Dickovick, J. T. 2014. "Foreign aid and decentralization: Limitation on impact in autonomy and responsiveness." *Public Administration and Development* 34 (3): 194–206.

Doherty, B. 2009a. "30 survivors huddle in shelter from the storm." http://www.theage .com.au/national/30-survivors-huddle-in-shelter-from-the-storm-20090212-8639.html.

Doherty, B. 2009b. "Black Saturday donations get tangled in red tape." http://www .theage.com.au/national/black-saturday-donations-get-tangled-in-red-tape-20090401 -9jsu.html.

Dosi, G. 1984. *Technical change and industrial transformation: The theory and an application to the semiconductor industry.* London: Palgrave Macmillan.

Drabek, T. E. 1985. "Managing the emergency response." *Public Administration Review* 45:85–92.

Drabek, T. E. 1986. *Human System Responses to Disasters: An Inventory of Social Findings.* New York: Springer-Verlag.

Drabek, T. E. 1987. "Emergent structures." In *Sociology of Disasters: Contribution of Sociology to Disaster Research*, ed. R. R. Dynes, B. De Marchi and C. Pelanda. Milan: Franco Angeli.

Drabek, T. E. 1989. "Disasters as non-routine social problems." *International Journal of Mass Emergencies and Disasters* 7 (3): 253–264.

Drabek, T. E. 2004. "Theories relevant to emergency management versus a theory of emergency management." Paper presented at the Annual Emergency Management Higher Education Conference, National Emergency Training Center, Emmitsburg, MD, June.

Drabek, T. E. 2005. "Predicting disaster response effectiveness." *International Journal of Mass Emergencies and Disasters* 23 (1): 49–72.

Drabek, T. E. 2007. "Social problems perspectives, disaster research and emergency management: Intellectual contexts, theoretical extensions, and policy implications." Paper presented at the Annual Meeting of the American Sociological Association, New York, August.

Drabek, T. E., and D. A. McEntire. 2002. "Emergent phenomena and multiorganizational coordination in disasters: Lessons from the research literature." *International Journal of Mass Emergencies and Disasters* 20 (2): 197–224.

Drabek, T. E., and D. A. McEntire. 2003. "Emergent phenomena and the sociology of disaster: Lessons, trends and opportunities from the research literature." *Disaster Prevention and Management* 12:97–112.

Drabek, T. E., and D. A. McEntire. 2003. "Emergent phenomena and the sociology of disaster: Lessons, trends and opportunities from the research literature." *Disaster Prevention and Management* 12 (2): 97–112.

Dunn, E. W., L. B. Aknin, and M. I. Norton. 2008. "Spending money on others promotes happiness." *Science* 319 (5870): 1687–1688.

Dutton, J. E. 2003. "Breathing life into organizational studies." *Journal of Management Inquiry* 12:5–19.

Dutton, J. E., P. J. Frost, M. C. Worline, J. M. Lilius, and J. M. Kanov. 2002. "Leading in times of trauma." *Harvard Business Review* 80 (1): 54–61.

Dutton, J. E., K. M. Workman, and A. E. Hardin. 2014. "Compassion at work." *Annual Review of Organizational Psychology and Organizational Behavior* 1:277–304.

Dutton, J. E., M. C. Worline, P. J. Frost, and J. M. Lilius. 2006. "Explaining compassion organizing." *Administrative Science Quarterly* 51 (1): 59–96.

Dynes, R. R. 1974. *Organized Behavior in Disaster.* Columbus: Ohio State University, Disaster Research Center.

Dynes, R. R. 1970. *Organized Behavior in Disaster.* Lexington, MA: Heath Lexington Books.

Dynes, R. R. 2003. "Noah and disaster planning: The cultural significance of the flood story." *Journal of Contingencies and Crisis Management* 11 (4): 170–177.

Dynes, R. R. 2005. *Community Social Capital as the Primary Basis for Resilience.* Newark: University of Delaware Disaster Research Center.

Dynes, R. R., E. L. Quarantelli, and G. A. Kreps. 1981. *A Perspective on Disaster Planning.* Columbus: Ohio State University, Disaster Research Center.

Dynes, R. R., and K. Tierney. 1994. *Disasters, Collective Behavior, and Social Organization.* Newark: University of Delaware Press.

Easterly, W. 2006. *The White Man's Burden: Why the West's Efforts to Aid the Rest Have Done So Much Ill and So Little Good.* New York: Penguin.

Easterly, W., and T. Pfutze. 2008. "Where does the money go? Best and worst practices in foreign aid." *Journal of Economic Perspectives* 22 (2): 29–52.

Eckhardt, J. T., and S. Shane. 2003. "Opportunities and entrepreneurship." *Journal of Management* 29 (3): 333–349.

Eckhardt, J. T., and S. A. Shane. 2013. "Response to the commentaries: The individual-opportunity (IO) nexus integrates objective and subjective aspects of entrepreneurship." *Academy of Management Review* 38 (1): 160–163.

Edmonds, K. 2013. "Beyond good intentions: The structural limitations of NGOs in Haiti." *Critical Sociology* 39:439–452.

Eikenberry, A. M., V. Arroyave, and T. Cooper. 2007. "Administrative failure and the international NGO response to Hurricane Katrina." *Public Administration Review* 67 (s1): 160–170.

Eisenhardt, K. M. 1989. "Building theory from case study research." *Academy of Management Review* 14 (4): 532–550.

Eisenhardt, K. M., and D. N. Sull. 2001. "Strategy as simple rules." *Harvard Business Review* 79 (1): 106–119.

Elbers, W., L. Knippenberg, and L. Schulpen. 2014. "Trust or control? Private development cooperation at the crossroads." *Public Administration and Development* 34 (1): 1–13.

Enander, A. 2010. "Human needs and behavior in the event of emergencies and social crises." In *Emergency Response Management in Today's Complex Society*, ed. L. Fredholm and A. L. Göransson, 31–37. Stockholm: Swedish Civil Contingencies Agency.

Engwall, M. 2003. "No project is an island: Linking projects to history and context." *Research Policy* 32 (5): 789–808.

Evans, D. S., and L. S. Leighton. 1989. "Some empirical aspects of entrepreneurship." *American Economic Review* 79 (3): 519–535.

Faulkner, R. R., and A. B. Anderson. 1987. "Short-term projects and emergent careers: Evidence from Hollywood." *American Journal of Sociology* 92:879–909.

Fergus, S., and M. A. Zimmerman. 2005. "Adolescent resilience: A framework for understanding healthy development in the face of risk." *Annual Review of Public Health* 26:399–419.

Fiet, J. O. 2002. *The Systematic Search for Entrepreneurial Discoveries*. Westport, CT: Quorum Books.

Figley, C. R. 2002. "Introduction." In *Treating Compassion Fatigue*, ed. C. R. Figley, 1–14. New York: Routledge.

Folkman, S., and J. T. Moskowitz. 2000. "Positive affect and the other side of coping." *American Psychologist* 55 (6): 647–654.

Folkman, S., and J. T. Moskowitz. 2004. "Coping: Pitfalls and promise." *Annual Review of Psychology* 55:745–774.

Forbes, D. P. 2005. "Are some entrepreneurs more overconfident than others?" *Journal of Business Venturing* 20 (5): 623–640.

Fox-Wolfgramm, S., K. B. Boal, and J. G. Hunt. 1998. "Towards an understanding of organizational adaptation: Inside the black box." *Administrative Science Quarterly* 43 (1): 87–126.

Fraser, L. 2009. Marysville marathon festival. https://sites.google.com/site/marysvillemarathonfestival.

Fredholm, L., and A. L. Göransson, eds. *Emergency Response Management in Today's Complex Society*, 31–72. Stockholm: Swedish Civil Contingencies Agency.

Fredrickson, B. L. 2001. "The role of positive emotions in positive psychology: The broaden-and-build theory of positive emotions." *American Psychologist* 56 (3): 218–226.

Fredrickson, B. L., R. A. Mancuso, C. Branigan, and M. M. Tugade. 2000. "The undoing effect of positive emotions." *Motivation and Emotion* 24 (4): 237–258.

Frost, P. J. 2003. *Toxic Emotions at Work: How Compassionate Managers Handle Pain and Conflict.* Boston: Harvard Business School Press.

Frost, P. J., J. E. Dutton, S. Maitlis, J. M. Lilius, J. M. Kanov, and M. C. Worline. 2006. "Seeing organizations differently: Three lenses on compassion." In *The Sage Handbook of Organization Studies,* ed. S. R. Clegg, C. Hardy, T. B. Lawrence, and W. R. Nord. London: Sage.

Fuchs, A., A. Dreher, and P. Nunnenkamp. 2014. "Determinants of donor generosity: A survey of the aid budget literature." *World Development* 56:172–199.

Gaglio, C. M. 1997. "Opportunity identification." In *Advances in Entrepreneurship, Firm Emergence, and Growth,* ed. J. A. Katz, 139–202. Greenwich, CT: JAI Press.

Galatzer-Levy, I. R., C. L. Burton, and G. A. Bonanno. 2012. "Coping flexibility, potentially traumatic life events, and resilience: A prospective study of college student adjustment." *Journal of Social and Clinical Psychology* 31 (6): 542–567.

Gartner, W. B. 1985. "A conceptual framework for describing the phenomenon of new venture creation." *Academy of Management Review* 10:696–706.

Gartner, W. B. 1988. "'Who is an entrepreneur?' is the wrong question." *American Journal of Small Business* 12 (4): 11–32.

Gartner, W. B., N. M. Carter, and P. D. Reynolds. 2010. "Entrepreneurial behavior: Firm organizing processes." In *Handbook of Entrepreneurship Research,* ed. Zoltan J. Acs and David B. Audretsch, 99–127. New York: Springer.

Garud, R., and P. Karnøe. 2003. "Bricolage versus breakthrough: Distributed and embedded agency in technology entrepreneurship." *Research Policy* 32 (2): 277–300.

Gazley, B. 2008. "Beyond the contract: The scope and nature of informal government–nonprofit partnerships." *Public Administration Review* 68 (1): 141–154.

George, G. 2005. "Slack resources and the performance of privately held firms." *Academy of Management Journal* 48:661–676.

Gersick, C. J., J. E. Dutton, and J. M. Bartunek. 2000. "Learning from academia: The importance of relationships in professional life." *Academy of Management Journal* 43 (6): 1026–1044.

Gimeno, J., T. B. Folta, A. C. Cooper, and C. Y. Woo. 1997. "Survival of the fittest? Entrepreneurial human capital and the persistence of underperforming firms." *Administrative Science Quarterly* 42 (4): 750–783.

Gioia, D. A., K. G. Corley, and A. L. Hamilton. 2013. "Seeking qualitative rigor in inductive research notes on the Gioia methodology." *Organizational Research Methods* 16 (1): 15–31.

Godfrey, P. C. 2005. "The relationship between corporate philanthropy and shareholder wealth: A risk management perspective." *Academy of Management Review* 30 (4): 777–798.

Goodman, R. A., and L. P. Goodman. 1976. "Some management issues in temporary systems: A study of professional development and manpower. The theater case." *Administrative Science Quarterly* 21:494–501.

Goss, D. 2005. "Entrepreneurship and 'the social': Towards a deference-emotion theory." *Human Relations* 58 (5): 617–636.

Gould, R. V., and R. M. Fernandez. 1989. "Structures of mediation: A formal approach to brokerage in transaction networks." *Sociological Methodology* 19:89–126.

Grabher, G. 2002a. "Cool projects, boring institutions: Temporary collaboration in social context." *Regional Studies* 36 (3): 205–214.

Grabher, G. 2002b. "The project ecology of advertising: Tasks, talents and teams." *Regional Studies* 36 (3): 245–262.

Granovetter, M. S. 1973. "The strength of weak ties." *American Journal of Sociology* 78:1360–1380.

Grant, A. M. 2008. "Does intrinsic motivation fuel the prosocial fire? Motivational synergy in predicting persistence, performance, and productivity." *Journal of Applied Psychology* 93:48–58.

Grant, A. M. 2012. "Leading with meaning: Beneficiary contact, prosocial impact, and the performance effects of transformational leadership." *Academy of Management Journal* 55:458–476.

Grant, A. M., and J. W. Berry. 2011. "The necessity of others is the mother of invention: Intrinsic and prosocial motivations, perspective taking, and creativity." *Academy of Management Journal* 54:73–96.

Grant, A. M., E. M. Campbell, G. Chen, K. Cottone, D. Lapedis, and K. Lee. 2007. "Impact and the art of motivation maintenance: The effects of contact with beneficiaries on persistence behavior." *Organizational Behavior and Human Decision Processes* 103 (1): 53–67.

Grant, A. M., and J. J. Sumanth. 2009. "Mission possible? The performance of prosocially motivated employees depends on manager trustworthiness." *Journal of Applied Psychology* 94:927–944.

Grégoire, D. A., P. S. Barr, and D. A. Shepherd. 2010. "Cognitive processes of opportunity recognition: The role of structural alignment." *Organization Science* 21 (2): 413–431.

Grégoire, D. A., and D. A. Shepherd. 2012. "Technology-market combinations and the identification of entrepreneurial opportunities: An investigation of the opportunity-individual nexus." *Academy of Management Journal* 55 (4): 753–785.

Grewal, R., and P. Tansuhaj. 2001. "Building organizational capabilities for managing economic crisis: The role of market orientation and strategic flexibility." *Journal of Marketing* 65:67–80.

Gross, J. J., and O. P. John. 2003. "Individual differences in two emotion regulation processes: Implications for affect, relationships, and well-being." *Journal of Personality and Social Psychology* 85 (2): 348–362.

Guha-Sapir, D., I. Santos, and A. Borde. 2013. *The Economic Impacts of Natural Disasters.* Oxford: Oxford University Press.

Guillaumont, P. 2010. "Assessing the economic vulnerability of small island developing states and the least developed countries." *Journal of Development Studies* 46 (5): 828–854.

Gulrajani, N., and K. Moloney. 2012. "Globalizing public administration: Today's research and tomorrow's agenda." *Public Administration Review* 72 (1): 78–86.

Gupta, S., and G. A. Bonanno. 2011. "Complicated grief and deficits in emotional expressive flexibility." *Journal of Abnormal Psychology* 120 (3): 635.

Hale, J. E., R. E. Dulek, and D. P. Hale. 2005. "Crisis response communication challenges building theory from qualitative data." *Journal of Business Communication* 42:112–134.

Hargadon, A. 2002. "Brokering knowledge: Linking learning and innovation." *Research in Organizational Behavior* 24:41–85.

Harris, J. D., H. J. Sapienza, and N. E. Bowie. 2009. "Ethics and entrepreneurship." *Journal of Business Venturing* 24 (5): 407–418.

Hart, S. L. 2005. *Capitalism at the Crossroads: The Unlimited Business Opportunities in Solving the World's Most Difficult Problems.* Upper Saddle River, NJ: Prentice Hall.

Hart, S. L., and C. M. Christensen. 2002. "The great leap: Driving innovation from the base of the pyramid." *MIT Sloan Management Review* 44 (1): 51–56.

Hatfield, E., J. T. Cacioppo, and R. L. Rapson. 1994. *Emotional Contagion: Studies in Emotion and Social Interaction.* New York: Cambridge University Press.

Hayek, F. A. 1945. "The use of knowledge in society." *American Economic Review* 35:519–530.

Haynie, J. M., and D. Shepherd. 2011. "Toward a theory of discontinuous career transition: Investigating career transitions necessitated by traumatic life events." *Journal of Applied Psychology* 96 (3): 501–524.

Haynie, J. M., D. A. Shepherd, and J. S. McMullen. 2009. "An opportunity for me? The role of resources in opportunity evaluation decisions." *Journal of Management Studies* 46 (3): 337–361.

Hayward, M. L., W. R. Forster, S. D. Sarasvathy, and B. L. Fredrickson. 2010. "Beyond hubris: How highly confident entrepreneurs rebound to venture again." *Journal of Business Venturing* 25 (6): 569–578.

Hayward, M. L., D. A. Shepherd, and D. Griffin. 2006. "A hubris theory of entrepreneurship." *Management Science* 52 (2): 160–172.

Hazen, M. A. 2003. "Societal and workplace responses to perinatal loss: Disenfranchised grief or healing connection." *Human Relations* 56:147–166.

Hazen, M. A. 2008. "Grief and the workplace." *Academy of Management Perspectives* 22:78–86.

Hébert, R. F., and A. N. Link. 1988. *The Entrepreneur: Mainstream Views and Radical Critiques.* New York: Praeger Publishers.

Hite, J. M., and W. S. Hesterly. 2001. "The evolution of firm networks: From emergence to early growth of the firm." *Strategic Management Journal* 22 (3): 275–286.

Hobfoll, S. E. 1989. "Conservation of resources." *American Psychologist* 44 (3): 513–524.

Hobfoll, S. E. 2001. "The influence of culture, community, and the nested-self in the stress process: Advancing conservation of resources theory." *Applied Psychology* 50 (3): 337–421.

Hobfoll, S. E., R. J. Johnson, N. Ennis, and A. P. Jackson. 2003. "Resource loss, resource gain, and emotional outcomes among inner city women." *Journal of Personality and Social Psychology* 84 (3): 632–643.

Hobfoll, S. E., and R. S. Lilly. 1993. "Resource conservation as a strategy for community psychology." *Journal of Community Psychology* 21 (2): 128–148.

Hobfoll, S. E., A. D. Mancini, B. J. Hall, D. Canetti, and G. A. Bonanno. 2011. "The limits of resilience: Distress following chronic political violence among Palestinians." *Social Science & Medicine* 72 (8): 1400–1408.

Hurlbert, J. S., V. A. Haines, and J. J. Beggs. 2000. "Core networks and tie activation: What kinds of routine networks allocate resources in nonroutine situations?" *American Sociological Review* 65 (4): 598–618.

International Crisis Group. 2013. *Governing Haiti: Time for national consensus, Latin America and Caribbean Report*. Brussels: International Crisis Group.

Ireland, R. D., M. A. Hitt, and D. G. Sirmon. 2003. "A model of strategic entrepreneurship: The construct and its dimensions." *Journal of Management* 29 (6): 963–989.

Jacobson, J. M. 2006. "Compassion fatigue, compassion satisfaction, and burnout: Reactions among employee assistance professionals providing workplace crisis intervention and disaster management services." *Journal of Workplace Behavioral Health* 21:133–152.

Janoff-Bulman, R. 1985. "The aftermath of victimization: Rebuilding shattered assumptions." In *Trauma and Its Wake*, ed. Charles R. Figley, 15–35. Bristol, PA: Brunner/Mazel.

Janoff-Bulman, R. 1989. "Assumptive worlds and the stress of traumatic events: Applications of the schema construct." *Social Cognition* 7 (2): 113–136.

Janoff-Bulman, R. 1992. *Shattered assumptions: Towards a new psychology of trauma*. New York: Free Press.

Jarillo, J. C. 1989. "Entrepreneurship and growth: The strategic use of external resources." *Journal of Business Venturing* 4 (2): 133–147.

Jellison, J. M., and J. Green. 1981. "A self-presentation approach to the fundamental attribution error: The norm of internality." *Journal of Personality and Social Psychology* 40 (4): 643–649.

Jensen, J., and W. L. Waugh. 2014. "The United States' experience with the Incident Command System: What we think we know and what we need to know more about." *Journal of Contingencies and Crisis Management* 22 (1): 5–17.

Jetstarmag. 2009, "Bringing a ray of happiness: A hero's holiday." *Jetstar News*. http://www.jetstarmag.com/story/jetstar-news/664/1.

Jobe, K. 2011. "Disaster relief in post-earthquake Haiti: Unintended consequences of humanitarian volunteerism." *Travel Medicine and Infectious Disease* 9 (1): 1–5.

Joseph, S., and P. A. Linley. 2005. "Positive adjustment to threatening events: An organismic valuing theory of growth through adversity." *Review of General Psychology* 9 (3): 262–280.

Kahneman, Daniel, and Dan Lovallo. 1993. "Timid choices and bold forecasts: A cognitive perspective on risk taking." *Management Science* 39:17–31.

Kaish, S., and B. Gilad. 1991. "Characteristics of opportunities search of entrepreneurs versus executives: Sources, interests, general alertness." *Journal of Business Venturing* 6 (1): 45–61.

Kandachar, P., and M. Halme. 2008. *Sustainability challenges and solutions at the base of the pyramid: Business, technology and the poor.* Sheffield: Greenleaf Publications.

Kanov, J. M., S. Maitlis, M. C. Worline, J. E. Dutton, P. J. Frost, and J. M. Lilius. 2004. "Compassion in organizational life." *American Behavioral Scientist* 47:808–827.

Kanov, J., E. H. Powley, and N. D. Walshe. 2017. "Is it ok to care? How compassion falters and is courageously accomplished in the midst of uncertainty." *Human Relations* 70 (6): 751–777.

Kapucu, N. 2011. "Collaborative governance in international disasters: Nargis cyclone in Myanmar and Sichuan earthquake in China cases." *International Journal of Emergency Management* 8 (1): 1–25.

Katila, R., and S. Shane. 2005. "When does lack of resources make new firms innovative?" *Academy of Management Journal* 48 (5): 814–829.

Katz, J., and W. B. Gartner. 1988. "Properties of emerging organizations. *Academy of Management Review* 13 (3): 429–441.

Kauffman, J., ed. 2013. *Loss of the Assumptive World: A Theory of Traumatic Loss.* New York: Routledge.

Kehr, H. M. 2004. "Integrating implicit motives, explicit motives, and perceived abilities: The compensatory model of work motivation and volition." *Academy of Management Review* 29 (3): 479–499.

Kelly, C. 1995. "A framework for improving operational effectiveness and cost efficiency in emergency planning and response." *Disaster Prevention and Management: An International Journal* 4 (3): 25–31.

Kelley, D. J., L. Peters, and G. C. O'Connor. 2009. "Intra-organizational networking for innovation-based corporate entrepreneurship." *Journal of Business Venturing* 24 (3): 221–235.

Keltner, D., and G. A. Bonanno. 1997. "A study of laughter and dissociation: Distinct correlates of laughter and smiling during bereavement." *Journal of Personality and Social Psychology* 73 (4): 687–702.

Kenis, P., M. Janowicz, and B. Cambré, eds. 2009. *Temporary Organizations: Prevalence, Logic and Effectiveness.* Cheltenham, UK: Edward Elgar Publishing.

Kenneally, C. 2009. "The inferno." *The New Yorker*, 46–57.

Kershaw, B. 1998. "Pathologies of hope in drama and theatre." *Research in Drama Education* 3 (1): 67–83.

Kiefer, J. J., and R. S. Montjoy. 2006. "Incrementalism before the storm: Network performance for the evacuation of New Orleans." *Public Administration Review* 66 (s1): 122–130.

Kirkels, Y., and G. Duysters. 2010. "Brokerage in SME networks." *Research Policy* 39 (3): 375–385.

Kirzner, I. M. 1997. "Entrepreneurial discovery and the competitive market process: An Austrian approach." *Journal of Economic Literature* 35:60–85.

220   References

Kissane, K. 2009. "Town burnt once by fire and again by tax rules." http://www.theage
.com.au/national/town-burnt-once-by-fires-and-again-by-tax-rules-20090426-ajej.html
Accessed 28 June 2013.

Kistruck, G. M., and P. W. Beamish. 2010. "The interplay of form, structure, and embeddedness in social intrapreneurship." *Entrepreneurship Theory and Practice* 34 (4):
735–761.

Klarreich, K., and L. Polman. 2012. "The NGO Republic of Haiti: How the international
relief effort after the 2010 earthquake excluded Haitians from their own recovery." *Nation,*
October 31.

Knack, S., and L. Smets. 2013. "Aid tying and donor fragmentation." *World Development*
44:63–76.

Knight, F. H. 1921. *Risk, Uncertainty and Profit.* New York: Hart, Schaffner and Marx.

Kobasa, S. C., and M. C. Puccetti. 1983. "Personality and social resources in stress
resistance." *Journal of Personality and Social Psychology* 45 (4): 839–850.

Kreps, G. A., and T. E. Drabek. 1996. "Disasters as non-routine social problems."
International Journal of Mass Emergencies and Disasters 14 (2): 129–153.

Kreps, G. A. 1984. "Sociological inquiry and disaster research." *Annual Review of Sociology*
10:309–330.

Kreps, G. A. 1990. "Organizing for emergency management." In *Emergency Management:
Principles and Practice for Local Government,* ed. T. E. Drabek and G. J. Hoetmer, 86–99.
Washington, DC: International City Management Association.

Kreps, G. A., and S. L. Bosworth. 1993. "Disaster, organizing, and role enactment: A
structural approach." *American Journal of Sociology* 99 (2): 428–463.

Kuckertz, A., and M. Wagner. 2010. "The influence of sustainability orientation on entrepreneurial intentions: Investigating the role of business experience." *Journal of Business
Venturing* 25:524–539.

Lagadec, P. 1996. "Un nouveau champ de responsabilité pour les dirigeants." *Revue
Française de Gestion* 108:100–109.

Laufer, R. 2007. "Crisis management and legitimacy: Facing symbolic disorders." In
International Handbook of Organizational Crisis Management, ed. C. M. Pearson, C. Roux-
Dufort and J. A. Clair. Thousand Oaks, CA: Sage.

Lazarus, R. S. 1998. "Coping theory and research: Past, present, and future." *Fifty Years
of the Research and Theory of R. S. Lazarus: An Analysis of Historical and Perennial Issues,*
366–388. Mahwah, NJ: Lawrence Erlbaum.

Lecy, J. D., H. P. Schmitz, and H. Swedlund. 2012. "Non-governmental and not-for-profit
organizational effectiveness: A modern synthesis." *Voluntas* 23 (2): 434–457.

Legg, K. 2010. "A year later, Marysville waits for a future." http://www.theaustralian
.com.au/news/nation/a-year-later-marysville-waits-for-a-future/story-e6frg6nf
-1225824893878.

Leleux, B., and B. Surlemont. 2003. "Public versus private venture capital: Seeding or
crowding out? A pan-European analysis." *Journal of Business Venturing* 18 (1): 81–104.

Lévi-Strauss, C. 1966. *The Savage Mind.* Chicago: University of Chicago Press.

Lewis, M. 2009. "From the ashes: Gold Coast getaway." Goldcoastbulletin.com.

Lichtenstein, B. B., K. J. Dooley, and G. T. Lumpkin. 2006. "Measuring emergence in the dynamics of new venture creation." *Journal of Business Venturing* 21:153–175.

Lilius, J. M., J. M. Kanov, J. E. Dutton, M. C. Worline, and S. Maitlis. 2011. "Compassion revealed: What we know about compassion at work (and where we need to know more)." In *Handbook of Positive Organizational Scholarship*, ed. K. S. Cameron and G. Spreitzer. New York: Oxford University Press.

Lilius, J. M., M. C. Worline, J. E. Dutton, J. M. Kanov, and S. Maitlis. 2011. "Understanding compassion capability." *Human Relations* 64:873–899.

Lilius, J. M., M. C. Worline, S. Maitlis, J. Kanov, J. E. Dutton, and P. J. Frost. 2008. "The contours and consequences of compassion at work." *Journal of Organizational Behavior* 29:193–218.

Lipshitz, R., and O. Strauss. 1997. "Coping with uncertainty: A naturalistic decision-making analysis." *Organizational Behavior and Human Decision Processes* 69 (2): 149–163.

Lissoni, F. 2010. "Academic inventors as brokers. *Research Policy* 39 (7): 843–857.

London, T. 2007. "A base-of-the-pyramid perspective on poverty alleviation." Working paper. Ann Arbor: The William Davidson Institute-University of Michigan.

London, T. 2008. "The base-of-the-pyramid perspective: A new approach to poverty alleviation." *Academy of Management Annual Meeting Proceedings* 2008 (1): 1–6.

London, T., and S. L. Hart. 2004. "Reinventing strategies for emerging markets: Beyond the transnational model." *Journal of International Business Studies* 35 (5): 350–370.

Long, W. A., and W. E. McMullan. 1984. "Mapping the new venture opportunity identification process." In *Frontiers of Entrepreneurship Research*, ed. J. A. Hornaday, F. A. Tardeley and K. H. Vesper. Wellesley, MA: Babson College.

Lundin, R. A., and A. Söderholm. 1995. "A theory of the temporary organization." *Scandinavian Journal of Management* 11 (4): 437–455.

Madsen, P. M., and Z. J. Rodgers. 2015. "Looking good by doing good: The antecedents and consequences of stakeholder attention to corporate disaster relief." *Strategic Management Journal* 36 (5): 776–794.

Magni, M., L. Proserpio, M. Hoegl, and B. Provera. 2009. "The role of team behavioral integration and cohesion in shaping individual improvisation." *Research Policy* 38:1044–1053.

Mair, J., and I. Marti. 2006. "Social entrepreneurship research: A source of explanation, prediction, and delight." *Journal of World Business* 41 (1): 36–44.

Mair, J., and I. Marti. 2009. "Entrepreneurship in and around institutional voids: A case study from Bangladesh." *Journal of Business Venturing* 24 (5): 419–435.

Maitlis, S. 2012. *Posttraumatic Growth: A Missed Opportunity for Positive Organizational Scholarship*. New York: Oxford University Press.

Maitlis, S., and S. Sonenshein. 2010. "Sensemaking in crisis and change: Inspiration and insights from Weick (1988)." *Journal of Management Studies* 47:551–580.

Majchrzak, A., S. L. Jarvenpaa, and A. B. Hollingshead. 2007. "Coordinating expertise among emergent groups responding to disasters." *Organization Science* 18 (1): 147–161.

Mann, S. 2009. "Findings highlight systematic failure." http://www.theage.com.au/national/findings-highlight-systemic-failure-20090817-enps.html.

Mansuri, G., and V. Rao. 2004. "Community-based and-driven development: A critical review." *World Bank Research Observer* 19 (1): 1–39.

Mansuri, G., and V. Rao. 2012. *Localizing Development: Does Participation Work?* Washington, DC: World Bank.

Marcum, C. S., C. A. Bevc, and C. T. Butts. 2012. "Mechanisms of control in emergent interorganizational networks." *Policy Studies Journal: The Journal of the Policy Studies Organization* 40 (3): 516–546.

Margesson, R., and M. Taft-Morales. 2010. *Haiti Earthquake: Crisis and Response.* Washington, DC: Congressional Research Service.

Marr, D. 2009. "A community's tough choices." http://www.theage.com.au/national/a-communitys-tough-choices-20090213-877j.html.

Marsden, P. V. 1982. "Brokerage behavior in restricted exchange networks." In *Social Structure and Network Analysis*, ed. P. V. Marsden and N. Lin. Thousand Oaks, CA: Sage.

Mason, C. M. 2007. "Informal sources of venture finance." In *The Life Cycle of Entrepreneurial Ventures*, ed. S. Parker, 259–299. New York: Springer.

Mason, C. M., and R. T. Harrison. 2000. "Investing in technology ventures: What do business angels look for at the initial screening stage?" In *Proceedings of the Twentieth Annual Entrepreneurship Research Conference: Frontiers of Entrepreneurship Research*, ed. P. D. Reynolds, E. Autio, C. G. Brush, W. D. Bygrave, S. Manigart, H. Sapienza, and K. D. Shaver, 293–304.

Maxwell, A. L., S. A. Jeffrey, and M. Lévesque. 2011. "Business angel early stage decision making." *Journal of Business Venturing* 26 (2): 212–225.

McEntire, D. A. 2007. *Disaster Response and Recovery: Strategies and Tactics for Resilience.* Hoboken, NJ: John Wiley & Sons.

McKenzie, D. 2009. "Six months on after bushfire." *Weekly Times Now.* http://www.weeklytimesnow.com.au/article/2009/08/07/99701_latest-news.html.

McMullen, J. S., and D. A. Shepherd. 2006. "Entrepreneurial action and the role of uncertainty in the theory of the entrepreneur." *Academy of Management Review* 31:132–152.

Mendonca, D., G. E. Beroggi, and W. A. Wallace. 2001. "Decision support for improvisation during emergency response operations." *International Journal of Emergency Management* 1 (1): 30–38.

Meyer, A. D. 1982. "Adapting to environmental jolts." *Administrative Science Quarterly* 27:515–537.

Meyerson, D., K. E. Weick, and R. M. Kramer. 1996. "Swift trust and temporary groups." In *Trust in Organizations: Frontiers of Theory and Research*, ed. R. M. Kramer and T. R. Tyler, 166–195. Thousand Oaks, CA: Sage.

Milovanovic, S. 2009. "Heaven to hell … and hopefully back." national/heaven-to-hell—and-hopefully-back-20090807-ebud.html.

Miles, M. B. 1964. "On temporary systems." In *Innovation in Education*, vol. 19, ed. M. B. Miles, 437–490. New York: Teachers College Bureau of Publications.

Miles, M. B. 1977. "Origin of concept temporary system." *Administrative Science Quarterly* 22:134–135.Miles, M. B., and A. M. Huberman. 1994. *Qualitative Data Analysis: An Expanded Sourcebook*. Thousand Oaks, CA: Sage Publications.

Miles, M. P., and J. G. Covin. 2002. "Exploring the practice of corporate venturing: Some common forms and their organizational implications." *Entrepreneurship Theory and Practice* 26:21–40.

Mileti, D. S. 1989. "Catastrophe planning and the grassroots: A lesson to the USA from the USSR." *International Journal of Mass Emergencies and Disasters* 7 (1): 57–67.

Mulford, C. L. 1984. *Interorganizational Relations: Implications for Community Development*. vol. 4. New York: Human Sciences Press.

Muller, A., and R. Kräussl. 2011. "Doing good deeds in times of need: A strategic perspective on corporate disaster donations." *Strategic Management Journal* 32 (9): 911–929.

Mushkatel, A., and L. F. Weschler. 1985. "Emergency management and the intergovernmental system." *Public Administration Review* 45:47–58.

Nahapiet, J., and S. Ghoshal. 1998. "Social capital, intellectual capital, and the organizational advantage." *Academy of Management Review* 23 (2): 242–266.

Neal, D. M., and B. D. Phillips. 1995. "Effective emergency management: Reconsidering the bureaucratic approach." *Disasters* 19 (4): 327–337.

Nelson, R. R., and S. G. Winter. 1982. "The Schumpeterian tradeoff revisited." *American Economic Review* 72 (1): 114–132.

New, A. S., J. Fan, J. W. Murrough, X. Liu, R. E. Liebman, K. G. Guise, C. Y. Tang, and D. S. Charney. 2009. "A functional magnetic resonance imaging study of deliberate emotion regulation in resilience and posttraumatic stress disorder." *Biological Psychiatry* 66 (7): 656–664.

Newbert, S. L. 2007. "Empirical research on the resource-based view of the firm: An assessment and suggestions for future research." *Strategic Management Journal* 28 (2): 121–146.

Newbert, S. L., and E. T. Tornikoski. 2013. "Resource acquisition in the emergence phase: Considering the effects of embeddedness and resource dependence." *Entrepreneurship Theory and Practice* 37 (2): 249–280.

Newcomer, K., L. E. Baradei, and S. Garcia. 2013. "Expectations and capacity of performance measurement in NGOs in the development context." *Public Administration and Development* 33 (1): 62–79.

Nicholls, A. 2010. "The legitimacy of social entrepreneurship: Reflexive isomorphism in a pre-paradigmatic field." *Entrepreneurship Theory and Practice* 34:611–633.

Nolen-Hoeksema, S. 1996. "Chewing the cud and other ruminations." *Ruminative Thoughts* 9:135–144.

Normann, R. 1977. *Management for Growth*. New York: Wiley.

Norris, F. H., M. J. Friedman, P. J. Watson, C. M. Byrne, E. Diaz, and K. Kaniasty. 2002. "60,000 disaster victims speak: Part I. An empirical review of the empirical literature, 1981–2001." *Psychiatry* 65 (3): 207–239.

Norris, F. H., and K. Kaniasty. 1996. "Received and perceived social support in times of stress: A test of the social support deterioration deterrence model." *Journal of Personality and Social Psychology* 71 (3): 498.

Obstfeld, D. 2005. "Social networks, the tertius lungens and orientation involvement in innovation." *Administrative Science Quarterly* 50 (1): 100–130.

Oh, C. H., and J. Oetzel. 2011. "Multinationals' response to major disasters: How does subsidiary investment vary in response to the type of disaster and the quality of country governance?" *Strategic Management Journal* 32 (6): 658–681.

Ong, A. D., C. Bergeman, T. L. Bisconti, and K. A. Wallace. 2006. "Psychological resilience, positive emotions, and successful adaptation to stress in later life." *Journal of Personality and Social Psychology* 91 (4): 730.

Oyserman, D., K. Terry, and D. Bybee. 2002. "A possible selves intervention to enhance school involvement." *Journal of Adolescence* 25 (3): 313–326.

Palmer, N. 2006. "An awkward threesome: Donors, governments and non-state providers of health in low income countries." *Public Administration and Development* 26 (3): 231–240.

Park, C. L., D. Edmondson, J. R. Fenster, and T. O. Blank. 2008. "Meaning making and psychological adjustment following cancer: The mediating roles of growth, life meaning, and restored just-world beliefs." *Journal of Consulting and Clinical Psychology* 76 (5): 863.

Park, C. L., and S. Folkman. 1997. "Meaning in the context of stress and coping." *Review of General Psychology* 1 (2): 115–144.

Parmigiani, A., and M. Rivera-Santos. 2015. "Sourcing for the base of the pyramid: Constructing supply chains to address voids in subsistence markets." *Journal of Operations Management* 33:60–70.

Patten, D. M. 2008. "Does the market value corporate philanthropy? Evidence from the response to the 2004 tsunami relief effort." *Journal of Business Ethics* 81 (3): 599–607.

Pattison-Sowden, M. 2009. "$4m for golf and bowls plan." *Upper Yarra Mail*, http://www.starnewsgroup.com.au/mail/upper-yarra/282/story/129063.html.

Patzelt, H., and D. A. Shepherd. 2011. "Recognizing opportunities for sustainable development." *Entrepreneurship Theory and Practice* 35:631–652.

Pearson, C. M., and J. A. Clair. 1998. "Reframing crisis management." *Academy of Management Review* 23:59–76.

Peduzzi, P., H. Dao, C. Herold, and F. Mouton. 2009. "Assessing global exposure and vulnerability towards natural hazards: The Disaster Risk Index." *Natural Hazards and Earth System Sciences* 9 (4): 1149–1159.

Peek, L. A., and D. S. Mileti. 2002. "The history and future of disaster research." In *Handbook of Environmental Psychology*, ed. R. B. Bechtel and A. Churchman, 511–524. New York: John Wiley and Sons.

Peksen, D. 2012. "Does foreign military intervention help human rights?" *Political Research Quarterly* 65 (3): 558–571.

Penner, L. A., J. F. Dovidio, J. A. Piliavin, and D. A. Schroeder. 2005. "Prosocial behavior: Multilevel perspectives." *Annual Review of Psychology* 56:365–392.

Penrose, E. T. 1959. *The Theory of the Growth of the Firm.* New York: Oxford University Press.

Peredo, A. M., and J. J. Chrisman. 2006. Toward a theory of community-based enterprise. *Academy of Management Review* 31 (2): 309–328.

Peredo, A. M. A., and M. McLean. 2006. "Social entrepreneurship: A critical review of the concept." *Journal of World Business* 41:56–65.

Perkins, M. 2009. "A community and its caring principle." TheAge.com, August 7, 2009. http://www.theage.com.au/national/education/a-community-and-its-caring-principle-20090807-ebto.html.

Pickering, J., and M. Peceny. 2006. "Forging democracy at gunpoint." *International Studies Quarterly* 50 (3): 539–560.

Powell, E. E., and T. Baker. 2011. "Beyond making do: Toward a theory of entrepreneurial resourcefulness." *Frontiers of Entrepreneurship Research* 31 (12): 2.

Powell, W. W., and L. Smith-Doerr. 1994. "Networks and economic life." In The Handbook of Economic Sociology, ed. N. J. Smelser and R. Swedberg, 368–402. Princeton, NJ: Princeton University Press.

Powley, E. H. 2009. "Reclaiming resilience and safety: Resilience activation in the critical period of crisis." *Human Relations* 62:1289–1326.

Powley, E. H., and S. K. Piderit. 2008. "Tending wounds: Elements of the organizational healing process." *Journal of Applied Behavioral Science* 44:134–149.

Prahalad, C. K. 2004. *The Fortune at the Bottom of the Pyramid: Eradicating Poverty through Profits.* Philadelphia: Wharton School Publishing.

Prahalad, C., and S. Hart. 2002. "The fortune at the base of the pyramid." *Strategy + Business* 26: 1–14.

Putnam, R. D. 2000. *Bowling Alone: The Collapse and Revival of American Community.* New York: Simon and Schuster.

Quarantelli, E. L. 1986. *Research Findings on Organizational Behavior in Disasters and Their Applicability in Developing Countries.* Newark: University of Delaware Disaster Research Center.

Quarantelli, E. L. 1988. "Disaster crisis management: A summary of research findings." *Journal of Management Studies* 25:373–385.

Quarantelli, E. L. 1996a. "Emergent behaviors and groups in the crisis time of disasters." In *Individuality and Social Control: Essays in Honor of Tamotsu Shibutani,* ed. K. Kwan. Greenwich, CT: JAI Press.

Quarantelli, E. L. 1996b. "The future is not the past repeated: Projecting disasters in the 21st century from current trends." *Journal of Contingencies and Crisis Management* 4 (4): 228–240.

Quinn, C. N. 2005. *Engaging Learning: Designing E-learning Simulation Games.* San Francisco, CA: John Wiley & Sons.

Reagans, R., and E. W. Zuckerman. 2001. "Networks, diversity, and productivity: The social capital of corporate R&D teams." *Organization Science* 12 (4): 502–517.

Reynolds, P., and B. Miller. 1992. "New firm gestation: Conception, birth, and implications for research." *Journal of Business Venturing* 7 (5): 405–417.

Ricketson, M. 2009. "Lucky club that avoided flames is the new heart of town." TheAge.com, February 19, 2009. http://www.theage.com.au/national/lucky-club-that-avoided-flames-is-new-heart-of-town-20090219-8co3.html.

Riding, A. L. 2008. "Business angels and love money investors: Segments of the informal market for risk capital." *Venture Capital* 10 (4): 355–369.

Rinpoche, S. 1992. *The Tibetan Book of Living and Dying.* London: Rider Books.

Rintoul, S. 2009. "Tourism boost on par for bushfire-devastated Marysville." *The Australian.* http://www.theaustralian.com.au/news/nation/tourism-boost-for-marysville/story-e6frg6nf-1225939389890.

Roberts, K. H., R. Bea, and D. L. Bartles. 2001. "Must accidents happen? Lessons from high-reliability organizations." *Academy of Management Executive* 15 (3): 70–78.

Rose, P. 2009. "NGO provision of basic education: Alternative or complementary service delivery to support access to the excluded?" *Compare: A Journal of Comparative Education* 39 (2): 219–233.

Ross, N. 2009. "'Dad's Army' saved 15 homes in Taggerty, bushfire commission hears." *Herald Sun.* http://www.heraldsun.com.au/news/dads-army-saved-15-homes-in-taggerty-bushfire-commission-hears/story-e6frf7jo-1225732506016.

Rossi, P. H., J. D. Wright, and E. Weber-Burdin. 1982. *Natural Hazards and Public Choice: The State and Local Politics of Hazards Mitigation.* New York: Academic Press.

Ryan, R. M., and E. L. Deci. 2000. "Self-determination theory and the facilitation of intrinsic motivation, social development, and well-being." *American Psychologist* 55 (1): 68–78.

Rynes, S. L., J. M. Bartunek, J. E. Dutton, and J. D. Margolis. 2012. "Care and compassion through an organizational lens: Opening up new possibilities." *Academy of Management Review* 37:503–523.

Sachs, J. 2005. *The End of Poverty: Economic Possibilities for Our Time.* New York: Penguin.

Scheier, M. F., and C. S. Carver. 1992. "Effects of optimism on psychological and physical well-being: Theoretical overview and empirical update." *Cognitive Therapy and Research* 16 (2): 201–228.

Schneider, S. K. 1992. "Governmental response to disasters: The conflict between bureaucratic procedures and emergent norms." *Public Administration Review* 52:135–145.

Schneider, S. K. 2014. *Dealing with Disaster: Public Management in Crisis Situations.* New York: Routledge.

Schnietz, K. E., and M. J. Epstein. 2005. "Exploring the financial value of a reputation for corporate social responsibility during a crisis." *Corporate Reputation Review* 7 (4): 327–345.

Schuller, M. 2007. "Haiti's 200-year ménage-a-trois Globalization, the state, and civil society." *Caribbean Studies* 35:141–179.

Seelos, C., and J. Mair. 2007. "Profitable business models and market creation in the context of deep poverty: A strategic view." *The Academy of Management Perspectives* 21 (4): 49–63.

Sen, G. 1999. "Engendering poverty alleviation: Challenges and opportunities." *Development and Change* 30 (3): 685–692.

Shah, R. J. 2012. *Building Resilience to Recurrent Crisis: USAID Policy and Program Guidance.* Washington, DC: U.S. Agency for International Development.

Shane, S. 2000. "Prior knowledge and the discovery of entrepreneurial opportunities." *Organization Science* 11:448–469.

Shane, S., E. A. Locke, and C. J. Collins. 2003. "Entrepreneurial motivation." *Human Resource Management Review* 13:257–279.

Shane, S., and S. Venkataraman. 2000. "The promise of entrepreneurship as a field of research." *Academy of Management Review* 25 (1): 217–226.

Shepherd, D. A. 2003. "Learning from business failure: Propositions of grief recovery for the self-employed." *Academy of Management Review* 28 (2): 318–328.

Shepherd, D. A., and D. R. DeTienne. 2005. "Prior knowledge, potential financial reward, and opportunity identification." *Entrepreneurship Theory and Practice* 29 (1): 91–112.

Shepherd, D. A., E. J. Douglas, and M. Shanley. 2000. "New venture survival: Ignorance, external shocks, and risk reduction strategies." *Journal of Business Venturing* 15 (5): 393–410.

Shepherd, D. A., J. M. Haynie, and J. S. McMullen. 2012. "Confirmatory search as a useful heuristic? Testing the veracity of entrepreneurial conjectures." *Journal of Business Venturing* 27 (6): 637–651.

Shepherd, D. A., J. S. McMullen, and P. D. Jennings. 2007. "The formation of opportunity beliefs: Overcoming ignorance and reducing doubt." *Strategic Entrepreneurship Journal* 1 (1–2): 75–95.

Shepherd, D. A., J. S. McMullen, and W. Ocasio. 2017. "Is that an opportunity? An attention model of top managers' opportunity beliefs for strategic action." *Strategic Management Journal* 38 (3): 626–644.

Shepherd, D. A., V. Parida, and J. Wincent. In press. "The surprising duality of jugaad: Low firm growth and high inclusive growth." *Journal of Management Studies.*

Shepherd, D. A., H. Patzelt, and M. Wolfe. 2011. "Moving forward from project failure: Negative emotions, affective commitment, and learning from the experience." *Academy of Management Journal* 54 (6): 1229–1259.

Shepherd, D. A., and T. A. Williams. 2014. "Local venturing as compassion organizing in the aftermath of a natural disaster: The role of localness and community in reducing suffering." *Journal of Management Studies* 51 (6): 952–994.

Shepherd, D. A., and T. A. Williams. 2018. "Hitting rock bottom after job loss: Bouncing back to create a new positive work identity." *Academy of Management Review* 43 (1): 28–49.

Shi, W., L. Markoczy, and G. G. Dess. 2009. "The role of middle management in the strategy process: Group affiliation, structural holes, and Tertius Iungens." *Journal of Management* 35 (6): 1453–1480.

Siegel, G. B. 1985. "Human resource development for emergency management." *Public Administration Review* 45:107–117.

Simon, M., and R. C. Shrader. 2012. "Entrepreneurial actions and optimistic overconfidence: The role of motivated reasoning in new product introductions." *Journal of Business Venturing* 27 (3): 291–309.

Sirmon, D. G., M. A. Hitt, and R. D. Ireland. 2007. "Managing firm resources in dynamic environments to create value: Looking inside the black box." *Academy of Management Review* 32:273–292.

Smith, N. R., and J. B. Miner. 1983. "Type of entrepreneur, type of firm, and managerial motivation: Implications for organizational life cycle theory." *Strategic Management Journal* 4 (4): 325–340.

Smith, S. C. 2012. "The Scope of NGOs and Development Programme Design: Application to Problems of Multidimensional Poverty." *Public Administration and Development* 32 (4–5): 357–370.

Sobel, R. S., and P. T. Leeson. 2006. "Government's response to Hurricane Katrina: A public choice analysis." *Public Choice* 127:55–73.

Sonenshein, S. 2014. "How organizations foster the creative use of resources." *Academy of Management Journal* 57 (3): 814–848.

Sonnentag, S., and A. M. Grant. 2012. "Doing good at work feels good at home, but not right away: When and why perceived prosocial impact predicts positive affect." *Personnel Psychology* 65 (3): 495–530.

Sørensen, M. 2007. "How smart is smart money? A two-sided matching model of venture capital." *Journal of Finance* 62 (6): 2725–2762.

Spiro, E. S., R. M. Acton, and C. T. Butts. 2013. "Extended structures of mediation: Reexamining brokerage in dynamic networks." *Social Networks* 35 (1): 130–143.

Stallings, R. A., and E. L. Quarantelli. 1985. "Emergent citizen groups and emergency management." *Public Administration Review* 45:93–100.

Stein, A. J., and H. R. Winokuer. 1989. "Monday mourning: Managing employee grief." In *Disenfranchised Grief: Recognizing Hidden Sorrow*, ed. K. Doka, 91–102. New York: Lexington.

Stephens, H. W. 1997. *The Texas City Disaster, 1947*. Austin: University of Texas Press.

Stevenson, H. H., and J. C. Jarillo. 1990. "A paradigm of entrepreneurship: Entrepreneurial management." *Strategic Management Journal* 11 (4): 17–27.

Stinchcombe, A. L. 1965. *Organizations and Social Structure*. Chicago: Rand McNally.

Stovel, K., and L. Shaw. 2012. "Brokerage." *Annual Review of Sociology* 38:139–158.

Strobl, E. 2012. "The economic growth impact of natural disasters in developing countries: Evidence from hurricane strikes in the Central American and Caribbean regions." *Journal of Development Economics* 97 (1): 130–141.

Stuart, T. E., S. Z. Ozdemir, and W. W. Ding. 2007. "Vertical alliance networks: The case of university-biotechnology-pharmaceutical alliance chains." *Research Policy* 36 (4): 477–498.

Sutcliffe, K. M., and T. J. Vogus. 2003. "Organizing for resilience." In *Positive Organizational Scholarship: Foundations of a New Discipline*, ed. K. S. Cameron, J. E. Dutton, and R. E. Quinn, 94–110. San Francisco: Berrett-Koehler.

Sydow, J., and U. Staber. 2002. "The institutional embeddedness of project networks: The case of content production in German television." *Regional Studies* 36 (3): 215–227.

Takeda, M. B., and M. M. Helms. 2006a. "'Bureaucracy, meet catastrophe': Analysis of the tsunami disaster relief efforts and their implications for global emergency governance." *International Journal of Public Sector Management* 19 (2): 204–217.

Takeda, M. B., and M. M. Helms. 2006b. "'Bureaucracy, meet catastrophe': Analysis of Hurricane Katrina relief efforts and their implications for emergency response governance." *International Journal of Public Sector Management* 19 (4): 397–411.

Taylor, J. B., L. A. Zurcher, and W. H. Key. 1970. *Tornado: A Community Responds to Disaster*. Seattle, WA: University of Washington Press.

Teague, B., R. McLeod, and S. Pascoe. 2010. *Victorian Bushfires Royal Commission*. Melbourne, Australia: Government Printer for the State of Victoria.

Teal, E. J., and A. B. Carroll. 1999. "Moral reasoning skills: Are entrepreneurs different?" *Journal of Business Ethics* 19 (3): 229–240.

Thomas, A., and L. Fritz. 2006. "Disaster relief, inc." *Harvard Business Review* 84 (11): 114–122.

Tierney, K. 2012. "Disaster governance: Social, political, and economic dimensions." *Annual Review of Environment and Resources* 37:341–363.

Tierney, K. J., M. Lindell, and R. Perry. 2001. *Facing the Unexpected: Disaster Preparedness and Response in the United States*. Washington, DC: Joseph Henry Press.

Tierney, K. J., and J. E. Trainor. 2004. *Networks and Resilience in the World Trade Center Disaster*. Buffalo, NY: University of Buffalo, Center for Earthquake Engineering Research.

Tilcsik, A., and C. Marquis. 2013. "Punctuated generosity how mega-events and natural disasters affect corporate philanthropy in US communities." *Administrative Science Quarterly* 58 (1): 111–148.

Tomazin, F. 2009. "We will rebuild Marysville's school." TheAge.com, February 12. http://www.theage.com.au/national/we-will-rebuild-marysvilles-school-20090212-863a.html.

Tugade, M. M., and B. L. Fredrickson. 2007. "Regulation of positive emotions: Emotion regulation strategies that promote resilience." *Journal of Happiness Studies* 8 (3): 311–333.

Tushman, M. L., and P. Anderson. 1986. "Technological discontinuities and organizational environments." *Administrative Science Quarterly* 31 (3): 439–465.

Ucbasaran, D., D. A. Shepherd, A. Lockett, and S. J. Lyon. 2013. "Life after business failure the process and consequences of business failure for entrepreneurs." *Journal of Management* 39 (1): 163–202.

Ucbasaran, D., P. Westhead, and M. Wright. 2009. "The extent and nature of opportunity identification by experienced entrepreneurs." *Journal of Business Venturing* 24 (2): 99–115.

Uhr, C., H. Johansson, and L. Fredholm. 2008. "Analysing emergency response systems." *Journal of Contingencies and Crisis Management* 16 (2): 80–90.

UN. "What are least developed countries (LDCs)?" UN.org. http://www.un.org/en/development/desa/policy/cdp/ldc_info.shtml.

USAID. 2015. "Working in crises and conflict." http://www.usaid.gov/what-we-do/working-crises-and-conflict.

Uzzi, B. 1996. "The sources and consequences of embeddedness for the economic performance of organizations: The network effect." *American Sociological Review* 61 (4): 674–698.

Van der Vegt, G. S., P. Essens, M. Wahlström, and G. George. 2015. "Managing risk and resilience." *Academy of Management Journal* 58 (4): 971–980.

Van Wart, M., and N. Kapucu. 2011. Crisis management competencies: The case of emergency managers in the USA. *Public Management Review* 13:489–511.

Villanueva, J., A. H. Van de Ven, and H. J. Sapienza. 2012. "Resource mobilization in entrepreneurial firms." *Journal of Business Venturing* 27 (1): 19–30.

Virany, B., M. L. Tushman, and E. Romanelli. 1992. "Executive succession and organization outcomes in turbulent environments: An organization learning approach." *Organization Science* 3:72–91.

Voorhees, W. R. 2008. "New Yorkers respond to the World Trade Center attack: An anatomy of an emergent volunteer organization." *Journal of Contingencies and Crisis Management* 16 (1): 3–13.

Wachtendorf, T. 2004. "Improvising 9/11: Organizational improvisation following the world trade center disaster." PhD diss. University of Delaware, Newark, DE.

Wan, W. P., and D. W. Yiu. 2009. "From crisis to opportunity: Environmental jolt, corporate acquisitions, and firm performance." *Strategic Management Journal* 30 (7): 791–801.

Waugh, W. L., and G. Streib. 2006. "Collaboration and leadership for effective emergency management." *Public Administration Review* 66:131–140.

Webb, G. 2004. "Role improvising during crisis situations." *International Journal of Emergency Management* 2 (1–2): 47–61.

Webb, J. W., G. M. Kistruck, R. D. Ireland, and D. J. Ketchen, Jr. 2010. "The entrepreneurship process in base of the pyramid markets: The case of multinational enterprise/nongovernment organization alliances." *Entrepreneurship Theory and Practice* 34 (3): 555–581.

Webb, J. W., L. Tihanyi, R. D. Ireland, and D. G. Sirmon. 2009. "You say illegal, I say legitimate: Entrepreneurship in the informal economy." *Academy of Management Review* 34 (3): 492–510.

Weerawardena, J., and G. S. Mort. 2006. "Investigating social entrepreneurship: A multidimensional model." *Journal of World Business* 41:21–35.

Weick, K. E. 1993. "The collapse of sensemaking in organizations: The Mann Gulch disaster." *Administrative Science Quarterly* 38:628–652.

Weick, K. E., and K. H. Roberts. 1993. "Collective mind in organizations: Heedful interrelating on flight decks." *Administrative Science Quarterly* 38:357–381.

Wenger, D. E. 1992. *Emergent and Volunteer Behavior during Disaster: Research Findings and Planning Implications.* College Station: Texas A&M University Hazard Reduction Recovery Center.

Wenger, D. E., E. L. Quarantelli, and R. R. Dynes. 1987. *Disaster Analysis: Emergency Management Offices and Arrangements.* Newark: University of Delaware, Disaster Research Center.

Westphal, M., and G. A. Bonanno. 2004. "Emotion self-regulation." In *Consciousness, Emotional Self-Regulation and the Brain,* ed. M. Beauregard, 1–34. Philadelphia: John Benjamin's Publishing.

Westphal, M., N. H. Seivert, and G. A. Bonanno. 2010. "Expressive flexibility." *Emotion* 10 (1): 92–100.

White, S. C. 1999. "NGOs, civil society, and the state in Bangladesh: The politics of representing the poor." *Development and Change* 30 (2): 307–326.

Wilkinson, G. 2009. "Black Saturday bushfire donations rot in storage." *National,* http://www.news.com.au/national-old/bush-fire-donations-rot-in-storage/story-e6frfkvr-1225811582677 (accessed June 28, 2013).

Williams, P. 2010. "If you don't know what to do, do something." Speakola.com, http://speakola.com/motivate/pete-williams-flowerdale-tedxcanberra-2010.

Williams, T. A., and D. A. Shepherd. 2017. "Mixed method social network analysis: Combining inductive concept development, content analysis, and secondary data for quantitative analysis." *Organizational Research Methods* 20 (2): 268–298.

Williams, T. A., and D. A. Shepherd. 2016a. "Building resilience or providing sustenance: Different paths of emergent ventures in the aftermath of the Haiti earthquake." *Academy of Management Journal* 59 (6): 2069–2102.

Williams, T. A., and D. A. Shepherd. 2016b. "Victim entrepreneurs doing well by doing good: Venture creation and well-being in the aftermath of a resource shock." *Journal of Business Venturing* 31 (4): 365–387.

Williams, T. A., and D. A. Shepherd. In press. "To the Rescue!? Brokering a Rapid, Scaled and Customized Compassionate Response to Suffering after Disaster." *Journal of Management Studies.*

Williams, T. A., D. A. Gruber, K. M. Sutcliffe, D. A. Shepherd, and E. Y. Zhao. 2017. "Organizational response to adversity: Fusing crisis management and resilience research streams." *Academy of Management Annals* 11 (2): 733–769.

Williamson, G. M., and M. S. Clark. 1989. "Providing help and desired relationship type as determinants of changes in moods and self-evaluations." *Journal of Personality and Social Psychology* 56 (5): 722–734.

Winborg, J., and H. Landström. 2001. "Financial bootstrapping in small businesses: Examining small business managers' resource acquisition behaviors." *Journal of Business Venturing* 16 (3): 235–254.

Winters, M. S., and G. Martinez. 2015. "The role of governance in determining foreign aid flow composition." *World Development* 66:516–531.

Worline, M., and J. E. Dutton. 2017. *Awakening Compassion at Work: The Quiet Power That Elevates People and Organizations*. Oakland, CA: Berrett-Koehler Publishers.

Wright, M., R. E. Hoskisson, L. W. Busenitz, and J. Dial. 2000. "Entrepreneurial growth through privatization: The upside of management buyouts." *Academy of Management Review* 25 (3): 591–601.

Wrzesniewski, A., C. McCauley, P. Rozin, and B. Schwartz. 1997. "Jobs, careers, and callings: People's relations to their work." *Journal of Research in Personality* 31 (1): 21–33.

Yang, T., and H. E. Aldrich. 2012. "Out of sight but not out of mind: Why failure to account for left truncation biases research on failure rates." *Journal of Business Venturing* 27 (4): 477–492.

Yates, J. F., and E. R. Stone. 1992. "Risk appraisal." In *Risk-taking Behavior*, ed. J. F. Yates, 49–85. Oxford, England: John Wiley.

Yin, R. K. 2008. *Case Study Research: Design and Methods*. Los Angeles: Sage Publications.

York, J. G., and S. Venkataraman. 2010. "The entrepreneur-environment nexus: Uncertainty, innovation, and allocation." *Journal of Business Venturing* 25 (5): 449–463.

Zacharakis, A. L., G. D. Meyer, and J. DeCastro. 1999. "Differing perceptions of new venture failure: A matched exploratory study of venture capitalists and entrepreneurs." *Journal of Small Business Management* 37 (3): 1–14.

Zahra, S. A., E. Gedajlovic, D. O. Neubaum, and J. M. Shulman. 2009. "A typology of social entrepreneurs: Motives, search processes and ethical challenges." *Journal of Business Venturing* 24:519–532.

Zanotti, L. 2010. "Cacophonies of aid, failed state building and NGOs in Haiti: Setting the stage for disaster, envisioning the future." *Third World Quarterly* 31:755–771.

Zhang, R., Z. Rezaee, and J. Zhu. 2010. "Corporate philanthropic disaster response and ownership type: Evidence from Chinese firms' response to the Sichuan earthquake." *Journal of Business Ethics* 91 (1): 51–63.

Index

Index   235

International connections, 188
Intrinsic motivation, 139–141
Itinerant (consulting) brokers, 103

Knowledge, 10, 17, 21, 23, 36–37, 41, 46,
50, 52, 56–58, 60, 66, 68, 74, 80, 82–83,
85–90, 95, 105–107, 109, 117, 123,
134–135, 150, 156, 189, 192, 195

Learning, 9, 20, 27, 31, 39, 47, 50–51, 58,
93–94, 118, 123, 145, 153, 159, 163, 171,
175, 178, 183, 188, 192, 195–196, 201
Least developed country (LDCs), 149,
151, 153–160, 163, 165, 167, 169, 171,
173, 175, 177, 179, 181, 183–189, 193
"Leave early" strategy, 4–5, 17–20
Legitimacy, 50, 99, 134
Level of analysis, 26, 28, 81, 144
Liaison brokers, 103
Listening to the locals, 189
Lobbying, 74, 170–173, 181
Local know-how, 56
Local know-what, 54
Local nonphysical resources, 54
Locals, 33, 43, 45, 56–57, 59, 61, 66, 68–72,
82, 93, 103, 141, 143, 174, 176, 183, 189,
196
Local venturing, 155–156, 184, 186–187
Logistics, 52–53, 55, 68–69, 83, 105, 200
Loneliness, 71, 84
Loss, 3, 5, 12–19, 27, 47, 54, 67, 75, 83,
85–86, 88–91, 95, 97, 98, 105, 114–116,
121, 124–125, 128, 130, 135–138, 145,
150, 151, 154, 162, 183, 188, 191, 192,
196, 197

Marysville and Triangle Development
Group (MATDG), 12, 55, 57, 60, 61,
65–66, 70–71, 74, 85
Marysville marathon, 72, 75, 90, 214
Marysville marathon festival, 75, 90, 214
Mateship, 100
Media, 24, 27, 54, 68, 85, 106, 146, 151
Men's shed, 100
Mindset, 30, 37, 164–167, 169, 175–176,
178, 181, 183, 186–188
MNCs, 154, 156, 158–159, 170, 185, 186
Motivations, 48, 138–139, 174, 200
Multinational corporations, 154, 158

Natural disasters, 43–44, 81, 94, 96, 145,
150, 152, 154–156

Neighborhood, 75, 91
Networks, 30, 32–37, 49, 56, 64, 77, 83, 95,
111, 122, 152, 155, 173
Nonlocal, 32–37, 60, 62–63, 69–70, 72,
76–77, 80
Noticing, 32, 35, 44, 100

Obstacles, 30, 32–37, 49, 56, 64, 83, 95, 111,
122, 152, 155, 173
Opportunities, 33, 50, 61, 70, 79–80,
85–86, 88, 90, 92–93, 96, 98, 102–103,
113–114, 119, 123, 132–133, 135, 137,
145–146, 155–159, 162, 164–170,
174–178, 183, 185–186, 188–189,
195–197, 199
Organizational emergence, 46, 50–51, 76, 78
Organizational slack, 79
Organizing, 10, 21, 23, 38, 44–48, 51, 55,
65, 67–70, 76–78, 82, 92, 94–97, 100–101,
103, 106, 112, 116–117, 119, 121, 128,
140, 146, 155–157, 168, 170, 172, 177,
187, 191, 193, 198–199
Overconfidence, 19, 135

Pathways, 114, 156, 165, 174, 184
Patriotism, 166–167, 171, 187
Physical, 7, 13–14, 26, 30, 33, 48, 52,
54–55, 59, 65, 67, 83, 95, 100, 102–103,
105, 109, 121–122, 124, 127, 137, 140,
163, 179, 189, 194
Plan, 1, 5, 8, 10, 21, 24, 28, 31, 34, 38–39,
48–49, 56, 60, 67–68, 70, 74–75, 82, 85,
90, 107, 126, 128, 142, 145, 147, 163, 178,
180, 192, 201
Policies, 21–22, 28, 48, 160
Poorest of the poor, 150, 153, 158
Port-au-Prince, 10, 154, 159–160
Positive psychology, 47
Potential opportunities, 80, 155–156, 164,
167, 170, 176, 196
Poverty alleviation, 156, 159, 184, 186
Power, 12, 19–20, 33, 68, 88, 139, 151, 153,
168, 170–172, 180, 187, 200
Preparedness, 2, 6, 11, 22, 24, 28, 40, 72,
75, 134, 143, 150, 191–193, 197–198
Procedures, 22, 24–25, 28–29, 31, 33,
48–49, 177
Process, 16, 18, 21, 24–28, 30, 33–34, 38,
44, 46, 49, 51, 54–55, 58–59, 63, 66,
69–71, 78, 82, 84, 95–96, 109, 115, 126–
127, 132–136, 140–141, 144, 150, 157–
158, 170, 178, 181, 186, 193–194, 200

Printed in the United States
by Baker & Taylor Publisher Services

Printed in the United States
by Baker & Taylor Publisher Services